ASSET & LIABILITY MANAGEMENT

A Synthesis of New Methodologies

ASSET & LIABILITY MANAGEMENT

A Synthesis of New Methodologies

THE KAMAKURA CORPORATION

Published by Risk Books, a specialist division of Risk Publications.

Haymarket House
28–29 Haymarket
London SW1Y 4RX
Tel: +44 (0)171 484 9700
Fax: +44 (0)171 930 2238
E-mail: books@risk.co.uk
Home Page: http://www.riskpublications.com

©Financial Engineering Ltd 1998

ISBN 1 899332 76 6 (hardback)
ISBN 1 899332 81 2 (softback)

British Library Cataloguing in Publication Data
A catalogue record for this book is available from the British Library

Risk Books Commissioning Editor: Conrad Gardner
Designer: Karen Raison

Desk editing and typesetting by
Special Edition, London.

Printed and bound in Great Britain by Bookcraft (Bath) Ltd, Somerset.

This book was published in association with The Kamakura Corporation.

FOREWORD

The discipline called asset and liability management (ALM) has gone through enormous changes since the term was first coined in the late 1960s and early 1970s. An accounting perspective originally dominated asset and liability management, with the forecasting of net income as the main objective. The late 1970s saw the implementation of the current mark-to-market perspective in a few leading institutions – the same was true for the ALM art known as "matched maturity transfer pricing". Concurrently, Mack Terry and his team at the Bank of America, soon followed by others at Continental Illinois, recognised that the management of interest rate risk should be the responsibility of a single unit within the financial institution – which is now standard practice. During the early 1980s, rapidly improving computer technology allowed mark-to-market risk management, net-income forecasting and transfer pricing to be undertaken with greater precision.

In the 1980s and the early 1990s, however, ALM lost its status as the focus for analytical finance and the emphasis on derivatives and the mathematics for their pricing and hedging supplanted it. This resulted in a concentration of analytical talent on trading floors and in the "middle office", generating a group of sophisticated risk managers with a level of analytical training much greater than that seen in traditional ALM. For many years thereafter, ALM practitioners were viewed by their trading-floor peers analogously to the way ALM experts view accountants!

However, by the mid-1990s the ALM discipline acquired a fresh infusion of analytics, talent and organisational responsibility. It began to be recognised that the mathematical tools used for the risk management of derivatives could be applied to the entire balance sheet. Moreover, the fairly staid credit risk assessment process was jolted by the complexities of derivative-related credit risk issues. Hence, more and more institutions now manage credit risk, interest rate risk and other trading floor-related concerns by using the same techniques via the same organisational unit. This book reflects this synthesis of ALM and derivative risk management procedures.

In the first chapter, Michael Ong provides a broad overview of the integrated approach to ALM and analyses traditional topics like interest rate risk and newer topics such as credit risk analytics and derivatives. In the second chapter, Jean-François Boulier applies a European perspective to the science of ALM and reviews the tools that have become essential to the practice of ALM. Emilio Barone continues this exposition on the essential tools of ALM in the third chapter, presenting a unified approach to value-at-risk calculations.

The fourth chapter is an extensive review of the term structure models used in risk management. Rajna Gibson, François-Serge Lhabitant, Nathalie Pistre and Denis Talay emphasise the critical issue of model risk, as we should be reminded that even the best models are only approximations to the actual movements of interest rates.

In the fifth chapter, Robert Jarrow and Donald van Deventer provide a critical analysis of the current interest rate risk and credit risk management procedures. An empirical comparison of the hedging performance of naive bond pricing models with Robert Merton's 1974 risky-debt model is provided. The authors conclude that a new class of credit models that explicitly incorporates interest rate risk is essential to accurately hedge and price (a portfolio of) securities with credit risk.

Derek Chen, Harry Huang, Rui Kan, Ashok Varikooty and Henry Wang take on the formidable task of reviewing the "state of the art" in credit risk modelling in the sixth chapter. The authors review 13 models, 10 of which were developed in the 1990s, and conclude from recent events that more research is required on two critical issues: the impact of liquidity, and the changes in correlation that occur in volatile market conditions.

In the seventh chapter, Shenglin Lu turns to alternative measures of volatility, one of the most critical parameters in the risk management discipline. In the eighth chapter, Tomasz Bielecki and Stanley Pliska deal with the most difficult issue that arises in the face of volatility: dynamic asset allocation. They derive a methodology for an optimal asset allocation strategy and test this methodology using US data.

In the final chapter, John McCann deals with one of the biggest hurdles for the practical implementation of the risk management discussed in earlier chapters. His contribution describes and explains the components of an enterprise-wide data warehouse and provides advice on when and how to implement a database for risk management.

Our knowledge of risk management has continued to advance because of the relentless devotion of its practitioners to studying the mysteries of how markets work. The authors of the present volume have contributed to this task, clarifying what we know about ALM risk management and, more importantly, what we would like to know but still cannot fully explain. For this, we thank them.

Robert A. Jarrow
Director of Research
The Kamakura Corporation

Donald R. van Deventer
President
The Kamakura Corporation

CONTENTS

AUTHORS

Emilio Barone is a bank executive in SanPaolo IMI and Professor of Financial Economics at the Luiss Guido Carli and Tor Vergata Universities in Rome. He has been head of the Financial Risks Analysis department and Head of Research at IMI (Istituto Mobiliare Italiano). He previously worked as an economist in the research department at the Banca d'Italia. He received his BA/MA in Economics from the La Sapienza University in Rome and has followed postgraduate studies at Yale University. He has published around 30 articles in scientific journals and is an associate editor of the *Journal of Banking and Finance*.

Tomasz R. Bielecki has been affiliated with the Department of Mathematics at the Northeastern Illinois University since 1995. He is the author of over 20 research papers and other publications in the areas of mathematical finance, stochastic control, stochastic processes and stochastic analysis. His current research involves the mathematical/ econometric aspects of financial decision-making and probabilistic aspects of default risk modelling and analysis.

Jean-François Boulier is a director at CCF and responsible for the Research & Innovation and Market Risks Management departments. Since 1989 he has been manager of the CCF fundamental research team, which applies a modern finance approach and mathematical techniques to investment banking, fund management and ALM, supported by a team of information engineers. He is editor of *Quants*, a periodical focusing on the application of quantitative models to practical finance. Before joining CCF in 1987 Jean-François was a senior researcher at CNRS, where he studied flow through porous media. He was appointed market risk manager in 1996. His specialisms include yield curve and interest rate risk, ALM, optimisation and risk control, embedded options, financial markets and derivative instruments, cost of capital, quantitative asset management and pension fund management. He graduated from the Ecole Polytechnique, Paris, and has a PhD in Fluid Mechanics from Grenoble. He is the author of many articles and contributions in quantitative finance. Jean-François is vice chairman of AFFI, a board member of AFGAP and chairman of the Research and Program Committee of INQUIRE Europe. He received the INQUIRE Europe award in 1993.

Derek Chen is a quantitative analyst at Global Quantitative Strategies, Credit Suisse First Boston, where he is responsible for developing quantitative trading strategies for corporate trading desks. Derek gained a PhD in Applied Mathematics and Computer Science in 1996 and an MS in Operations Research in 1993 from Carnegie Mellon University.

Rajna Gibson is Professor of Finance at the Ecole des HEC, University of Lausanne, and a member of the Swiss Banking Commission. She holds a graduate degree in business administration and a PhD in Finance from the University of Geneva. She was previously assistant professor of finance at Groupe HEC Paris and visiting scholar at the Anderson Graduate School of Management (UCLA) and Stern Business School (New York University). She has published two books and a large number of articles in leading financial research journals. Her research interests include option pricing theory and its application to financial and real contingent claims, pricing and management of interest rate-linked derivative instruments, as well as the regulation of derivative markets.

Harry Huang is Vice President and Global Quantitative Strategist at Credit Suisse First Boston. His responsibilities at CSFB include research and development of quantitative strategies and models for fixed-income trading, sales and risk management. Harry holds a PhD in Economics from the University of Chicago.

Robert Jarrow is the Ronald P. and Susan E. Lynch Professor of Investment Management at the Johnson Graduate School of Management, Cornell University. He is a managing director and the director of research at Kamakura Corporation. He was the 1997 IAFE/SunGard Financial Engineer of the year. He is a graduate of Duke University, Dartmouth College and the Massachusetts Institute of Technology. Robert is renowned for his pioneering work on the Heath–Jarrow–Morton model for pricing interest rate derivatives. His current research interests include the pricing of exotic interest rate options and credit derivatives, as well as investment management theory. His publications include four books, *Options Pricing, Finance Theory, Modelling Fixed Income Securities and Interest Rate Options*, and *Derivative Securities*, as well as over 70 publications in leading

finance and economic journals. Robert is currently co-editor of *Mathematical Finance* and an associate editor of the *Journal of Financial and Quantitative Analysis, Review of Derivatives Research, Journal of Fixed Income, The Financial Review, The Journal of Derivatives*, the *Journal of Risk, Journal of Financial Engineering*, and *The Review of Futures Markets*. He is an advisory editor for *Asia-Pacific Financial Markets*.

Rui Kan is currently Head of Global Quantitative Strategies at Credit Suisse First Boston, where he is responsible for the management of a group involved in the design of quantitative strategies for the firm's fixed-income trading desks and clients. Prior to this he worked at Deutsche Bank. He has a PhD in Finance from Stanford University and a MS in Physics from Princeton University.

François-Serge Lhabitant is Professor of Finance at the Training Center for Investment Professionals (Zurich) and at Thunderbird, the American Graduate School of International Management (Glendale). He received a BSc, a MSc and a PhD in Finance from the Ecole des HEC, University of Lausanne, and an engineering degree in computer science from the Swiss Federal Institute of Technology. His main research interests are in mutual funds and contingent claims performance evaluation and in the pricing

and hedging of options in the presence of model risk. François-Serge has written many articles on information systems, risk management and performance evaluation.

Shenglin Lu is vice president, Merrill Lynch Fixed Income Research. Prior to joining Merrill Lynch in 1995 he was an assistant professor at the University of Michigan. He holds a PhD in Mathematics from the Courant Institute of Mathematics Science, which he completed in 1992. His current responsibilities include the quantitative analysis of yield curves and credit curves, modelling and development of interest rate- and credit-sensitive products including derivatives, bond options, and the volatility-relative values and strategies in fixed-income debt markets.

John McCann is currently a managing director in the senior management team of Global Technology at CIBC World Markets, where his responsibilities include architecture, data and design issues, along with sponsorship of major infrastructure projects. At present he is engaged in the initial advocacy and structuring of an enterprise-wide data warehouse initiative at CIBC World Markets. In 1996/97 he headed the implementation of a new global financial system, with London as the first site. During 1995 he headed Global Technology activities in the US. Before that assignment, he was responsible for the development and implementation of CIBC WG's global real-time credit limit management system. He joined CIBC WG in 1992 after two years managing the acquisition of a front office bond-trading system with ABN in Amsterdam. Prior to that he was with Toronto Dominion Bank, where he was last responsible for the re-engineering of the Bank's financial and business planning and measurement systems; he was also responsible for the implementation of the original consumer-lending Credit Scoring system at TD. John holds a BMath in Pure Mathematics from the University of Waterloo and a MSc in Mathematics from the University of Toronto.

Michael K. Ong is head of Enterprise Risk Management for ABN-AMRO Bank. He was previously head of the Corporate Research Unit for First Chicago NBD Corporation, where his unit supported the bank in their global risk management. Prior to this Michael was in charge of the Market Risk Analysis Unit and was responsible for quantitative research in the First Chicago Capital Markets Group. Before joining First Chicago NBD he was responsible for quantitative research at Chicago Research and Trading Group (now NationsBanc-CRT). Michael is an adjunct professor at the Stuart School of Business of the Illinois Institute of Technology, where he designed the quantitative portion of the Financial Markets and Trading. He is

a member of the editorial boards of the *Journal of Financial Regulation and Compliance* and the *Journal of RISK* and is a referee for trade and academic journals. He has written articles and contributed book chapters to industry publications, given many presentations and chaired industry conferences. Michael received a BS degree in Physics, cum laude, from the University of the Philippines and a MA in Physics, a MS in Applied Mathematics, and a PhD in Applied Mathematics from the State University of New York at Stony Brook.

Dr Nathalie Pistre is Professor of Finance at Ceram and works in the INRIA research group OMEGA. Her research area is stochastic dominance applied to derivatives valuation, incomplete markets, and asset and liability management. She teaches portfolio and risk management, international financial markets, and financial strategy at Ceram, HEC (France), and HEC-Lausanne. Her most recent publication is a paper on stochastic dominance arguments and the bounding of generalised concave option prices, published in *The Journal of Futures Markets*, September 1998.

Stanley R. Pliska is the CBA Distinguished Professor of Finance at the University of Illinois at Chicago. He is the founder and editor of the academic journal *Mathematical Finance*, and author of about 50 research papers and other

publications, including the textbook *Introduction to Mathematical Finance*. He is noted for his important paper "Martingales and Stochastic Integrals in the Theory of Continuous Trading" (jointly with J. M. Harrison), and his current research interests involve applications of stochastic control theory to financial decision-making problems. Stanley has a BS from the Massachusetts Institute of Technology and a PhD from Stanford University. He is the Executive Secretary of the Bachelier Finance Society, a new society for academics and practitioners with research interests in the area of financial mathematics.

Dr Denis Talay received the 'Habilitation à diriger des recherches' in 1991. Since 1983 he has been an INRIA researcher and since 1991 he has been Directeur de Recherche. In 1992 he became responsible for scientific research with the INRIA research group OMEGA. His research areas are the approximation of stochastic processes, probabilistic methods for the numerical solvution of partial differential equations (Monte Carlo methods, stochastic particle methods, and ergodic methods), and financial mathematics. He serves on the editorial board of *Finance and Stochastics* and of *Monte Carlo Methods and Applications*. He teaches probability theory, the simulation of stochastic processes and financial mathematics at the Ecole Polytechnique (France), University Paris 6 (France),

HEC (France), and in the FAME doctoral Program (Switzerland).

Donald R. van Deventer is currently president of the Kamakura Corporation, which he founded in 1990. His emphasis is on the expansion of the company's software product lines and its international risk management and financial advisory businesses. He is the author of *Financial Risk Management in Banking* (with Dr Dennis Uyemura) and *Financial Risk Analytics: A Term Structure Model Approach for Banking, Insurance and Investment Management* (with Kenji Imai). Donald was senior vice president in the investment banking department of Lehman Brothers (then Shearson Lehman Hutton) from 1987 to 1990. From 1982 to 1987 he was the treasurer for First Interstate Bancorp in Los Angeles and also served as senior planning officer for acquisitions, new ventures and corporate strategy. Prior to this, Donald was a vice president in the risk management department of Security Pacific National Bank. He holds a PhD in Business Economics from the Harvard University Department of Economics and the Harvard Graduate School of Business Administration, and a degree in mathematics and economics from Occidental College.

Ashok P. Varikooty is principal at Flatiron Capital Investment Inc. He was formerly Director of Global Quantitative Strategies at Credit Suisse First Boston, where he was responsible for the management of a group involved in the design of quantitative investment strategies for the firm's proprietary trading desks and the firm's clients. He has also worked with Salomon Brothers Inc and SEI Inc.

Henry Wang is a PhD candidate in Finance at Columbia University and works part time at the Global Quantitative Strategies Group at Credit Suisse First Boston.

1

Integrating the Role of Risk Management in ALM

Michael K. Ong*
ABN AMRO Bank

I f asset and liability management – commonly abbreviated to the acronym ALM – is the single most important financial risk management function of an institution, does it not behove the institution to summon its most talented resources from throughout the enterprise to come together in unity to manage and control its financial destiny? This chapter tacitly assumes an enlightened answer to the question and draws attention to non-traditional ways of conducting the ALM function in an integrated, enterprise-wide risk management framework.

ALM is about the trade-off between risk and reward. Why take risks if there is no reward? Therefore, ALM is also about taking risk in innovative ways to achieve the desired reward. The discussion that follows attempts to introduce meaningful risk and return measures that are not traditionally used in asset and liability management.

Most important of all, the financial market has an uncanny ability to reinvent itself time and time again. Institutions that are skillful in adapting to this evolution stand a better chance of surviving market upheavals. Hence, the management of assets and liabilities should never be a process that is performed in isolation without the use of innovations in the capital markets. This chapter highlights such innovations as value-at-risk, asset securitisation and credit derivatives.

The ABCs of ALM

Asset and liability management always starts with an analysis of the balance sheet – what is in it and what is not. Items not included in the balance sheet are called "off-balance-sheet items". Both on- and off-balance-sheet items are then carefully accounted for one by one.

The balance sheet is a statement of the financial position of a business enterprise which reports major categories and amounts of assets, liabilities (ie, claims on those assets) and stockholders' equity and their interrelationship at a specific point in time.

By regulatory requirements, all institutions have to conform to accounting standards when analysing their balance sheets. In its Statement of Financial Accounting Concepts (SFAC), the Financial Accounting Standards Board (FASB) defined the three elements of the balance sheet as:

❏ *Assets*: probable future economic benefits obtained or controlled by a particular entity as a result of past transactions or events.

❏ *Liabilities*: probable future sacrifices of economic benefits arising from present obligations of a particular entity to transfer assets or provide services to other entities in the future as a result of past transactions or events.

❏ *Equity*: the residual interest in the net assets of an entity that remains after deducting its liabilities.

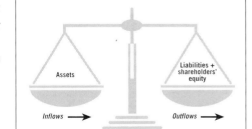

1. The balance sheet

Assets

Liabilities + shareholders' equity

Inflows ⟶

Outflows ⟶

The author expresses his gratitude to Thanh Tran for the outstanding graphics work.

The major categories of assets, liabilities, and equities are classified according to *liquidity* – that is, their *expected* use in operations or conversion to cash in the case of assets – and time to maturity (ie tenor) for liabilities.

Within the assets group, there are two major classifications:
❏ *Current assets*: assets which are expected to be converted to cash or used within one year (or one operating cycle).
❏ *Long-term assets*: assets which are expected to provide benefits and services over periods longer than a year.

A similar classification holds for liabilities:
❏ *Current liabilities*: obligations the firm is expected to settle within one year (or one operating cycle).
❏ *Long-term liabilities*: obligations the firm has to repay more than one year later.

Current assets in the balance sheet include cash and cash equivalents, marketable equity securities, receivables, inventories, and prepaid expenses. Long-term (or non-current) assets include property, equipment, investments in affiliated companies, and intangibles such as brand names, patents, copyrights and goodwill.

Short-term bank debt, the current portion of long-term debt and capitalised leases, accounts payable to suppliers, accrued liabilities (eg, debts owed to employees), interest, and taxes payable are classified under current liabilities. Long-term debt, capitalised lease obligations, pension obligations, and other liabilities such as deferred income taxes and minority interests in net assets of consolidated affiliates constitute non-current liabilities.

Stockholders' equity follows a similar pecking order with regard to their priority in liquidation.

The analysis of liquidity – with emphasis on *expected use and tenor* – relies heavily, therefore, on the distinction between current and long-term classification. With this understanding, the ALM process has become universally known as a system of *timely* matching of cash inflows and outflows – that is, of liquidity management. The terms "gap analysis" and "duration analysis" quickly enter the picture. This was the prevailing wisdom until the 1970s. While this viewpoint was necessary when assessing the financial wellbeing of an institution, was it, however, sufficient? In retrospect the answer is obviously not.

Expectation and the measurement of assets and liabilities

One quickly observes from the definitions given above the emergence of a common theme – *expectation*. From the assets side, there is an expected future usage theme, and on the liabilities side, the expected payment or settlement of an obligation at some future time.

The tunnel vision created, however, by the accounting standards through the definitions of the various elements in the balance sheet forces the analysis of the balance sheet in terms of accounting yields rather than on the more prudent "expected economic returns" or "risk-adjusted returns" basis.

In addition, the expectation in usage (for assets) and in settlement (for liabilities) at some future point in time necessarily requires a paradigm for measuring the elements in the balance sheet. Many elements of the balance sheet are, however, difficult to measure in terms of market value; thus, most elements of the balance sheet are reported at historical cost (ie, the exchange or replacement price at acquisition date). In some cases – accounts receivable, for example – reserve for bad debt adjusts the reported amount to an approximate net realisable value. Generally speaking, current market values are not reflected in the balance sheet prior to the realisation of a sale or other transaction.

Accounting income is measured on the basis of the *accrual* concept. In financial reporting, the determination of which cashflows are included, when and how the changes in asset values are measured, and which changes in assets are to be included in income is bound by accounting rules and principles known as the "generally accepted accounting principles" (GAAP). However, the accrual basis of accounting allocates cash-flows to time periods other than those in which they occur. Recognition of gains or losses must normally await the disposal of the assets or the settlement of the liabilities.

Assigning cash inflows and outflows to appropriate accounting periods belies the institution's ability to assess its expected cashflows, thereby weakening the *predictive* ability of the balance sheet that it was originally meant to have.

Clearly, the ALM function of an institution is not meant to be limited to income accounting. ALM is, indeed, a far more general concept than dutifully conforming to accounting standards. We need, therefore, a broader perception of what the asset and liability management function really is within an institution, instead of confining ourselves to a myopic precept of timely accounting of in-and-out flows – even though cashflow matching is necessary.

Objectives of ALM

What are the objectives of an ALM function within the institution? The ALM function is not simply about risk protection. It should also be about enhancing the net worth of the institution through opportunistic positioning of the balance sheet. The more leveraged an institution, the more critical is the ALM function within the enterprise. The ALM process allows an institution to take on positions that, without such a function, would be deemed too large.

The following points address some of the fundamental objectives that an asset and liability management function must strive to include.

❑ The ALM process must preserve and enhance the net worth of the institution.
❑ ALM is a quantification of the various risks in the balance sheet.
❑ The ALM function must streamline the management of regulatory capital.
❑ ALM should provide liquidity management within the institution.
❑ ALM should actively and judiciously leverage the balance sheet.

These objectives – although stated quite broadly – tacitly assume a financial accounting framework, but they do not highlight accounting as the ultimate goal. Proactively taking a stance to quantify risk and streamlining management processes with the ultimate goal of preserving the institution and enhancing its net worth, through whatever means, deviates from the traditional wisdom about ALM.

In the subsections that follow I elaborate on each objective and highlight the more modern thoughts on asset and liability management in the light of recent advances in risk measurement techniques in the capital markets. The target audience is primarily financial institutions whose key function is to act as financial intermediaries.

PRESERVATION AND ENHANCEMENT OF NET WORTH

Perhaps the single most important function of the ALM function is to preserve and enhance the net worth of an institution through whatever means are available to it. The objectives do not limit the scope of the ALM functionality to mere risk assessment but expand the process to the taking on of risks that might conceivably result in an increase in economic value of the balance sheet.

Asset liability management should focus on managing the net worth of the institution under *uncertainty* while satisfying certain *constraints*. The uncertainty may take the form of interest rates movements, volatility in portfolio earnings, and general economic conditions; while the constraints can be driven primarily by regulatory requirements, corporate appetite for risk, and expected levels of performance and returns. The ability to balance the uncertainty with the constraints while maintaining (or even increasing) the net economic value of the institution is the primary concern of ALM.

In fact, after all is said and done, the asset and liability management function indeed serves as the single most important risk management

2. Fundamental objectives of ALM

Quantification of the various **risks** in the balance sheet		Provide **liquidity management** within the institution
	Preserve and enhance the **net worth** of the institution	
Actively and judiciously **leverage** the balance sheet		Streamline the **management** of regulatory capital

function of the institution, encompassing both reactive and proactive stances against market movements and projected market conditions. The phenomenal growth in risk management and risk measurement techniques in recent years is no longer confined to the capital markets alone. Under the auspices of the ALM function, an institution can prudently integrate and borrow proven technical methods from the capital markets and engage in what can truly be called *enterprise-wide* risk management.

QUANTIFICATION OF RISKS IN THE BALANCE SHEET

The delicate juggling act required in the preservation and enhancement of its net worth presupposes an institution's ability to measure thoroughly all the myriad manifestations of risks on- and off-balance sheet. What are these risks? All are, in fact, well known to us and, to a large extent, many of them are quantifiable.

The balance sheet, which represents the financial position of the enterprise as a whole, contains a wide variety of risk elements and their interrelationships to one another. The major components of risk, illustrated in Figure 3, vary widely in scope and are by no means trivial.

As the financial markets continue to become more transparent, two important phenomena begin to emerge:
❏ Objective statistical measures of risk are rapidly supplanting traditional asset and liability analyses.
❏ Mark-to-market valuation of asset and liabilities becomes more readily available as markets become more liquid and better established.

These two developments allow a significant portion of the embedded risks in a financial institution's balance sheet to be adequately quantified and they therefore facilitate prudent risk management. Consequently, institutions which primarily serve as financial intermediaries can take on larger amounts of risky assets and yet be able to transform them into relatively safer ones by means of diversification and specific expertise in market and credit risk management. Due to continued advancement in commoditisation and its ensuing liquidity, even manufacturing companies may soon be able to apply advanced ALM methodology to their balance sheets through the clever use of commodity and equity swaps and other derivatives.

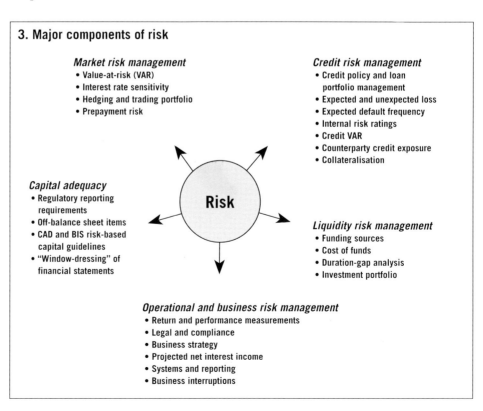

3. Major components of risk

Market risk management
• Value-at-risk (VAR)
• Interest rate sensitivity
• Hedging and trading portfolio
• Prepayment risk

Credit risk management
• Credit policy and loan portfolio management
• Expected and unexpected loss
• Expected default frequency
• Internal risk ratings
• Credit VAR
• Counterparty credit exposure
• Collateralisation

Capital adequacy
• Regulatory reporting requirements
• Off-balance sheet items
• CAD and BIS risk-based capital guidelines
• "Window-dressing" of financial statements

Risk

Liquidity risk management
• Funding sources
• Cost of funds
• Duration-gap analysis
• Investment portfolio

Operational and business risk management
• Return and performance measurements
• Legal and compliance
• Business strategy
• Projected net interest income
• Systems and reporting
• Business interruptions

Furthermore, the two developments in the market did not arrive unnoticed within regulatory circles. As a consequence of the increasing ability to use mark-to-market valuation and statistical quantification of risks (primarily market risk and credit risk), new regulatory rules were enacted. This action also partly stems from the uniform outcry of financial institutions asking for the mandate to begin using their own internal models for risk measurement and capital attribution.

MANAGEMENT OF REGULATORY CAPITAL

The main idea behind regulatorily mandated risk-based capital adequacy guidelines is a direct association of capital reserves requirement and the credit risk inherent in the assets held by financial institutions. More recently, risk-based capital adequacy requirements have been extended to include the market risk activities undertaken by an institution. The wisdom is that, other things being equal, institutions holding a riskier portfolio must have higher capital reserves levied against them.

Depending on how an institution leverages its balance sheet and how it circumvents the interpretation of these capital adequacy guidelines, the capital requirement across similar types of institutions can vary widely.

On its introduction on May 1993, the Financial Accounting Standards Board (FASB) statement no. 115 forced many financial institutions to rethink how their portfolios were managed for income, liquidity and control of interest rate risk. How did this happen? The answer is simple. Prior to FASB 115, accounting restrictions governing the sale of investments allowed many financial institutions to follow a buy-and-hold investment strategy, whereby securities are held to maturity except for certain permissible sales and transfers in the event of a deterioration in an issuer's credit quality. Under FASB 115, securities in the investment portfolios must be classified as one of the following:

❏ *Hold-to-maturity* (HTM): debt securities which are intended to be held to maturity and whose valuations are reported at amortised costs.

❏ *Trading securities*: debt and equity securities purchased for short-term gains and for which assets are required to be marked-to-market for reporting purposes.

❏ *Available-for-sale* (AFS): debt and equity securities which are neither intended for trading nor held to maturity and whose valuations are reported at fair market values net of tax effects.

Placing an asset in the appropriate category has significant ramifications as far as an institution's ability to manage interest rate and liquidity risks and its flexibility in leveraging the balance sheet are concerned. While the HTM classification makes it difficult for the institution to manage interest rate risk actively through the investment portfolio and limits the institution's flexibility in providing liquidity management, it can ignore market volatility and has significantly less capital fluctuation. The opposite is true of the AFS classification, which introduces capital volatility and requires more active management of the investment portfolio but provides greater flexibility in interest rate and liquidity management.

Depending on how well it is capitalised, a financial institution may need to make tough decisions when classifying its assets for the purposes of managing its regulatory capital requirement. To reduce capital volatility during an upward-sloping rate cycle, for instance, it may want to shorten the duration of the AFS securities or reduce the size of the overall investment portfolio.

It is also interesting to note that the FASB 115 ruling applies only to the assets side of the ALM process. There is no similar provision for the liabilities side of the balance sheet.

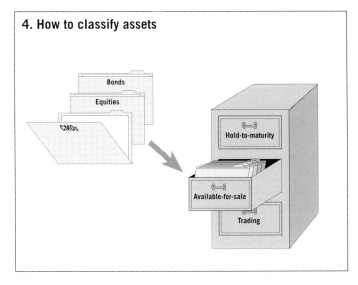

4. How to classify assets

Bonds

Equities

CMOs

Hold-to-maturity

Available-for-sale

Trading

LIQUIDITY MANAGEMENT

Every financial institution requires a certain amount of liquidity to meet its short-term liability payments. Although in principle this implies either the need for access to quick short-term and low-cost funding or to have assets with sufficiently short-term cashflows, a combination of both is ideal since low-cost funding might not be available all the time. The role of the ALM process is to ensure that the short-term in- and outflows process in the balance sheet is carefully balanced to prevent a funding crisis.

Classifying too many assets as available for sale results in too much capital risk. Classifying too few as AFS may result in decreased liquidity in the investment portfolio. In many ways, therefore, financial institutions are faced with a double-edged sword in providing liquidity and, yet, still being able to protect their capital. Liquidity management and the streamlining of regulatory capital in the ALM process is, therefore, one and the same issue.

Liquidity provided by the AFS securities should be determined by periodically analysing a combination of: the fluctuating cycles for loan demands; run-offs in deposits; quick and cheap access to funding sources; the purchase of Federal Reserve Board funds and other money market investments; and the overall economic outlook.

ACTIVELY LEVERAGING THE BALANCE SHEET

Why take risks if there is no reward? Why balance the balance sheet if the ultimate purpose is simply the mere act of balancing? There has got to be a profitable side to risk management, and this is where asset and liability management comes in.

ALM is an insurance policy that allows financial institutions to assume intermediation risk. In their intermediary and fiduciary roles, institutions assume primarily two principal kinds of risks – interest rate risk and credit risk – among other business risks. Relative to its competitors, an institution actively and judiciously shifts positions (either through trading activities or asset reclassification) within the balance sheet and off-balance sheet, capitalising on its:

❑ superior internal expertise in market risk and credit risk analyses and risk management systems for measurement and control;
❑ superb delivery system and funding access at lower costs;
❑ excellent management of regulatory and economic capital;
❑ proper use of risk-adjusted return methodology;
❑ cutting-edge quantification of the embedded optionality in the balance sheet to hedge against prepayment risk; and
❑ prudent use of derivatives to hedge against portfolio risk.

The institution does this with the aim of deriving a significant advantage, *vis-à-vis* its competitors, in leveraging its own balance sheet, thereby enhancing its value while, at the same time, assuming only a reasonable level of risk.

Required components of ALM

The balance sheets of financial institutions, in particular, have become increasingly complex over the past several years. This is a direct consequence of: increased interest rate volatility; intense competition due to deregulation; the introduction of regulatory risk-based capital requirements; technological advances in systems and risk measurement; product innovations in the capital markets; and increased general awareness of the myriad elements of financial risk. The increase in the sophistication and complexity of the balance sheet presents new challenges for modern asset and liability management. As a consequence, the ALM process can no longer be undertaken in isolation within an archaic accounting framework.

To carry out the objectives of the asset and liability management function within a totally integrated, enterprise-wide risk management context, fundamental components must be in place within the institution. These can be seen as divided into two types – traditional and non-traditional. The traditional components of ALM encompass the old GAAP accounting mentality – which is still useful but is deficient and highly inadequate.

TRADITIONAL ALM

The traditional ALM function normally consists of the following elements:

❏ Interest rate risk management
    ❏ Net interest income sensitivity analysis
        ❏ Maturity-gap analysis
    ❏ Net portfolio value sensitivity analysis
        ❏ Duration-gap and convexity analyses
    ❏ Scenario analyses of the above
        ❏ Prepayment modelling
❏ Liquidity and funding report
❏ Hedge report
❏ Risk limits and compliance reports
❏ Capital requirement reports
    ❏ Solvency status
    ❏ Leverage ratios
    ❏ Regulatory capital ratios

[handwritten note: No B/Sheet forecast? history +]

These traditional elements are well known and self-explanatory. For instance, maturity-gap analysis measures the dollar difference (or gap) between the absolute values of the assets and liabilities that are sensitive to interest rate movements. The objective of this analysis – other than to assess the relative interest rate sensitivities of the assets and liabilities – is to determine the risk profile of the institution arising from changes in interest rate levels.

The commonly used "gap ratio", defined as

$$\text{Gap ratio} = (\text{Interest rate-sensitive assets})/(\text{Interest rate-sensitive liabilities})$$

measures whether there are more interest rate-sensitive assets than interest rate-sensitive liabilities. A gap ratio of greater than one, for example, indicates that when interest rates are rising the return on assets (ROA) will rise faster than funding costs, resulting in a more highly spread income. A gap ratio of less than one signals a rising funding cost, which must be dealt with as a matter of urgency. Other ratios can easily be formed for risk assessment purposes.

Duration-gap analysis, on the other hand, assesses the impact of the net worth of the institution due to interest rate changes by focusing on the changes in the market value of either assets or liabilities. That is because duration measures the percentage change in the market value of a single security given a one percentage change in the underlying yield of the security. The duration gap is, therefore, normally defined as

$$\text{Duration gap} = (\text{Duration of assets}) - w \times (\text{Duration of liabilities})$$

where w is the percentage of assets funded by liabilities. Clearly, the duration gap indicates the effects of the change in the *net* worth of the institution – the greater the duration gap, the greater is the interest rate exposure of the institution.

For institutions whose balance and off-balance sheets contain a disproportionately large percentage of securities with embedded optionalities (ie prepayment options) – for example, mortgage-backed securities, CMOs, extendible or cancellable swaps, mortgage pipelines and loan servicing, loan commitments, and money-market instruments with embedded put options – it is also traditionally recognised that convexity analysis should be used in addition to duration analysis.

We shall see later that these two analytic measures – duration and convexity – are still insufficient. It becomes imperative that a modern and non-traditional ALM function also utilise an option-adjusted spread (OAS) analysis.

As far as interest rate risk management of the balance sheet is concerned, the traditional function naively simulates interest rate paths by randomly "shocking" the yield curve, which could result in totally unrealistic scenarios. The non-traditional wisdom borrows interest rate term structure modelling techniques from the capital markets and takes into account mean reversion and other nuances. It simulates interest rate paths that are arbitrage-free – that is, interest rates and volatilities which are consistent with market observation.

The traditional liquidity and funding reports, hedge report and capital requirement reports, as well as other limits or compliance reporting, are still very important but are limited in function. They can act as sentinels for the institution by flagging short-term cashflows and highlighting liquidity problems, in determining actions required in the buying and selling of hedge instruments, and in the monitoring of risk limits or egregious failure to comply with either internal policies or regulatory guidelines. However important and useful they are, these reports are still relatively *ex post facto* tools rather than the more forward-looking and proactive engagement that is required in an institution's risk management. As such, they are likely to be less able to project correctly *expectation* in the proper usage of assets and the timely settlement of liabilities, which is what the balance sheet is supposed to do.

NON-TRADITIONAL ALM

As required supplements to the traditional asset and liability process, I suggest the following more proactive and projective non-traditional ALM elements:

❏ Redefined role of the treasurer and asset and liability committee (ALCO)
❏ Option-adjusted spread (OAS) analysis
   ❏ Arbitrage-free interest rate scenarios
❏ Integrated enterprise-wide risk management
   ❏ Integrated view of credit risk and market risk
      ❏ Value-at-risk methods
      ❏ Introduction of new risk measures
   ❏ Risk-adjusted return performance measurement
      ❏ Economic capital
      ❏ Risk models of loss
   ❏ Portfolio optimisation
❏ Credit risk management
   ❏ Asset securitisation programme
   ❏ Expanded role of credit derivatives
   ❏ Collateral management systems

Role of the treasurer and ALCO

The balance sheet is a portfolio of the institution's assets counterweighted by its liabilities. Should not the treasurer, who, in principle, functions as a portfolio manager on behalf of the institution, use modern portfolio analytical tools to assess his or her projections of scenarios and the like?

The term "treasurer" is taken here to mean the treasury management function within the institution. The asset and liability committee (ALCO) is, by definition, a group of risk managers from various areas of the enterprise who assist the treasurer in the risk management process. The role of the modern treasurer needs to be redefined to reflect recent technological innovations in the capital markets. The treasurer can no longer continue to be just a bean counter.

The modern treasurer, while acting as the institution's chief portfolio manager, should also be the chief strategic guru of the enterprise. He should, therefore, have an in-depth knowledge of the credit processes and trading activities of the institution, possess superlative expertise in the capital markets and be very adept in the interpretation of requirements imposed by the regulatory bodies.

Regulatory bulletins and guidelines issued by such bodies as the Federal Deposit Insurance Corporation (FDIC), Office of the Comptroller of the Currency (OCC), the Securities and Exchange Commission (SEC), the Office of Thrift Supervision (OTS), the Bank for International Settlements (BIS) and the Federal Reserve Board are sometimes confusing and inconsistent and very often are indecisive and ambiguous. The treasurer must be skillful in interpreting and arbitraging some of these regulatory edicts, especially regarding capital requirements, without unduly jeopardising the safety of the institution or alienating the supervisory authorities. He is a highly skilled tightrope walker with two faces.

The treasurer is also the great communicator and educator on the subject of risk within the enterprise. In January 1997 the BIS outlined a number of principles ("Principles for the Management of Interest Rate Risk") for use by supervisory authorities when evaluating banks' interest rate risk management processes. Sound interest rate risk management involves the application of four basic elements in the management of assets, liabilities and off-balance-sheet instruments, namely: appropriate oversight by the Board and senior management; adequate risk management policies and procedures; appropriate risk measurement and monitoring; and comprehensive internal controls and independent external audits.

The treasurer should clearly act as an ombudsman and communicate all the above points across the enterprise, thereby ensuring its safety. In essence, the modern treasurer is also an institution's "risk czar".

Although the treasurer is not a soothsayer capable of predicting interest rate movements and future market changes, he or she must have at their disposal a variety of analytical portfolio tools. The first and foremost of these is an option-adjusted spread analysis toolkit, after which new risk measures for portfolio management have to be introduced.

Option-adjusted spread analysis

The idea behind an option-adjusted spread (OAS) analysis is now well established. It was first widely used in the mortgage-backed securities market to analyse the effect of the embedded prepayment optionality on the yield of these securities.

Fixed-income instruments which have embedded call features cannot be compared to each other on an absolute-yield basis but only according to their option-adjusted spreads. The OAS technique allows instruments to be compared on a risk-adjusted basis. In this context, the OAS methodology is very much a measure of *relative risk* rather than one of relative yield.

Embedded options in fixed-income instruments shroud the true yields of these instruments. To assess the relative value of these option-embedded securities, it is important to determine what their yields would be in the absence of embedded options. The option-adjusted spread is calculated as the spread over comparable risk-free rates (eg, Treasury security yields) that have no embedded options, no embedded credit risk and minimal liquidity constraints. The calculated option-adjusted spread does not say anything about the relative richness or cheapness of the security being analysed; instead, it measures the extent to which the security's expected rate of return exceeds risk-free returns.

The option-adjusted spread allows comparison of the *relative* value of two similar securities with different credit risk, dissimilar liquidity constraints, and different embedded call or put features. Other things being equal, the security with the higher OAS offers the investor a higher level of compensation for taking on the embedded risks in the security.

Application of the OAS methodology is no longer confined to the mortgage-backed industry. Its usefulness in comparing the relative value of embedded optionality can also be extended to measure the embedded risk in the balance sheet. For the most part, the assets and liabilities in the balance sheet contain risks very similar to those embedded in fixed-income securities. The balance sheet and fixed-income securities are both highly sensitive to interest rate movements, and both are highly susceptible to embedded optionalities that could leverage the valuation in some unusual or unexpected manner.

Many institutions (Procter & Gamble, Banc One, Orange County, etc) have run into serious trouble with their balance sheets while in search of higher yields through highly leveraged structured derivative products. Very often, as evidenced by well-publicised press coverage of the ensuing collapse, a high current yield was unable to compensate appropriately for the embedded risks in the instruments placed in the balance sheet. A traditional ALM process is definitely not able to pick up advance signals of imminent danger. "What were the treasurers thinking?" outside observers would have to ask loudly.

Schematics of an OAS model

A schematic diagram of how the OAS methodology works is displayed in Figure 5. Briefly, an OAS model is driven by an interest rate path generator. The interest rates are generated in a "no-arbitrage" fashion consistent with market observations and constrained to the current term structure and volatilities of interest rates. This means that the generated paths are calibrated to the current market prices of benchmark instruments (for example Treasuries, interest rate options, etc). On average, the simulated rate for a given period will be consistent with that period's forward rate and implied volatility. The generated paths, being consistent with the market, imply that they are possible outcomes weighted by their likelihood of occurrence.

Once these paths or scenarios are generated, cashflows within each scenario can be generated in accordance with their prepayment or amortisation schedule and other embedded contractual requirements. Very briefly, to determine the OAS of a security, for instance, one needs to solve iteratively for the spread over the Treasury rates as the average of all the present values of the cashflows, under all possible scenarios, that equate to the market observed price of the security.

Mathematically, the OAS is that number in the following equation

$$\frac{1}{N}\sum_{s=1}^{N}\left[\sum_{t=1}^{T}\frac{CF_t^{(s)}}{\prod_{i=j}^{j}\left(1+y_t^{(s)}+OAS\right)}\right]$$

which equates to the fair market-quoted price of, say, a mortgage-backed security. The number of scenarios in the formula above is N and $y_t^{(s)}$ is the corresponding t-period Treasury rate under scenario s. A typical OAS simulation judiciously chooses from 200 to 500 scenarios. The first summation in the formula above is the average over these chosen N scenarios. The inner summation is nothing but the present value calculation of the cashflows over one specific scenario, adjusted for the OAS.

Excellent discussions of the OAS method applied to the analysis of balance sheets are widely available in the literature.

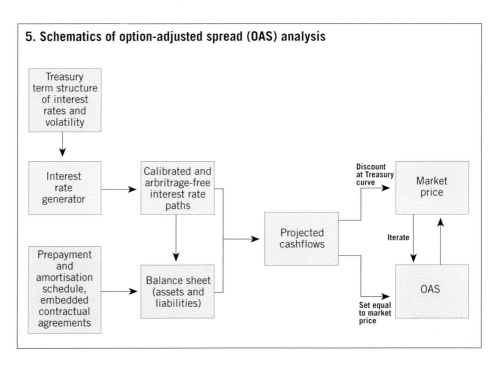

5. Schematics of option-adjusted spread (OAS) analysis

Failure of traditional ALM

Criticisms levied against the accounting mentality of the traditional ALM are well founded. The most prominent of these are summarised below.

First, traditional ALM methods overemphasised the management of short-term net interest income and failed to recognise the *potential* change in the net market value of the balance sheet. An OAS framework attempts to correct this deficiency, thereby allowing the recognition of our underlying theme concerning the role of risk management in ALM – the expected usage of assets and the projected settlement of liabilities.

Second, scenario analysis is widely used in traditional ALM, but, more often than not, the interest rate scenarios generated are not arbitrage-free – that is, they are inconsistent with the market expectation of future interest rates and volatilities. The resulting traditional "shocks" to the term structure of interest rates are, therefore, not realistic. Traditional shocks, consisting generally of "shift", "twist" and "butterfly", are necessary but are highly insufficient! The projection of cashflows and net income streams on the basis of these unrealistic scenarios results in an unrealistic view of future outcomes.

Third, income simulation is almost synonymous with traditional ALM. But what does it really do? The objective of such a simulation is, of course, to maximise earnings potential over a desired horizon, the horizon normally being one or two years out. Beyond that, a simplistic simulation introduces more errors – which render the exercise useless. In most instances the income simulation fails to capture the risk beyond the horizon and it also fails realistically to capture the risk over the horizon. In both cases there is reward measurement but no corresponding risk measurement. As modern balance sheets become more dynamic and complex both long-term and short-term earnings projections become very important. This will, therefore, require different kinds of risk measures so that risks due to horizon effects can be appropriately quantified.

New risk and return measures: integrating market risk and credit risk

The OAS method is just one of the important tools for non-traditional ALM. It needs to be supplemented by other risk and return measures that are capable of quantifying risks in a portfolio context.

Generally speaking, the ALM process (as we may already have discovered earlier) involves a juggling act with three sub-portfolios – the credit-related portfolio, the investment portfolio and the trading portfolio. Each of these has its own unique quirkiness in accounting treatment, taxation, composition and valuation and in its value-generating philosophy. Under the current philosophy of risk-managing the balance sheet in an enterprise-wide perspective and keeping in mind the single mandate of the ALM function – to preserve and to enhance the net worth of the institution – it is mandatory to have a framework with which to measure their embedded risk *and* return on a *level playing field*.

Given their natural composition, these three general sub-portfolios simultaneously have embedded within them both of the major components of risk – market risk and credit risk. It is, therefore, also important to look at these two components in an *integrated* manner.

In the next section I shall discuss the risk-adjusted performance measurement framework, which represents an attempt to quantify the risk and return measurement of seemingly disparate portfolios on a more comparative and even basis. The return measures generally come under the acronym RAROC – risk-adjusted return on capital. For the moment, however, I shall list some of the more non-traditional risk and return measures used in balance sheet risk management.

What follows, then, is a list of some important risk and return measures that should be applied to these portfolios. Each needs to be calculated to obtain an accurate picture of the risk and return profile of the entire balance sheet.

RISK MEASUREMENT

Value-at-risk (VAR)

The market risk component of the portfolios can be readily captured by the corresponding VAR of the portfolio. VAR, being the uncertainty of the change in value of the portfolio, represents the potential loss with a predetermined level of confidence. Because the parameters of any internal VAR model are dictated by regulatory bodies, an *annualised* VAR number also represents the amount of required risk-based capital for undertaking market risk activities in a given portfolio. The market risk embedded in the investment and the trading portfolios can be measured via a VAR framework. Keep in mind that both duration and convexity analyses are automatically embedded in a good VAR framework; therefore, these traditional risk measures are not highlighted in this discussion. Currently, there is impetus in the market to develop value-at-risk measurements for credit risk.

Expected loss

For market risk the expected loss is zero. However, since expected loss is related to default characteristics, this means that the high-yield assets in the investment portfolio, the credits in the credit-related portfolio, and the counterparty credit risk in the trading portfolio require provisions for expected loss. In this context, the expected loss measures the *anticipated* loss of the portfolios associated with the failure of the issuer of the security or the counterparty of the transaction or the obligor of the loan to deliver what was promised. The expected loss of a portfolio is proportional to the total exposure of the portfolio and the probability of default.

Unexpected loss

The risk at the horizon (for either the short term or the long term) is due to *unanticipated* changes in the value of the portfolio. The main source of unanticipated risk is the occurrence of default and credit migration. The unexpected loss, defined as the standard deviation of the value at the horizon, is the appropriate measure to capture this unanticipated risk of loss. Technically, VAR is the unexpected loss in the trading portfolio associated with the unanticipated changes in market rates and other risk factors. It is the unexpected loss that requires economic or risk capital to be set aside so that portfolio activities can be engaged in (economic capital is defined in the following section on return measurement). A measurement of unexpected loss at both the individual asset and the portfolio level is necessary to gauge the uncertainty in the portfolio accurately.

Risk contribution

The unexpected loss of a given portfolio is the weighted average of all the risk contributions from each and every asset in the portfolio, taking into account diversification (ie correlation) and concentration effects. The risk contribution is a measure of the undiversified risk of an asset in the portfolio – ie, the amount of risk that is not diversified away by the portfolio. An asset's risk contribution is dependent on the characteristics and the exposures within the current portfolio. Changing the exposure amounts in the portfolio will generally change the risk contribution. Risk contribution can also measure the incremental effect of a single asset on the overall risk profile of the portfolio.

The risk contribution of an asset is closely related to the asset's beta – viz, Beta = (Risk contribution of asset)/(Unexpected loss of portfolio).

Expected spread

The expected spread (in dollar terms) of an asset in the portfolio is the expected income (ie, total income less expected loss) over and above the cost of funds. The expected spread represents the "real" amount of money earned from holding the asset in the portfolio. The expected spread of the portfolio can likewise be determined as a weighted average of the individual spreads in the portfolio.

RETURN MEASUREMENT

Because regulatory capital is not the proper substitute for risk or economic capital, the return measures listed below will refrain from using it as a denominator. Furthermore, any return measure – however cleverly concocted – can only be constructed from a combination of several predefined risk measures. Therefore, the inability to agree on a set of prudent risk measures when assessing the risks embedded in any of the three sub-portfolios can only result in constructing return measures that have no bearing on the actual risks of the portfolios. Risk and return are, indeed, intertwined from the perspective of this frame of mind.

Economic capital

Capital is a determinant of return measures, but a capital number that does not appropriately take into account the risk-taking activities of an institution cannot properly measure the risk and return profile of the institution. Regulatory capital is one such inadequate capital measure and is, therefore, unable to protect the institution from insolvency.

As market conditions deteriorate further, financial losses of catastrophic magnitude are bound to occur more frequently. This corresponds to an *extreme loss* situation. The question is: "What level of capital is necessary for the bank to sustain extreme or - catastrophic losses?" The answer to this question lies in the economic capital. Briefly, economic capital is the number of standard deviations away from the expected loss necessary to prevent the institution from becoming insolvent in the event of extreme losses in the institution's portfolio due to default or other market risks. The necessary cushion is the amount of capital the institution must set aside to provide for such disastrous market conditions. Other names for economic capital are "risk capital" or "capital-at-risk".

Risk-adjusted return

Such provision can easily be achieved through any RAROC-type initiative either at portfolio or at transaction level. The risk-adjusted return is simply the expected spread (in dollar terms) over economic capital. RAROC can be calculated for individual assets and on a portfolio basis. Both return measures have to be used when determining relative value. The risk-adjusted return framework, by virtue of its provisioning for expected loss regardless of the nature of the assets, indeed puts the three portfolios on a level playing field.

Modified Sharpe's ratio

Defined as the expected spread divided by the unexpected loss, the modified Sharpe's ratio represents return per unit risk. On a plot of expected spread versus unexpected loss, assets to the left of the Sharpe's ratio line have higher return per unit risk than the average portfolio. Those lying to the right of the line have lower returns per unit risk and, thus, should have their weights in the portfolio reduced. In essence, the modified Sharpe's ratio measures the reward-to-volatility trade-off. Volatility, in this context, is adequately represented by the unexpected loss. Because the numerator is the expected spread, the modified Sharpe's ratio is also a risk-adjusted performance measure.

It should be noted that both RAROC and the modified Sharpe's ratio are risk-adjusted return measures relative only to one's own portfolio, regardless of external market pricings. They put the three sub-portfolios on an *internal* level playing field. Therefore, when used blindly in an enclosed environment, the results can be quite myopic. To avoid such internal short-sightedness, a benchmark-based return measure needs to be developed. This is discussed next.

Appraisal ratio

If any of the three portfolios is an active portfolio and is benchmarked by some passive market indexes (for instance, high-yield securities in the investment portfolio and credit derivatives in the trading portfolio), the appropriate return measure is the appraisal ratio, defined as the alpha of the portfolio divided by the unexpected loss of the portfolio. The alpha of the portfolio is simply the difference between the "fair" return of the benchmark portfolio and the actual expected rate of return of the active portfolio. In other words, alpha is the expected "abnormal" return. Consequently, the function of the appraisal ratio is to appraise (ie measure) the relative value of holding the active portfolio *vis-à-vis* the benchmark portfolio.

There are other return measures, but they tend to be variants of the three mentioned above.

Risk-adjusted return performance measurement

Once all the necessary measures concerning market risk and credit risk have been properly integrated and quantified (including the difficult issue of determining economic capital), it becomes important to develop tools for assessing the performance of the institution's balance sheet, including the sub-portfolios mentioned earlier. The profitability of the investment or trading activities that are subject to intrinsic credit risk and market risk can only be appropriately and fairly analysed on a *risk-comparable* basis if the returns are measured in conjunction with the specific risks undertaken by these value-generating activities. The process that places returns on a comparable playing field is known as "risk adjustment". The return calculated using risk adjustment is called the risk-adjusted return on capital, or RAROC. We will take this as a generic term for risk adjustment using economic capital as the proper capital measure.

As the name implies, the risk adjustment is performed on both the revenue and capital components of the equation. On the revenue side, the "cost or expenses" of doing business needs to be taken into account. The cost, from a credit default risk perspective, is the expected loss from engaging in credit-providing activities. Other expenses include tax provisions and transactions expenditure. Capital is appropriately replaced by risk or economic capital. Observe that, as described in the previous section, we have deliberately incorporated the unexpected loss component (incurred under extreme loss conditions) into the capital determination. Since the institution (in the enterprise-wide sense) also engages in activities other than those which induce credit risk, the capital must, in principle, also incorporate other risks, such as market risk, operational risk, etc. In principle, other forms of conceivable, but quantifiable, risk can easily be included without loss of generality.

Without going into too much detail, the ingredients of the RAROC equation can be simply defined as shown in Figure 6. The numerator, representing the return component, consists of revenue information, "expenses" in the broadest sense, transfer pricing among the different risk-taking activities, and the expected losses associated with each of these activities. The denominator, on the other hand, represents the amount of capital needed for the institution to sustain a desired credit rating commensurate with the level of risk it is taking. This capital cushion is risk or economic capital.

Portfolio optimisation

Once all the risk and return measures for determining the profitability and risk profile of the balance sheet are in place, a corresponding optimisation of the balance sheet needs to be undertaken. In line with the primary objectives of the ALM function within the institution, such an exercise really has only three objectives: to obtain maximum diversification; to enhance profitability; and to maintain optimal capital adequacy.

The optimisation process allows the treasurer judiciously to reclassify the assets and liabilities in the balance sheet and off-balance sheet by swapping low return-to-risk assets with high return-to-risk assets, while keeping capital adequacy (both economic and regulatory) as a constraint. Strategic

---

6. The RAROC equation

$$\frac{\text{Risk-adjusted return}}{\text{Risk or economic capital}} = \frac{\begin{array}{l}\text{Revenues} \\ \pm \text{ Treasury transfer prices} \\ - \text{ Expenses} \\ - \text{ Expected losses}\end{array}}{\begin{array}{l}\text{Capital for unexpected losses} \\ \quad \bullet \text{ Credit risk} \\ \quad \bullet \text{ Market risk} \\ \quad \bullet \text{ Operational risk} \\ \quad \text{etc}\end{array}}$$

decisions either to lever or to de-lever the balance sheet require optimisation of the arbitrage opportunity between regulatory and economic capital.

Investment or trading decisions either to purchase or to sell assets should also be a by-product of optimising the profitability profile without unduly disturbing the other constraints – for example, the risk contribution of these assets to the portfolio or increasing economic or regulatory capital requirements.

In fact, a full-blown optimisation of the balance sheet is not a simple task. Because in practice portfolio investment decision processes occur under conditions of uncertainty, the optimisation technique becomes, mathematically, what is known in operations research as a "multiperiod stochastic dynamic programming problem". The topic is, however, beyond the scope of this chapter; nevertheless, it is enlightening to highlight a few important factors and constraints that need to be considered.

In practical optimisation for asset and liability management, the starting point is the market prices of securities as set by the capital markets. As market prices are based on expectations of future cashflows, the description of these uncertain future cashflows can be modelled adequately using stochastic programs that are consistent with these observed market prices. This is the same arbitrage-free condition required in the OAS simulation discussed earlier. In addition, these capital markets factors include asset-class assumptions, economic scenarios and time horizons.

The two other factors pertain to the balance sheet – asset factors and liability factors. They are normally in the form of constraints. The ALM optimisation problem, in summary, requires the following factors and their associated constraints:

❏ *Capital markets factors*: time horizon, economic scenario and assumptions about asset class.
❏ *Asset factors*: asset-type constraints, minimum income requirement, inflationary sensitivity of new asset flows, net economic surplus in relation to the present value of loss payouts and FASB 115 asset classification.
❏ *Liability factors*: forecast business mix, inflation sensitivity of liability flows, loss ratio volatility, etc.

The number crunching required in this kind of balance sheet optimisation cannot be underestimated. In fact, in April 1996, IBM and Risk Management Technologies (RMT) announced their agreement to develop and market the world's first massively parallel-processing asset liability and data warehouse solution as a response to global demands for this kind of service.

ALM has, indeed, come a long way since the antediluvian "gap" analysis.

Credit risk management

One of the fundamental roles that financial institutions play in the market place is to act as financial intermediaries. In so doing they have to invest in illiquid financial assets which, by their very nature, require vast amounts of information. Furthermore, as such assets cannot be readily traded in the capital markets, it behoves an institution to engage actively in the risk management of these illiquid entities.

Given a fixed capital structure, a financial institution can either hedge away the associated illiquid risks by using offsetting transactions in the capital markets (which is not always possible at low cost) or by radically revising its investment policies. Therefore, faced with illiquid risks, the capital budgeting process and risk management functions of the institution become one and the same.

The most straightforward example of such an illiquid asset held in the institution's balance sheet is a loan extended to a company. The counterparty credit risk associated with the off-balance-sheet trading activities is another example – albeit less subtle and less recognisable at first glance but, nevertheless, a risk to reckon with.

Unlike market risk, credit risk is, in general, difficult to hedge or unload. Credit risk, as mandated by the supervisory bodies, requires regulatory capital; and credit risk is by far the largest consumer of risk-based capital in a financial institution's balance sheet.

Therefore, a discussion of one of the primary objectives of the ALM function – to stream-line the management of regulatory capital – cannot be considered without addressing the important issue of credit risk management.

In introducing the non-traditional risk and return measures (specifically, unexpected loss and risk contribution) earlier, allusion was made to the importance of credit risk man-agement in the ALM process. More concretely, in the light of the ALM objectives for the management of regulatory capital and the enhancement of net worth, two items that need to be addressed are asset securitisation and the role of credit derivatives in the balance sheet. These vehicles are potential mitigants of credit risk in the balance sheet, and both have the potential either to reduce or to allow the arbitrage of regulatory capital.

ASSET SECURITISATION

In addition to the significant product innovations in capital markets in recent years, finan-cial institutions in particular have begun to securitise those illiquid assets in their balance sheets which are difficult to unload in the capital markets. Second, in view of the increased constraints – both external and internal – on their capital structure, the secu-ritisation of illiquid assets has been seen by many financial institutions as a means of offering capital relief. To a lesser extent, credit derivatives also offer some kind of capital relief, but credit derivatives are primarily viewed as a hedge against credit risk and a tool for enhancing return on capital.

Asset securitisation broadly refers to the process whereby loans, receivables and other illiquid assets in the balance sheet with similar characteristics are packaged into interest-bearing securities that offer attractive investment opportunities. Sometimes the securitised assets are collateralised to enhance the yields of the securities.

The securitisation of assets is not new, but only recently has it begun to be viewed as a tool for balance-sheet risk management. From the issuing institution's perspective, as well as providing capital relief, the securitisation of illiquid assets is viewed as a means of:
❏ reducing leverage in the balance sheet;
❏ improving overall credit quality;
❏ enhancing asset performance;
❏ broadening funding sources and reducing funding costs;
❏ lessening the need for asset management; and
❏ satiating yield-hungry investors.

As the illiquid assets in the securitisation programmes of many financial institutions are generally loans, the reduction of leverage in the balance sheet and the issues attending credit risk management and capital requirements are the most important.

The highly successful securitisation of the mortgage markets lends much credibility to current innovation in the securitisation of illiquid assets. Judging by the explosive growth of asset securitisation programmes, it seems that big financial institutions have learned the power of the vehicle quickly. Without the securitisation vehicle, the traditional sale of whole loans as a funding source requires a tremendous amount of due diligence, primarily because of the credit quality of the packaged loans. Also, in most cases the investors bear the default risk of such loans. However, by using securitisation as the vehicle, the burden of due diligence is passed from the issuing institution to the underwriters involved in the distribution of the securitised assets. Furthermore, since the securitised assets are agency-rated, they are considerably less risky than whole loans and, therefore, they normally trade at higher prices in the secondary markets. These higher proceeds translate into lower funding costs to the issuing institution than are incurred in the execution of whole loans.

Regulatory and economic capital arbitrage
From a balance-sheet perspective, the big secret about asset securitisation is that illiquid assets such as whole loans, which might otherwise have to be classified as hold-to-maturity, can now be repackaged, securitised, collateralised, yield-enhanced and then jettisoned (at least partially) from the balance sheet into the capital markets. This virtually

amounts to an arbitrage between regulatory and economic capital in its purest form. Of course, the regulators are hovering keenly over this "window-dressing" activity like vultures and, predictably, may soon issue new regulations to plug some of the loopholes. But who is to blame?

The increasing use of asset securitisation is a clever response by many financial institutions to the risk-based capital adequacy guidelines mandated by the various regulatory bodies, and the guidelines imposed on financial institutions generally place a higher risk weight on loans than on securities. Therefore, to lower its regulatory capital, a financial institution can either buy securitised assets rather than whole loans or initiate an asset securitisation programme. Either way, this immediately reclassifies the illiquid assets into a lower category of risk weighting, resulting in a lower regulatory capital requirement.

Furthermore, the introduction of FASB 115 requires institutions to classify as available-for-sale and to mark-to-market all securities they might ever sell as part of their ALM process. Because the ruling does not apply to whole loans, the last few years have seen an increase in the acquisition of whole loans by banks. These illiquid assets need, in turn, to be placed into an asset securitisation vehicle so that they can be jettisoned from the balance sheet as a means of reducing regulatory capital.

THE ROLE OF CREDIT DERIVATIVES
Within the risk management framework of the ALM process, credit derivatives are beginning to play a very important role. Financial institutions, in particular, are now using credit derivatives to manage the credit risk in their balance sheets. Among the areas witnessing rapid growth in today's changing credit market landscape are:
❑ Primary – loan syndication.
❑ Secondary – institutions making markets specifically for yield pick-up.
❑ Tertiary – credit-portfolio and balance-sheet management in banks.

Credit derivatives are widely used today as part of the overall loan-syndication strategy. In preparation for a turn in the credit cycle, syndication agents are using these derivatives to entice an ever increasing number of hedge funds into an already crowded loan market.

The preferred vehicle is usually a "total return swap", whereby the investor (generally a hedge fund) puts up collateral and borrows (up to several times the amount of the collateral) from the lender at a substantial premium. In return, the investor receives the cashflows linked to the total return of an underlying asset (normally a loan or a high-yield bond). Since the investor is leveraged, his return is substantially high. In addition, the investor also receives the yield on the collateral pledged, which is usually a risk-free instrument such as Treasuries. The lender, on the other hand, receives the substantial premium on the investment-grade loan to the investor while, at the same time, reducing his exposure to the underlying asset.

Through the total return swap vehicle the arranger bypasses the upfront fees normally required of ordinary loans in the primary market and receives a relatively wide margin on a high-grade loan to the hedge fund. Both sides appear to benefit from the transaction.

Credit risk concentration and the credit paradox
Why do banks continue to find it beneficial to use credit derivatives in their balance-sheet management function even though undertaking the process often results in a loss?

The simple answer lies in what is collectively known as the "credit paradox". A credit portfolio that is not well diversified will generally be characterised by an excess in the two portfolio risk measures – expected loss and unexpected loss – relative to a more diversified portfolio of similar size and other characteristics. This is because the credit losses in the portfolio are highly correlated and the risk of default between individual obligors is not sufficiently mitigated by portfolio effects.

Unlike going for volume in market risk, it is not "cheaper" to accept more credit risk since the institution needs to charge an increasingly larger credit spread as its exposure to a specific obligor rises. The larger spread is required to compensate the institution for the increase in the expected and unexpected losses arising from an increase in exposure to the obligor. However, banks rarely charge more in the hope of retaining their good relationship with the borrower. In fact the opposite is true – relationship managers normally argue for higher levels of exposure as a means of retaining lead-bank status with the client or as a hedge to receiving more lucrative business down the road. A problematic paradox hereby exists, resulting in significant concentration risk for the bank.

Three factors that contribute to concentration risk in the balance sheet are considered below.

❑ *Specialisation* Most financial institutions, because of their expertise or lack of it, tend to specialise in specific industries or geographical areas. This causes their credit portfolios to be concentrated on clusters of clients that tend to have similar default characteristics and whose businesses tend to be highly correlated with the economic cycles to which they are currently subject. This means that specialised institutions can normally operate only within the scope of their natural markets and have a very difficult time matching their origination capacity with their objectives for diversification. Consequently, the more specialised an institution, the greater the dilemma posed by concentration risk in the balance sheet.

❑ *Credit trends* As a result of the direct issuance of securities to investors and capital-raising in the capital markets, larger corporations have succeeded in bypassing bank financing, leaving a concentration of less credit-worthy borrowers who do not have easy access to the capital markets for financing. As a result, some institutions are beginning to have a disproportionate concentration of lower-quality borrowers in their portfolios.

❑ *Relationship* To preserve a cozy client relationship in the hope of generating more non-credit related business down the road, many institutions have wrestled with the dilemma of increasing commitments to individual borrowers beyond what is considered profitable for the institutions. Consequently, faced with the inability to directly offload the larger credit exposures, many institutions take on substantial concentration risk with specific borrowers.

Given these factors which collectively contribute to the credit paradox phenomenon, financial institutions are turning quickly to the credit derivatives market for solutions. Even though the early indications are that banks are not so successful in using the credit derivatives vehicle to alleviate their concentration risk, the resulting capital relief allows banks to generate earnings elsewhere. For now, it appears that the newly released capital and the new opportunities it creates have compensated adequately for the loss incurred in using credit derivatives.

In tandem with the asset securitisation vehicle, credit derivatives potentially allow a substantial amount of credit risk and its associated concentration effects to be removed from the balance sheet. The amount of credit relief and capital reduction depends highly on the embedded tranches in the asset securitisation and the kinds of credit derivatives that are structured.

It seems that – provided there is no regulatory intervention – financial institutions have at their disposal a huge arsenal of innovative products enabling them to align their capital structure with the businesses they engage in while at the same time allowing a shift of the credit content of their balance sheets to more favourable positions.

Credit derivatives and regulatory capital

Credit derivatives are the first mechanism through which credit instruments can be executed with reasonable liquidity and without the risk of a short squeeze. Credit derivatives, except when embedded in structured notes, are off-balance-sheet instruments. As such, they offer considerable flexibility in terms of leverage. Amazingly, the degree of leverage is defined and controlled by the user.

Because of the absence of a credit repo market, the return on capital offered by bank loans has been unattractive to institutions that do not enjoy access to unsecured financ-

USING CREDIT DERIVATIVES TO MANAGE REGULATORY CAPITAL AND RETURNS

Consider two banks, each funding a $10 million BBB-rated corporate loan. The current Libor rate is 5.625%. The regulatory capital requirement for loans is 8% of the appropriate risk weighting. The risk weighting is 100% if the counterparty is a corporate and 20% if the counterparty is another OECD bank.

Figure A shows each bank going its separate way, financing the corporate loan at Libor plus 0.375%. Each bank must put up $800,000 of its own equity. Bank 1 (higher quality) and Bank 2 (lower quality) fund, respectively, at Libor less 0.20% and Libor plus 0.25%. The returns on regulatory capital are, respectively, 12.6% and 7.4%.

Figure B shows the two banks using a credit swap to end up in a "win–win" situation. The better-rated Bank 1 funds the $10 million loan and swaps the credit risk out to the lower-rated Bank 2 via a default put. Bank 1 is now exposed to the default risk of the lower-rated Bank 2 instead of that of the corporate. The new risk weighting for Bank 1 is 20% and the required regulatory capital is now reduced to $160,000. As a result, Bank 1's return on regulatory capital increases to 17.9% although its net revenue decreases. In addition, having effectively "hedged" this credit exposure, Bank 1 can now free up credit lines and continue to lend to a valued customer even though it would exceed the original credit limits.

Bank 2 also wins. In return for receiving the put premium of $37,500 per annum, the lower-rated Bank 2 takes on the $10 million default risk of the corporate and has to put up $800,000 as equity capital. Investing the $37,500 in Treasury bills (assuming a rate of 5.29%), the bank increases its revenue to $79,800 and improves its return on capital to 10.0%.

The credit swap, of course, sits off-balance sheet and is subject to daily mark-to-market, and should therefore be passed to the trading portfolio for risk management.

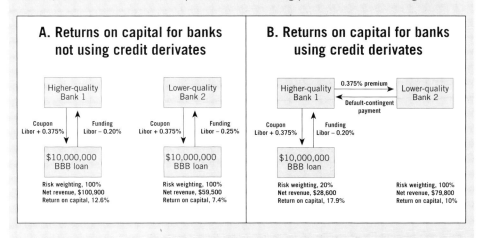

A. Returns on capital for banks not using credit derivates

Higher-quality Bank 1

Coupon Libor + 0.375% — Funding Libor − 0.20%

$10,000,000 BBB loan

Risk weighting, 100%
Net revenue, $100,900
Return on capital, 12.6%

Lower-quality Bank 2

Coupon Libor + 0.375% — Funding Libor − 0.25%

$10,000,000 BBB loan

Risk weighting, 100%
Net revenue, $59,500
Return on capital, 7.4%

B. Returns on capital for banks using credit derivates

Higher-quality Bank 1 — 0.375% premium → Lower-quality Bank 2
← Default-contingent payment

Coupon Libor + 0.375% — Funding Libor − 0.20%

$10,000,000 BBB loan

Risk weighting, 20%
Net revenue, $28,600
Return on capital, 17.9%

Risk weighting, 100%
Net revenue, $79,800
Return on capital, 10%

ing. However, by taking on exposure to bank loans using, say, a total return swap (eg, receiving the net proceeds of the loan after financing), a hedge fund can both synthetically finance the position more cheaply and avoid the administrative costs of direct ownership of the asset. The bank, on the other side, potentially stands to benefit from a reduction in regulatory capital usage and thereby achieve better return on capital. The degree of leverage achieved using this total return swap example will depend on the amount of upfront collateralisation and the underlying structure of the swap. The user controls this leverage.

The example presented in the panel (a modification of an illustration given by Wong and Song in "A Loan in Isolation", published in the June 1997 issue of *Asia* RISK) demonstrates the effect of return on regulatory capital when a simple credit derivative swap is used.

Some final thoughts

Asset and liability management has come a long way from its original archaic accounting mindset. Given the complexity of modern balance sheets, this chapter has argued for the introduction of more non-traditional ALM processes alongside the traditional ones. The ALM function needs to be performed from an integrated and enterprise-wide risk management perspective in addition to satisfying traditional GAAP principles. The major components of risk in the balance sheet – market risk and credit risk – can only be adequately assessed in an integrated portfolio management framework using the correct risk measures.

It comes as no surprise that the management of the balance sheet evolves alongside innovations in the capital markets such as value-at-risk, asset securitisation and credit derivatives. After all, the ALM processes of institutions cannot be undertaken in isolation, away from current developments in the those markets.

Financial institutions, in particular, may be the most efficient generators of loans because of their superior access to corporations, yet they are not always the best holders of these loans since credit risk increases exponentially with concentration. This credit paradox – a phenomenon associated with the fact that the spreads required to take on larger amounts of the same credit risk increase dramatically with concentration – forces banks to take on larger amounts of credit exposure in search of larger spreads and, hence, to expose themselves to a higher probability of suffering from default. In addition, the lack of a centralised portfolio management function within these large institutions, together with the absence of astute regulatory guidance, has not encouraged banks to look at returns from credit-embedded portfolios on a risk-adjusted basis and in a more unified framework.

This chapter is a call for attention to this matter and outlines the necessary risk and return measurement tools required to achieve a more coherent approach to asset and liability risk management in a more non-traditional manner. It also calls for more innovative methods of mitigating both market and credit risks embedded in the balance sheet by moving some of these risks around and swapping them out through the creative use of collateralisation, mark-to-market, risk-adjusted return performance measures, credit derivatives or other mechanisms.

2

Selected ALM Issues

Jean-François Boulier*

Crédit Commercial de France

T he technique known as asset liability management (ALM) has enjoyed remarkable popularity in recent years. From its origins as an actuarial and cashflow matching technique, ALM has grown into a conceptual framework for financial management – and a professional activity in its own right.

In a world governed by financial markets and physical commodities, it is vital to analyse objectively the economic effects of price movements on balance sheets, earnings growth and enterprise value. The constituency of ALM users goes beyond financial institutions and banks, and now includes pension funds. In the near future companies are bound to adopt it. And individuals will surely find it attractive for investment decision-making and income planning.

ALM specialists are now recognised as fully fledged professionals. In the banking industry they have found a niche between capital market divisions and management control divisions (in France) or alongside strategic divisions (in other European countries). They have also carved a place for themselves in public life, as witnessed by the constant stream of seminars and conferences devoted to ALM, either directly or indirectly. Professional bodies are thriving in several countries, including AFGAP in France, NALMA in the USA and ALMA in the United Kingdom. Lastly, and significantly, ALM is now being taught not only as part of a broader curriculum but also as a discipline in its own right.

CCF did pioneering work in adapting ALM methods to the French environment. A feasibility study was carried out in the period 1985–86, shortly after France deregulated its money market. In 1987 a prototype unit began to lay the groundwork for ALM and to adapt the tools that the bank would later need. But it was not until 1989 that the asset–liability department actually implemented an original approach based on the development of proprietary information systems. CCF's Research and Innovation Department (DRI) has investigated the possibilities of either applying ALM to banking requirements or adapting the underlying concepts to other environments. Some of the DRI's research has been outlined in various issues of *Quants* or at scientific financial conferences. The areas covered include securitisation and prepayment options (*Quants* no. 4; D'Andria, Boulier and Elie, 1991), embedded options (Boulier and Schoeffler, 1992; Boulier, 1996) and the modelling of dynamic management with stochastic interest rates (Jerad and Sikorav, 1992). Issue 12 of *Quants* examined an ALM-based methodology for pension fund investment strategies (Boulier, Florens and Trussant, 1995; and Boulier, Michel and Wisnia, 1996), while issue 23 explained how fuzzy calculus could be used to take account of unknown due dates in a cashflow matching context.

The purpose of this paper, which is a revised version of issue 24 of *Quants*, is to examine, in the most accessible way possible, key issues involved in ALM and its application. We provide three examples of how the technique relies on financial modelling. Through these case studies, which deal with different fields (and can be read separately), we hope to illustrate the diversity of techniques and applications of ALM. First,

---

The author wishes to thank C. Chambron, who was co-author of the original version of this paper, which appeared in Quants *no. 24.*

we discuss the advisability of exposing a bank to interest rate risk. We then give a description of a capital allocation method based on the Markowitz model. Finally, we rely on simulations to analyse the attractions and risks of increasing the equity investments of a life insurance company.

ALM: background and current issues

This part of our study examines, in an intentionally non-technical manner, the principal aspects of asset liability management in its present form in Europe. Since the main users of ALM are bankers, we intend to start with their concerns before moving on to other specialist fields, such as insurance and pension financing. We have divided this part into four sections: the first attempts to define the aims of ALM; the second retraces its history and examines the role played by associations such as AFGAP; the third draws up a list of the most commonly used methods (without relying on mathematical formalisation); and the fourth examines some of the challenges currently facing practitioners of ALM, particularly in terms of methodology.

DESCRIPTION

Asset liability management has three main aims, which vary in importance depending on the businesses that use the technique and on their maturity. The aims are to analyse economic risks (chiefly market risk), to choose appropriate strategies (eg, whether to hedge exposure) and to monitor the implementation of those strategies. For companies, the main concern – in theory – is to maximise shareholder value. In practice, however, this can vary depending on how the company's shareholders, creditors and management view the process of maximisation. In other words, the company's exposure must be decided upon rationally, accepted by all those concerned, and be applied optimally. This all goes to show the importance of information processing, both internally depending on the type of product and the volumes handled, and externally depending on the market opportunities involved. Moreover, the overriding concern of ALM teams is the quality of their information, which must be exhaustive, accessible and easy to model.

Analysis

When analysing market risk, commercial banks traditionally focus on three types of exposure: interest rate risk, currency risk and liquidity risk. Later on, we will look at other risks (eg, credit risk) and how they interact (counterparties, embedded options). For domestic banks, only the first and third types have any direct consequences. Interest rate risk stems from the fact that interest rates paid to depositors and yields earned on loans can change at different speeds. Take the example of a bank that grants a long-term loan at a fixed rate of interest and refinances it with deposits (which involves collection costs) and certificates of deposit (at market rates). There is no certainty that the interest it pays will be lower than the interest it receives. This risk shows up in many ways: in accounting flows (net banking income), the market value of the bank's products, futures contracts (which depend on the horizon) and, naturally, in share and bond prices. Moreover, depending on the product, interest rate risk manifests itself in very different ways. This can be seen in the simple example of fixed-rate and variable-rate loans. With fixed-rate loans the bank can anticipate its future flows with certainty on condition that the payment dates coincide, which is not always the case. In practice, this is not always the case. As a result, the bank relies on cashflow matching methods, which we will examine in the next section (under the heading "Future rate expectations and the persistence effect"). With a variable-rate loan the flows are not always known in advance (unless the lender uses a highly accurate matching method). However, if we look at fair market values – ie, the value of the credit flows discounted at market rates – we observe that variable-rate loans vary less than fixed-rate ones. As regards income flows and their economic value, everything depends on the geometry of the flows and on market conditions. In the third section, "Capital allocation", we discuss and model the process of taking interest rate risk, sometimes called transformation risk.

Liquidity risk – the bane of every banker's life – is more difficult to identify and measure. In a nutshell, liquidity risk is the danger of not finding a lender in the market. In practice, the aim is to avoid paying too dearly for liquidity, with the ultimate risk being that the market will not lend money under any circumstances or at any price. What are the underlying mechanisms? The state (the benchmark issuer) borrows for a given period and at a certain rate. Private issuers such as banks borrow at a higher rate, which includes a margin. This is because they are prone to default – unlike the state, which can always raise taxes to pay off its debts. The margin, therefore, is the incremental cost to the issuing bank and reflects either investor perception of its creditworthiness or the degree to which investors are already saturated with credit risk. As an initial approximation, that margin is the annual probability of default multiplied by the collection rate (corresponding to what the issuer's default would cost the investor) plus a risk premium, which depends on the uncertainty of the information and the liquidity of the security. From a technical perspective, liquidity risk management is much less advanced and thus demands a considerable amount of common sense as well as theoretical know-how. There are three basic requirements: the issuer must make an accurate assessment of its cash requirements; it must be present in numerous markets, including foreign ones; and it must operate a financial public relations policy that minimises the "risk premium".

We need to paint a broader picture of the economic risks that affect banks, even though the process of measuring and controlling such risks is not always an integral part of ALM. Clearly, the oldest and most significant form of exposure is credit risk. Even though it differs from the risks described above, it is clearly related to interest rate risk. First, as regards variable-rate loans, a rise in interest rates can force a borrower to default. And because it eliminates expected income flows, default can create market risk and thus interfere with the management of interest rate risk. Other risks that warrant consideration include the behaviour of a bank's customers in the presence of so-called embedded options, the right to certain types of loan, the right to withdraw deposits, and the right of refund. In the case of non-bank activities, other assets such as equities or property give rise to risks. And we have not even addressed the need for insurance companies to control their liability risks, or operational risks of all sorts. Last but not least, the practice of analysing competitive pressures should become more widespread. After all, lending and borrowing margins are core considerations for any merchant whether he is distributing or collecting.

Control strategies
A bank can react to (or pre-empt) a given situation in many different ways. It generally falls to the finance department of a bank or financial institution to draw up and implement suitable strategies.

Some of those strategies are purely financial, such as the decision to rely on maturity transformation. Similarly, selecting the percentage of equities in an insurance company's portfolio involves the same type of decision. Other strategies give greater emphasis to the distribution side. For example, in the case of leasing transactions, if the "tax advantage market" is prepared to offer higher margins on a durable basis having taken into account the cost of funds, it may be worth the bank's while to develop this activity. We note that the decision involves operational factors that do not come within the bailiwick of the finance department, even though that department will assess the broad economic interest. A more proactive strategy may consist in designing new products. For example, when the yield curve is steeply sloped it offers the opportunity of selling capped variable-rate loans to a certain segment of the customer base.

Responsibility for ALM is generally devolved to two entities: on the one hand, a department tasked with analysing, preparing and implementing strategy; and on the other, a committee comprising representatives of general management and the various specialist arms, which is in charge of financial decision-making and, in certain cases, product development. Dealing rooms are entrusted with the task of putting these decisions into practice; depending on the institution, they either deal only for their own account or have a discrete investment banking operation. The entity in charge of operations can, in certain cases, tolerate a degree of latitude, in the same way that investors will accept a tracking error from a fund manager who manages their money by means of a benchmark. Taken to its extreme, ALM can be a profit centre with a delegation of market risk.

All this comes at a cost in terms of expertise and information technology, not to mention a slew of procedures that limit the flexibility of an institution's departments. But it is obviously vital in a competitive world where, for private companies, unearned income is a thing of the past. ALM teams, like the practitioners of any other applied discipline, must strike the right note of compromise in their analyses (given the cost of obtaining exhaustive information). Likewise, their recommendations must be easily understood throughout the company and have a reasonable chance of success.

BACKGROUND

So recent is the technique of ALM that the word "history" seems inappropriate. However, its roots can be found in the practice of planning and matching cashflows, commonly found in project financing and long employed by specialised financial institutions.

The approach was formalised by the British and, more particularly, the American financial world. In terms of risk modelling, it dates back to the early 1980s and the introduction of measures such as duration and cashflow volatility. In terms of corporate management, too, it can be found in the concept of decentralised banking, which is diametrically opposed to one-stop, universal banking. In France ALM first appeared in the late 1980s and, as we recalled in the introductory overview, was originally developed by medium-sized private banks before spreading to the rest of the economy. Interestingly, the advance of ALM was not prompted by regulatory constraints. Life insurance companies tried to adapt the concept, but they ran into several difficulties. The most significant hurdle is the accounting "maze" specific to the insurance industry. The second is the fact that insurance company assets and liabilities are diversified and non-fungible, meaning that they cannot naturally be represented as flows as they can in the banking world. The third problem – without wishing to be overly polemical – is the relevance of ALM in state-run companies. Recently, retirement funds, private pension funds and employee benefit organisations – often acting at the behest of consultants – have looked into ALM with a view to using it for strategic asset allocation (see *Quants* no. 12). The actuaries conferences organised by the AFIR show the extent to which the pension industry is becoming increasingly aware of the importance of ALM.

Much of the credit for spreading the word about ALM lies with the Association Française des Gestionnaires Actif Passif (AFGAP), founded in 1989 by CCF, the Compagnie Bancaire and a handful of other pioneers. Today, AFGAP has one 120 members, two-thirds of whom are drawn from the banking industry, one-fifth from insurance companies and the remainder from businesses and consultancies. AFGAP's contacts with its counterparts abroad show that France and the UK are probably among the most advanced nations in terms of ALM for banking applications. However, such is the banking culture in countries like the Netherlands and Switzerland that institutions in those countries have already adopted approaches based on asset liability management, albeit under a different name. Several of the topics covered in this chapter have already been discussed at AFGAP meetings.

METHODS

Strictly speaking, there is no economic or financial theory of asset liability management. Having subsumed a number of complementary methods, ALM can be likened to a box of tools used by practitioners of the art. For a more detailed description of these methods see Bessis (1995) and Dubernet (1996). We intend to examine the three main approaches: gap analysis, duration analysis and simulations.

The first method, gap analysis, is widely used. It consists in taking the present balance sheet situation and projecting two factors into the future: on the one hand, the capital flows received or paid out; and on the other, the interest received or paid. The diagram of the differences for the different maturities is called the treasury gap. Products are usually pooled into categories that are as homogeneous as possible, with ranges of dates that are as detailed as necessary. The analysis then seeks to update future financing or investment requirements. The gap can be narrowed by means of transactions in the "physical" market (issuance, investment). And although interest rate risk can be eliminated by the use of derivatives, liquidity risk may persist if gap analysis reveals a borrowing requirement.

Second, duration analysis aims to identify the impact of a change in market conditions – chiefly, the term structure of interest rates – on several items on the balance sheet or the profit and loss (P&L) account. Consequently, it forms an excellent fit with the first method. However, it is often considered to be "theoretical", either because it has not yet been properly adapted to actual requirements or because it constitutes an "economic" viewpoint that has no direct consequences in accounting terms. At least, not in the imme-diate future….

The third method, simulation, is rapidly becoming the only tool that allows the future to be introduced into factors that are either internal (eg, production) or market-related (interest rate movements). Initially deterministic and scenario-based, simulations rely increasingly on stochastic modelling of environment variables. This involves generating a large number of random samplings to quantify the probability distribution of a result or an accounting (or financial) quantity at a certain horizon. This approach is widely used by consultants as a basis for the asset allocation recommendations they make to pension funds or insurance companies. It allows the user to take into objective consideration the uncertainty related to equities, which, while offering higher yields than bonds, are never-theless more volatile.

CURRENT ISSUES

Aside from the operational management aspects, which are not addressed in this study, there are a several questions of principle which, in our view, tend to exercise users of ALM techniques.

First and foremost is the question of capital allocation, which will be discussed in the third section. Another key issue, covered in the fourth section, is the selection of the pro-portion of equities that insurance companies should hold in their investment portfolios. But there are many other questions: the correlation (or lack thereof) between accounting data and economic information, transfer pricing (ie, how to represent the cost of banks' raw material), the use of derivatives by insurance companies and pension funds, and the links with credit risk and with the regulatory approach to market risk. Then there are time-honoured issues such as the modelling of demand deposits, which will become increasingly important – at least for French banks – in the context of the euro.

Before tackling the two main issues, and at the risk of oversimplification, we thought it would be useful to examine the subject that is most traditionally associated with ALM, namely interest rate risk. We have approached it from a practical angle that makes it possible to identify the attractions and risks of maturity transformation. Moreover, the current slope of the yield curve (with a gap of more than 3% in early October 1998 between money market rates and 10-year zero coupon yields) makes this topic all the more relevant.

Riding the yield curve

Riding the yield curve is a strategy that enables an investor to earn a higher rate of return by buying longer-dated bills and selling them before they mature. The attraction of matu-rity transformation is that yield curves are generally upward-sloping: there is a yield "premium" for longer-dated investments. If interest rate conditions remain unchanged, or if they are sufficiently stable, an investor may find it more profitable to choose a maturity that exceeds his holding period. By riding the yield curve, investors get a higher starting rate and a capital gain when they sell their investment… on condition that interest rates have not risen in the meantime.

The aim of this part of our study is analyse the returns and risks associated with maturity transformation from the viewpoint of a corporate treasurer assessing his results on the basis of market value. We first compute the rate of return, the risks and the Sharpe ratio of this well-known strategy using the term structure of French interest rates at the beginning of October 1998. We then consider the effect of leverage and examine how the "persistence" of the yield curve affects the results. We conclude with a short, empirical test to examine the efficacy of the strategy in the past.

DEFINING AND ANALYSING THE STRATEGY

When an investor's maturity differs from his horizon, he is exposed to two types of risk: reinvestment and/or capital gain and loss.

Consider the example of a treasurer who has a certain sum at his disposal for six months. If he buys a three-month certificate of deposit (CD), he runs a reinvestment risk because he does not know the rate at which he will invest his funds three months hence. Conversely, if he buys a one-year CD, he does not know the price at which he can sell it when the six months are up and he is therefore exposed to the risk of capital gain/loss.

Riding the yield curve is a strategy that consists in buying paper with a maturity longer than the investment horizon. The aim is to realise an "extra" return vis-à-vis an investment with a maturity that coincides with his holding period. The investor must take into consideration not only the upward slope of the current yield curve for the maturities in question but also the expected level of interest rates when the position is closed out.

Example

The data used in this example are those for October 1, 1996. The treasurer buys a four-year bond with a par value of Ffr1,000. Interest is paid annually at a rate of 5%. Given the slope of the yield curve, the price paid for the bond is

$$\frac{50}{1.0382} + \frac{50}{(1.0415)^2} + \frac{50}{(1.0457)^3} + \frac{1050}{(1.05)^4} = 1001.82$$

Consider the situation one year later, when he receives his first Ffr50 coupon. We assume that there has been no change in the yield curve. Our treasurer then decides to liquidate his position, which he does at the following price:

$$\frac{50}{1.0382} + \frac{50}{(1.0415)^2} + \frac{1050}{(1.0457)^3} = 1012.52$$

He has therefore received 1012.52 + 50 = Ffr1062.52. Reasoning in terms of the return over one year, it is as though he invested Ffr1001.82 for a year at a rate equivalent to $(1062.52 - 1001.82)/1001.82 = 6.06\%$. Over the same period a one-year investment would have returned just 3.82%: our treasurer has made a profit out of his ride.

The calculation is based on the assumption that future interest rates are unchanged. If rates had risen, the investment would have returned less than 6.06% and could even have fallen below the one-year rate. In this case, a riding strategy would have resulted in a loss.

Reciprocally, the steeper the curve's upward slope at the outset, the lower the interest rates when the position is liquidated (the horizon) and the higher the return to the strategy.

Computing the return to the strategy

Generally speaking, we consider an investor who has a certain sum for a period H. He could invest it immediately at the spot rate, R_H, over this period. However, he makes forecasts concerning $R(H, M)$, the rate of maturity M – H that will prevail at date H. He thus anticipates that the rate will be R_a (where the subscript a indicates "anticipated"), which is low.

So he decides to invest in an instrument with maturity M, greater than H. At H, his expectation proves to be correct so he closes out his position, selling his security for the residual period at the price prevailing in the market at H. Assuming actuarial rates (see also Figure 1), the return on this transaction over the period H, denoted R_g (where g indicates "gain"), verifies

$$\left(1 + R_g\right)^H \times \left(1 + R_a\right)^{M-H} = \left(1 + R_M\right)^M \tag{1}$$

From this, we work out the explicit formula that gives us the payoff:

$$R_g = \left(1 + R_a\right) \times \left[\frac{1 + R_M}{1 + R_a}\right]^{\frac{M}{H}} - 1 \tag{2}$$

Observing that the returns are small relative to (1), we can write a linear formula that approximates R_g:

$$R_g = R_M + \left(R_M - R_a\right)\frac{M - H}{H} \tag{3}$$

This is valid for money market rates and actuarial rates.

The future yield curve and the ride strategy

To make formula (3) more meaningful, we can draw the yield curve that would result in a preset return curve at the end of the year. Using (3), we express the future rate as a function of the return:

$$R_a = R_M + \left(R_M - R_g\right)\frac{H}{M - H} \tag{4}$$

Equation (4) allows us to establish a link between the future curve and the return to the strategy. It is illustrated in the following three examples, which illustrate how the choice of strategy is implicitly linked to a precise expectation of future rates.

Reproducing the yield at maturity (Figure 2) We will now try to determine what the shape of the curve must be in one year's time for the return (for different maturities, M) to coincide with the initial yield on an instrument with maturity M. As equation (4) shows, the configuration in question is the initial curve, with a one-year shift to the left along the x-axis. We want $R_g = R_M$, which gives us $R_a = R_M$. This is equivalent to a shift of a period H.

Identical return (Figure 3) In order for the return to the riding strategy to be the same for all maturities, what shape must the yield curve be one year later? This corresponds to the situation where an investor is indifferent between the "horizon equals maturity" strategy and riding the curve. Thus, the future yield curve is the forward curve defined by equation (4) with $R_g = R_H$.

Naive forecast of yield curves (Figure 4) We will now examine what the return curve looks like if the one-year curve remains unchanged. This scenario results in a return curve that sits above the initial yield curve. We obtain it by shifting the initial curve to the left and adding a term that is proportional to the difference $R_M - R_H$.

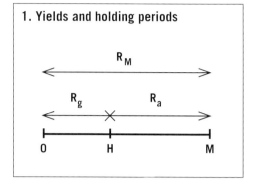

1. Yields and holding periods

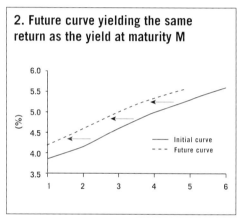

2. Future curve yielding the same return as the yield at maturity M

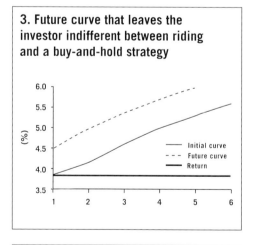

3. Future curve that leaves the investor indifferent between riding and a buy-and-hold strategy

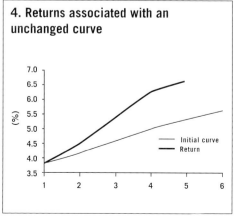

4. Returns associated with an unchanged curve

Risk measurement

The risk of riding the curve is that the investor will get a lower return than he would from a buy-and-hold strategy. Our risk quantification method is based on the value, R_a^*, of the future rate at date H that ensures a zero payoff (meaning an incremental return relative to a buy-and-hold investment) from the riding technique. With $R_g = R_H$ in (3), we have

$$R_a^* = R_M + \left(R_M - R_H\right) \frac{H}{M - H} \tag{5}$$

The threshold future rate R_a^* (for example) corresponds to the initial value of the forward rate between H and M. Ex post, we find that the more R_a^* exceeds R_a, the higher the real rate of return on the transaction, and vice versa.

We have two more strategy evaluation tools at our disposal. The first is a trading performance index known as the Sharpe ratio, which takes the form of a risk/return ratio. The return to the strategy is the average excess return over the riskless rate of interest. Risk is measured by the variability or standard deviation, σ_g, of the strategy's return. The higher the ratio, the better the performance. The Sharpe ratio is defined as follows:

$$SR = \frac{E\left(R_g\right) - R_H}{\sigma_g} \tag{6}$$

The second indicator is called the margin of safety (Dyl and Joehnk, 1981), which is a relative deviation:

$$MS = \frac{R_a^* - R_a}{R_a} \tag{7}$$

The margin of safety measures the fluctuation of the future rate that would eliminate the profit derived from the strategy.

Risk associated with a simple curve

To introduce our first interest rate risk model, we assume that the initial yield curve is an ascending straight line with slope p per year. With R_0 as the overnight rate, the yield on maturity, m, is given by

$$R_m = R_0 + p \times m \tag{8}$$

On the future curve, we make the following assumption regarding the yields on the maturity, M − H:

$$R_a = R_{M-H} + \varepsilon \tag{9}$$

where ε is a random variable with zero expectation and standard deviation σ. In other words, we suppose that the current curve is the best possible forecast of the future curve and that the future curve is subject to translation risk.

Thus, the average return is written

$$\bar{R}_g = R_0 + p \times (2M - H) \tag{10}$$

The future rate that ensures a zero payoff is

$$R_a^* = R_0 + p \times (2M + H) \tag{11}$$

The Sharpe ratio is

$$RS = \frac{2pH}{\sigma} \tag{12}$$

Table 1. Ex-ante characteristics of the riding strategy for different maturities at October 1, 1996		
Maturity, M (years)	Yield at M, R_M (%)	Return on ride, $\bar{R}_g$ (%)
2	4.2	4.5
3	4.6	5.4
4	5.0	6.2
5	5.3	6.7

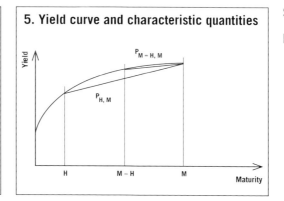

5. Yield curve and characteristic quantities

The margin of safety is

$$MS = \frac{2pH}{R_0 + p \times (M-H)} \tag{13}$$

As the above formulae show, the steeper the curve (while remaining positive), the more compelling the strategy. This is because the return, the margin of safety and the Sharpe ratio all increase as the curve steepens.

Also, when the yield curve is upward-sloping the average return can be increased by extending the maturity, M, of the investment, while the Sharpe ratio remains unchanged. However, we must not jump to hasty conclusions as a result of this observation, which depends heavily on our modelling of the curve and its attendant risks. If the riding strategy is to be successfully fine tuned, those risks must be carefully analysed.

Risk associated with a real curve

The yield curve is now described by an equation such as $R_m = f(m)$ (Figure 5). Also, we will assume a naive expectation, as defined by equation (9).

Denoting by $p_{a,b}$ the slope of the chord joining the points of the curve for maturities a and b, the mean return is

$$\bar{R}_g = f(M) + p_{M-H,M} \times (M-H) \tag{14}$$

In this case, the Sharpe ratio is written

$$RS = \frac{H}{\sigma} \times \left(P_{M-H,M} + P_{H,M}\right) \tag{15}$$

We applied the above calculations to the curve at October 1, 1996, once again under the naive expectation assumption. Table 1 shows the ex-ante results of the strategy. The horizon, H, is one year and the maturity, M, of the investment varies.

LEVERAGE

Thus far, we have focused solely on the example of an investor with no liability constraints. His choices are based on the maturity of the securities that form his asset base and on the fact that he must liquidate the position at a given date. We can apply the same approach to a more realistic situation: an investor with something more than shareholders' equity on the liabilities side of his balance sheet. We will model those liabilities (excluding equity) by means of a loan with a maturity H, which is our investor's horizon. The initial amount, A, of the assets can be decomposed thus:

$$A = \underset{\text{Equity}}{\alpha A} + \underset{\text{Loan}}{(1-\alpha)A} \tag{16}$$

Once again, R_g is the return on the riding strategy associated with a horizon H and an investment with an initial maturity M. At H, the date on which the positions are closed out, we have

$$\text{Assets} = A \times (1 + R_g)^H \qquad (17)$$

$$\text{Liabilities} = (1 - \alpha) \times A \times (1 + R_H)^H \qquad (18)$$

If R'_g is the return to the lending and borrowing transaction (16), we can write

$$(1 + R_g)^H A - (1 - \alpha)(1 + R_H)^H A = \alpha(1 + R'_g)^H A \qquad (19)$$

which, after linearisation, gives us

$$R'_g = R_g + \underbrace{\frac{1 - \alpha}{\alpha}}_{\text{leverage}}(R_g - R_H) \qquad (20)$$

Equation (20) shows that if the rate of return, R_g, is greater than R_H (the liability rate), the return is greater than that earned by investing the equity alone. The supplemental terms come from the loan. This produces *leverage*. Naturally, a higher rate of return goes hand in hand with greater risk. Not only that, but the Sharpe ratio of this type of transaction is identical to a non-leveraged transaction.

Returning to the first example in this section (the four-year bond), we will take a proportion of shareholders' equity such that $\alpha = 10\%$. The excess return obtained through leverage is

$$(1 - 0.1) \times (6.06\% - 3.82\%) / 0.1 = 20.16\%$$

– in other words, three times greater than the non-leveraged return (6.06%). Remember, however, that we made this calculation within the framework of a naive forecast. Furthermore, the volatility of this result is ten times greater than it would be without leverage.

FUTURE RATE EXPECTATIONS AND THE PERSISTENCE EFFECT

As we have seen, the choice of strategy is directly related to expectations of future rates. The most common expectations call for no change in the yield curve or, alternatively, a future curve identical to the current forward curve. In the latter case, the transformation is based on equation (4) with $R_g = R_H$. When the initial curve is upward-sloping, the forward yield curve is above the initial curve. Conversely, when the curve is inverted forward rates are lower than initial rates.

The *persistence factor* quantifies the curve's tendency to keep its initial shape. A persistence factor of 1 indicates an expectation of an unchanged future curve, whereas a factor of 0 indicates that we are expecting the forward curve.

Generally speaking, we assume that the future yield curve can be characterised by a persistence factor, k, as per the equation

$$\text{Future rate} = k \times \text{Initial rate} + (1 - k) \times \text{Forward rate} \qquad (21)$$

When the persistence factor varies from 0 to 1, it generates a continuous spectrum of curves within an envelope bounded by the initial curve and the forward curve (the persistence factor can also be negative or greater than one).

We will now return to the material covered earlier. When an investor's expectations can be summarised by a persistence factor, k, the expected return, $R_g(k)$, is easy to compute: it is equal to the average of the returns on the two preceding curves weighted by the coefficients k and $k - 1$. Noting that $R_g(0) = R_H$, we have

Table 2. Actual results of the strategy with the filter MS > 0%

Horizon, H, is three months. Results, for three-month holding periods, have been annualised

Maturity (years)	1988–92 Frequency, MS > 0 (%)	1988–92 Success rate (%)	1988–92 Excess return (%)	1988–92 Sharpe ratio	1992–96 Frequency, MS > 0 (%)	1992–96 Success rate (%)	1992–96 Excess return (%)	1992–96 Sharpe ratio
M = 1	8.2	44.5	−0.7	−0.39	77.5	53.3	0.5	+0.25
M = 2	9.4	53.3	−0.4	−0.25	81.4	56.8	1.3	+0.28
M = 3	10.8	68.6	0.6	+0.33	78.8	58.8	2.0	+0.27
M = 5	12.8	65.7	2.8	+0.93	82.3	64.4	3.4	+0.26
M = 10	17.7	51.8	4.7	+1.23	85.3	67.5	7.0	+0.44

Table 3. Effect of the filter on the success rate

Horizon, H, is one month; maturity, M, is one year

Margin of safety	Frequency of observation (%)	Success rate (%)	Average return over the period (%)	Standard deviation
MS > 0%	77.3	71.5	3.2	5.6
MS > 5%	32.4	72.6	3.3	3.1
MS > 10%	3.1	66.7	0.7	6.4

6. Returns to the riding strategy as a function of maturity with different persistence factors

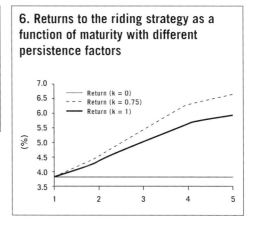

$$R_g(k) = k \times R_g(1) + (1 - k) \times R_H \qquad (22)$$

where $R_g(1)$ corresponds to the return earned under a naive-expectation scenario. Figure 6 shows the returns on riding strategies for three persistence factors 0, 0.75 and 1.

EMPIRICAL TEST

To test the efficacy of the riding strategy, we carried out an empirical study over two discrete periods: 1988–92 and 1992–96. We smoothed the yield curves with the Vasicek–Fong method and used weekly data. We then computed the return to the strategy using actual rather than expected rates. Thus, the study is based on ex-post returns.

An inequality condition on the margin of safety acts as a sort of filter through which we examined the success rate of the riding strategy (ie, the number of times that the excess return is positive). Table 2 shows the statistics for each period. The first column gives the frequency, or number of times that the margin of safety was positive. Under this condition we then counted the success rate, or the number of times the strategy really paid off. The table also shows the average returns and the Sharpe ratios, once again under the condition MS > 0%. Table 3 shows how the choice of filter influences the strategy's success rate (in terms of both frequency and average return).

The period 1988–92 was not ideal for riding: it is characterised by high but mainly flat yield curves. Better results were obtained in the second period, 1992–96, chiefly towards the end of 1995 and during 1996. Here, the curves are generally steeply sloped, a factor that is reflected in the frequency of the event MS > 0%.

OBSERVATIONS AND CONCLUSIONS

The strategy we have just described is both well-known and time-served – in the early 1990s, for example, it enabled US banks to return to profitability. However, although efficient, it nevertheless involves an element of risk. Adopting an accounting method based on rediscount rates rather than market values naturally modifies the perception of risk and return. This study goes beyond the framework that we initially adopted. However, we are still dealing with the same phenomenon, construed in two different ways. Naturally, the smoothing that results from the accounting method helps to attenuate the short-term variability of the results. For periods that are much longer than the smoothed period we can expect comparable volatilities.

In short, the return obtained through maturity transformation depends on the slope and persistence of the yield curve. Whereas the slope can be observed, persistence is more random. At current levels the Sharpe ratios raise the question of the degree of maturity transformation that a bank can introduce into its management policies. This depends on other opportunities that may arise and on the bank's capital allocation strategy, which we discuss in the next section.

Capital allocation

Allocating factors of production is a key concern for any company. Moreover, to protect the currency and the financial market, which are public goods, the regulatory authorities in charge of banks and insurance companies have imposed capital adequacy requirements. For many years the French financial industry (banks and insurance companies alike) was under the wing of the state and was therefore less concerned with return on equity than other sectors of the economy more exposed to foreign competition. But with privatisation, gradual deregulation and the prospect of a unified market underpinned by a single currency, France's bankers and insurers have become acutely aware of the need for capital allocation strategies and measures of return on equity.

We intend to look at the principle of capital allocation, by which we mean the process whereby a bank apportions its equity among different business units. Such an approach also makes it possible to gauge the level of profitability that each unit must achieve to ensure the optimum business structure. We will discuss the underlying principles and compute, on the basis of simple cases, the resulting allocations. This will be done for didactic purposes, using a loan portfolio, and also to assess the advisability for a commercial bank of engaging in maturity transformation. We conclude by discussing the difficulties and the limits of this method.

OPTIMISING A BUSINESS PORTFOLIO

The basic idea is simple: commercial banks, international banks and financial holding companies have to manage portfolios of business activities. Since managers seek to satisfy the demands of private shareholders, it is only natural that they should use classic portfolio optimisation methods. For example, the aim of a particular allocation structure will be to maximise profit for a given level of risk. Our first task is to define the requisite level of profitability for each line of business.

The profitability of an activity is the net income from activity I divided by the capital, C, allocated to it over a given period of time (one quarter, one year or more):

$$R = \frac{I}{C} \tag{23}$$

Net income is equal to total income minus capital losses and expenditure. Expenditures include: interest expense, overheads and outlays on plant and equipment (property, IT systems, etc). In the case of a loan, the rate of return is equivalent to the net interest rate minus current expenditure due to the loan, minus capital expenditure, minus the default rate for the life of the loan.

Now, assuming the presence of competition and random economic factors, we will assume that the rates of return of the different lines of business are random variables. We will assume, for example, that they are Gaussian multivariate. Consequently, they are wholly determined by their mean and their variance–covariance matrices. Under these circumstances the average return on a loan will be

$$\frac{\text{(Average interest rate – Current and Capital expenditure – Average default rate)}}{\text{Capital requirement}}$$

What are the risks? Under reasonable assumptions, randomness can stem only from changes in interest rates and the default rate. The covariance between two lines of business is simply a measure of the random factors common to both.

For example, in the case of a loan to two different borrowers, we will consider the covariances of the interest rates and of the default rate. If there is no interest rate risk and if the margin is stable (ie, no variation due to competition on the margin), the only relevant factor will be the covariance between the default rates of the two borrowers. Here, that covariance is equal to the standard deviations of the borrowers' default rates multiplied by their default correlation coefficients.

Consider a bank with N lines of business. We denote by: r_i the average profitability of business i (i = 1, ... , N); by $\sigma_{i,j}$ the covariance of businesses i and j ($\sigma_{ii} = \sigma_i^2$ is the variance of business i); and by α_i the proportion of total capital allocated to business i.

Under these circumstances, the optimal allocation in the case of risk-averse management is obtained by solving the maximisation of the utility

$$\max \sum \alpha_i \bar{r}_i - \frac{a}{2} \sum \alpha_i \alpha_j \sigma_{i,j}$$

$$\sum \alpha_i = 1 \quad \text{and} \quad \alpha_i \geq 0 \tag{24}$$

where a is the coefficient of the manager's aversion to risk. If we do not know this risk aversion but we do know the maximum level of risk, then a represents the coefficient of the constraint (maximal risk) in the Lagrangian.

This optimal allocation principle corresponds to Markowitz's theory, discussed in *Quants* no. 2. In practice, the indicator we are seeking to optimise is the expected return on a portfolio of businesses less a cost corresponding to the uncertainty of the return. That cost stems from two factors – one objective (the variability of the results), the other subjective and specific to the shareholder, measuring his or her fear of uncertainty.

ONE BANK, TWO LINES OF BUSINESS
We will illustrate this approach using a simplified example of a bank with two lending activities. We assume that the two business units in question lend to large companies, considered to be reliable, and to smaller firms, which are more risk-prone. The loans made to large companies carry a margin of 80 basis points (net of default), reflecting a higher level of safety than loans to small companies, which have a margin of 120 bp. Conversely, the uncertainty on the net margin is higher for smaller companies – we have assumed a normal distribution (implying a well-diversified portfolio) with a standard deviation of 1.6% – whereas the standard deviation for the large companies is assumed to be two times smaller (0.8%). We have also assumed that the two uncertainties are decorrelated. From the standpoint of the present Cooke ratio, there is no difference between the two types of loan, which both require a capital adequacy ratio of 8%.

When establishing the ratio of margins to equity, we deduce from these assumptions that the returns to the two lines of business are characterised by

$$r_1 = 10\%, \qquad \sigma_1 = 10\%$$
$$r_2 = 15\%, \qquad \sigma_2 = 20\%$$
$$\rho = 0$$

The solution to the problem of maximisation, presented in (23), is expressed by a proportion, α, invested in large-company loans such that

$$\alpha = \frac{r_1 - r_2 + a\left(\sigma_2^2 - \rho\sigma_1\sigma_2\right)}{a\left(\sigma_1^2 + \sigma_2^2 - 2\rho\sigma_1\sigma_2\right)} \tag{25}$$

or 0 (respectively 1) if the above value is negative (greater than 1). When the calculations are complete we find that

$$\alpha = 0.8 - \frac{1}{a} \tag{26}$$

Thus, for a low level of risk aversion (ie, 2) 30% of the capital is invested in loans to large companies and 70% in loans to small ones. If risk aversion is high (we will assume it to be infinite), 80% is invested in the first line of business. For the two businesses, respectively, the return on capital invested is 13.5% and 11% and the volatility of the results is 14.3% and 8.9%. In the second case diversification (the portfolio effect) made it possible to achieve an activity with an overall level of profit higher than that earned from the first business alone and with a lower level of risk. To that end, 20% of the portfolio consisted of loans to small companies.

APPLICATIONS: SHOULD COMMERCIAL BANKS PRACTISE TRANSFORMATION?
The economic principle of capital allocation will now be applied to an issue of concern to retail and investment banks. We will look at the attraction of maturity transformation for a bank that has earned a certain margin on its loan. To do this, we will analyse the relative appeal of interest rate risk and credit risk.

Interest rate risk is often considered to be superfluous in a commercial bank's conventional lending business. Using the results obtained in the second section, we will try to optimise a commercial bank's exposure to interest rate risk. We have assumed that the capital of our bank exceeds the mandatory level imposed by the Cooke ratio in view of the loans it has extended. The margins the bank earns on its credit business are exposed to default risk, modelled in the same way as in the example given immediately above. We are interested in the refinancing aspect: should the bank borrow in the market – matching the maturities of its loans with those of its borrowings – or should it transform the maturities? And if so, in what proportions?

This yield curve model has been deliberately simplified. We assume that the curve remains positive with slope d/S_m (Figure 7) and that the short-term rate is random, normally distributed with mean i (its initial value) and standard deviation σ_i/S_m. S_m is merely a point of reference on the curve. A difference (gap) in the duration of the assets and liabilities produces a gain related to the slope of the curve. However, it also carries an interest rate risk that we can identify by means of the current values of the asset and liability streams. We are therefore dealing with an economic approach to maturity transformation, not an accounting approach.

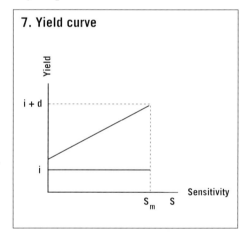

7. Yield curve

Denoting the nominal amount of the assets as A, the nominal amount of the liabilities as B, shareholders' equity as $C = A/B$ and their actuarial sensitivities as S_A, S_B and S_C, we have

$$S_c = \frac{S_A A - S_B B}{A - B} \qquad (27)$$

The return on shareholders' capital C is the difference between the income stream from the assets and the costs; that is to say, in terms of income:

$$A\left(i + \frac{dS_A}{S_m} + m\right) - AS_A\Delta i - A\Delta m \qquad (28)$$

where m is the margin, Δi the (random) variation of short rates and Δm the (random) variation of the margin, which is assumed to have zero mean and standard deviation σ_m.

And, in terms of cost:

$$B\left(i + \frac{dS_B}{S_m}\right) - BS_B\Delta i + E \qquad (29)$$

where E is the overhead, which for expositional ease we will not take into account. Hence, the return is computed as

$$r = i + \frac{dS_c}{S_m} + \left(\frac{m\Lambda}{C} - S_c\Delta i - \frac{A}{C}\Delta m\right) \qquad (30)$$

The terms can be easily interpreted. The margin on the loan is enhanced by the leveraged impact A/C (in terms of return and risk) and the payoff from the transformation is proportional to S_c/S_m with an interest rate risk proportional to S_c. Consequently, the sensitivities to interest rate risk and credit risk are A/C and S_c. We assume them to be decorrelated.

On average

$$\bar{r} = i + \frac{dS_c}{S_m} + \frac{mA}{C} \qquad (31)$$

and the volatility, σ, of the results is such that

$$\sigma^2 = \left(\frac{A}{C}\right)^2 \sigma_m^2 + \left(\frac{S}{S_m}\right)^2 \sigma_i^2 \qquad (32)$$

Lastly, we assume that there are regulatory constraints affecting credit risk and "structural" interest rate risk (not currently the case). Hence

$$C = bA + \frac{tS_a}{S_m} \qquad (33)$$

The problem remains the maximisation of $\bar{r} - 0.5a\sigma^2$. The solution can be found in Boulier (1994). When t is zero (no capital for the structural risk) the optimal sensitivity of the equity is

$$S_c^* = \frac{S_m d}{a\sigma_i^2} \qquad (34)$$

That sensitivity corresponds to the situation where the capital is invested entirely in a portfolio with sensitivity S_c^*. Only when the capital is "rationed" will a comparison between risks and returns come into play.

Let us look at some numerical values:

$$d = 1\%, \quad \sigma_d = 7\%, \quad S_m = 7$$

corresponding to an annualised standard deviation of 1% for i,

$$m = 1\%, \quad \sigma_m = 0.5\%$$

and

$$b = 8\%, \quad t = 8\%$$

the first corresponding to Cooke risks with a 100% weighting, the second corresponding broadly to twice the equity requirement calculated as a market risk according to Bank for International Settlements standards.

Table 4 provides optimal values for the sensitivity of the shareholders' equity, S_c, as a function of the level of equity, C, expressed as a percentage of assets (rows) and aversion to risk, a (columns). As can be seen, it is mainly a that influences exposure to interest rate risk. If a is low, the

Table 4. Optimal sensitivity of equity as a function of shareholders' equity, C, and risk aversion, a

a	8	8.5	C 9	10	12
0.5	6.3	6.4	6.5	6.6	6.8
1.0	3.2	3.2	3.3	3.3	3.4
2.5	1.31	1.32	1.33	1.34	1.37
5.0	0.68	0.68	0.68	0.69	0.69

Table 5. Optimal sensitivity of equity as a function of σ_m and a

a	σ_m (%)				
	0.1	0.2	0.5	1	2
1	6.2	6.2	6.5	6.5	7.1
10	0.63	0.63	0.68	0.85	1.5

sensitivity to interest rates is strong. Conversely, if a is high, interest rate risk is negligible. Note, however, that $S_C = 6.3$ corresponds to a very small difference $S_B - S_A = 0.13$ for $S_A =$ five years (ie, an asset with a maturity of around 12 years for loans with constant monthly repayments).

The substitution effect between interest rate risk and credit risk is clearly in evidence in Table 5, where we have varied the parameter σ_m, the uncertainty of the credit margin. For a strong aversion (a = 5), the exposure S_C increases significantly with σ_m. We would have obtained the same result (from a qualitative perspective) if m had decreased or if d had increased. In periods when the yield curve is steeply sloped and visibility on interest rates is good, the bank is encouraged to increase its reliance on maturity transformation.

IMPLEMENTATION AND CRITICISMS

The capital allocation process described above involves several types of difficulty. We will not go into detail regarding implementation *sensu stricto*; instead, we will try to identify the most important points and then take a more critical look at the process.

Difficulties of implementation

The economic approach we adopted was, from the beginning, outside the field of accountancy. The task of reconciling the two fields can prove difficult for several reasons. First, the perception of interest rates varies according to whether assets are marked to market. Second, it seems necessary to allocate default provisions for each entity. In France, this is generally done ex post, which reduces the visibility of economic results. Lastly (although this is not particular to the problem we are describing), we must consider the accounting mechanisms that are used to amortise goodwill on new acquisitions as well as any exceptional profit (or loss) generated when a business is discontinued. This is important inasmuch as all these items are relevant to an analysis of return on assets.

The second type of difficulty stems from information and communication. Allocation is based on the outlook for profitability and risk. Practitioners of the Markowitz optimisation technique know that results are sensitive to inputs. This constitutes an important issue, to which operational management must make as objective a contribution as possible. This is almost certainly easier in a mature line of business, where margins are stable. However, in today's highly competitive environment such situations are infrequent. Much skill is required to get across the underlying logic and to acquire and process relevant information (fuzzy calculus, discussed in *Quants* no. 23, can be useful for this). However, the figures are unlikely to be extremely precise. True, frequent monitoring and analysis of the (economic) results of the businesses can help. But, like all information relating to the past, it is not enough because the allocation is naturally made ex ante and not ex post.

The third type of difficulty stems from employee incentive and compensation schemes. This is best exemplified by the bonuses paid to trading-room staff. These are clearly useful, but they can lead to a markedly different application of the bank's choice. The same problems doubtless apply to compensation based on credits "sold". First, the cost of such compensation is not always taken into account: if the managers of a subsidiary receive stock options, for example, how does the parent company calculate this cost? Such sums can in some cases be identified – witness the case of Microsoft, which has declared an amount corresponding to nearly 10% of its market capitalisation!

Criticisms

A number of criticisms can be levelled at this approach. From an economic viewpoint, at least three objections are germane.

First, is there any point in considering that the bank is risk-averse and must operate a risk management policy that is consistent with its objectives? As theory shows, maximising shareholder value involves maximising the risks taken by the company. In contrast, the regulatory or market authorities restrict or penalise risk-taking to some extent. Answering that criticism does not come within the ambit of this study. It is nevertheless a fact that a growing number of bank chairmen are trying to limit the volatility of earnings.

Another critical question involves the investment horizon. Should a bank reject a new line of business on the grounds that it will take three years to reach maturity? On what joint horizon can shareholders' equity be compared? The question also arises when determining the risk-aversion coefficient, the importance of which was seen earlier in this section.

Finally, there are bound to be quasi-monopolistic situations in which the approach would no longer be appropriate because profitability can increase until such time as a competitor arrives.

Under these circumstances the nature of the risk differs enormously. The same remark applies in the case of cartelisation. When determining strategy in such situations, it is necessary to consider the way in which the other party reacts to the bank's decision. This, too, lies outside the scope of our study.

PERTINENT FINDINGS

With competitive pressures encouraging practitioners to take risks, which are the sole source of performance, it is necessary to find a discipline to govern risk-taking. We have just presented a rational method for achieving that objective, a method that is well known to investors because it forms the underpinnings of business portfolio optimisation.

However, adapting it to the context of capital allocation raises a number of difficulties – accounting practices, acquisition of information on choices, criteria, etc – which must be dealt with by management.

The most pertinent findings of our simplified examples are threefold: that diversification (in a known business area) is beneficial, that the activity mix changes depending on the market (eg, margin, credit risk, yield curve) and that the skill of the workforce (ability to profit from market anomalies, to screen borrowers, etc) must be taken into account. While this may seem obvious, an approach such as ours makes it possible to pin numbers on to what would otherwise be an intuitive understanding.

Sensitivity of a life insurer's earnings to asset allocation

Although the above considerations may help to answer questions of strategy, it must not be forgotten that, on a day-to-day basis, asset liability management depends heavily on the regulatory framework and accounting mechanisms. To assess the impact of these two factors, we will analyse the balance sheet and P&L account of a life insurance company to determine how the percentage of equities in the asset portfolio can affect profitability in the short and long term. To do so, we must take into account the regulatory and accounting constraints that affect the choice of asset allocation. However, our aim is not to model French insurance accounting mechanisms as a whole but only those which impact on the asset allocation strategy. In this section we present initial results obtained from the simulation tool used by the Financial Engineering Department of CCF Gestion.

For French savers, the attraction of life insurance products – tax-advantaged, flexible and profitable – remained undimmed for many years. In 1994 they generated total premium income of Ffr331 billion. Today, with the decline in bond yields, returns on life-insurance media are less attractive and insurance companies are looking for ways to make up for the loss of yield. They are motivated by the fact that a decline in returns on life insurance products will, in the medium to long term, result in an outflow of funds. A number of industry professionals are now taking a cautious interest in the equity market. In France, equities have traditionally earned much higher returns than fixed-income instruments (Figure 8). Moreover,

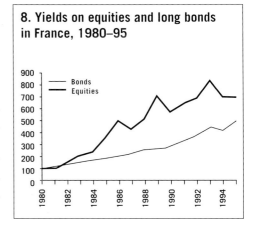

8. Yields on equities and long bonds in France, 1980–95

current economic conditions suggest that the yield gap is likely to widen still further in the coming years.

After a brief look at insurance companies' current portfolios, we will examine the accounting constraints that govern investment choices. We will also consider the security mechanisms required by the regulatory authorities to smooth the profits distributed to both policyholders and insurers. In the last part of the section we present the results of our simulations.

LIFE INSURERS' PORTFOLIOS: THE CURRENT SITUATION IN FRANCE
Structure of insurance company investments
Looking at the insurance industry (life and non-life) in France, we observe that bond holdings have risen sharply since 1980 and now account for between 50% and 60% of total investments. Conversely, property investments have been on a relative downtrend, dropping from 20% to 10% between 1980 and 1993. During the same period the proportion of equities has hovered at around 20%.

Regarding the asset allocation of life insurers alone, bond holdings account for the larger proportion (64% in 1993). Non-life insurance, in contrast, has an equivalent proportion of equities (37%) and bonds (38%), whereas property accounts for just 14% of the portfolio.

This segmentation can be fine-tuned still further according to the age of the insurance company. Older companies have substantial reserves (a profit participation reserve and a special depreciation reserve, the objectives of which are discussed later), which give them greater latitude to invest in high-yield media such as equities without compromising returns to policyholders. Conversely, younger companies tend to have a larger proportion of fixed-income instruments because they have to ensure sustainable returns throughout the life of their policies.

A technical and legal conception of the insurance business still prevails, even today, and this tends to relegate investment activities to second place. Moreover, the state intervenes in different ways, influencing insurers' investment policies with a view to ensuring guaranteed financing. Recently, however, the context has changed. And, with the development of cross-border service provision, insurers now have to add a financial dimension to their strategies to maintain competitiveness.

Within the European Union regulations have changed radically in the past few years. Our aim is not to examine the content of the new framework; merely to stress that, owing to regulatory constraints, insurers now have greater freedom.

Causes of overweighting of fixed-income investments
There are several reasons for the overweighting of fixed-income products. The main ones are outlined below.

Treasury management Assets and liabilities are easier to match when the portfolio is invested in bonds. Also, there has been a strong demand in recent years for guaranteed-return contracts. These are designed around fixed-rate bonds with the same maturity as the contracts themselves because the future cashflows correspond to defined amounts.

Flexibility Policyholders can terminate their contracts and pocket the proceeds at any time, a situation that is easier to manage through fixed-income investments. For this reason, life insurers limit their investments in volatile instruments.

Accounting mechanisms The absence of provisions for unrealised capital losses on bonds, negotiable debt instruments, loans and time deposits (an accounting mechanism that we will describe later on) encourages insurers to opt for this type of investment. This is particularly true for younger companies, which have almost no unrealised capital gains.

Consequences of overweighting

The long-term yields of insurers who invest heavily in the bond markets could decline because equities outperform fixed-income investments in the long run. Moreover, with the recent downtrend in interest rates, bond yields will become less and less attractive.

For these reasons, insurance companies must identify precisely the proportion of equities that they can hold (while respecting the interests of their shareholders and insureds) in view of the prevailing regulatory and accounting regulations.

ACCOUNTING MECHANISMS FOR APPROPRIATION OF EARNINGS

We will attempt to describe simply the regulatory and accounting framework within which French life insurers conduct their financial management. The accounting and underwriting rules are restrictive to the point that they constitute the main factor influencing asset allocation. For example, current accounting practices require that insurance companies set aside a provision for unrealised losses on equities, but there is no equivalent requirement for bonds. This rule clearly favours fixed-income investments. Consequently, it is vital for fund managers working on behalf of insurance companies to be aware of the relevant accounting mechanisms if they are to make the appropriate asset allocation.

Insurers' regulatory commitments to policyholders

Life insurance contracts fall into two broad categories: those denominated in francs, which offer guaranteed returns; and those that are unit-linked, which in general do not contain a guaranteed revaluation clause. In this study we will concentrate solely on the first type of contract, which have attracted higher levels of outstandings.

Life insurance contracts in French francs provide a benefit (capital or annuity) with a fixed term in return for a premium. This benefit is computed by means of a technical interest rate. Owing to the dual impact of regulatory pressures and intense competition, companies seek to offer policyholders more than just the guaranteed minimum yield (which, moreover, is capped by the regulations currently in force). This extra return is not simply a plus for policyholders; it is also a key factor in growing the business: policyholders are the first to benefit from higher yields, which will be used to revalue their investment.

An insurer's liabilities are primarily composed of mathematical reserves (MR), which represent the contracts that bind the company to its policyholders. Every year these contracts are revalued on the basis of the minimum guaranteed rate, at least.

In terms of commitments, the insurer offers its policyholders a minimum return composed of two elements: a minimum guaranteed rate and a share of the company's profits. The minimum rate is capped by law to protect both sides from unrealistic promises. For contacts in excess of eight years, the rate cannot exceed a predetermined level (in 1995, this was 3.5% or 60% of the yield on government paper, or TME). Profit sharing is mandatory: an insurance company is required to pay out to policyholders at least 85% of the financial income generated during the year (coupons, dividend and capital gains). This profit share (PS) is immediately credited to policyholders and is then transferred to mathematical reserves. It can also be added to reserves by adding to the profit participation reserve (PPR).

The regulations also impose solvency requirements to ensure that the insurer adopts a responsible approach to management. The aim of the solvency margin is to require insurance companies to hold a minimum level of wealth, proportional to their business volume, to enable them to cope with contingencies or with an unexpected shortfall in underwriting reserves. The margin is computed on the basis of shareholders' equity, the *Réserve de Capitalisation* (the provision for unrealised capital loss exposures) and potential capital gains. It must be equivalent to 4% of MR for franc-denominated contracts and 1% for unit-linked contracts.

Provisions used to smooth earnings

To help insurers to manage their appropriation of earnings, the regulatory framework depends primarily on two notions: the *Réserve de Capitalisation* and the profit participation reserve.

Réserve de Capitalisation The purpose of this reserve is to provide for the depreciation of an insurance company's assets and a decline in its income. It covers depreciable transferable securities that come within the scope of article R332-19 of the French Insurance Code – ie, securities that will be redeemed at a certain value and that generate a fixed level of income. They are valued at their acquisition price. When such securities are sold the reserve is adjusted so that the rate of return is equivalent to that expected when they were acquired.

At end 1995 the *Réserve de Capitalisation* represented between 0.5% and 1% of provisions and may account for as much as 3% of MR.

Profit participation reserve The other balance sheet item that can be used to smooth earnings is the PPR, (which, in volume terms, is larger than the *Réserve de Capitalisation*). It is used by most insurers that do not distribute the bulk of their financial income each year. Accordingly, they allocate the portion of undistributed profit share to the PPR. Broadly, the PPR is topped up either by capital gains on equities or whenever the returns on the overall portfolio are sharply higher than the company's or the market's expectations. The reserve forms a sort of safety cushion, which is used when adverse market conditions prevent the insurer from revaluing policyholders' contracts at the agreed rate. Notwithstanding this arrangement, each insurance company has considerable latitude when setting up its PPR. The only legal constraint is that the contents of the reserve must be redistributed to policyholders within eight years.

At end 1995 the PPR represented between 1% and 3% of MR. It can be used to offset the effects of a decline in the value of riskier assets such as equities.

Mechanism of apportioning earnings between insurers and policyholders

An insurance company can fulfil its role only to the extent that policyholders entrust it with their funds. For this reason, both its underwriting results (ie, results related to output, including commissions and overheads) and its financial results should logically be apportioned between the company and its policyholders on an equitable basis. Further, life insurers are required by law to allocate to policyholders a minimum portion of the financial income from investments.

If companies have considerable latitude in allocating the amount remaining once the minimum guaranteed rate has been paid to policyholders, they can use the PPR to amortise capital losses on equities. Conversely, it can be topped up solely with part of the potential gains realised on the equity market.

SIMULATION ASSUMPTIONS

After describing briefly the reasons that prompted us to develop a simulation tool, we present the principal assumptions and operating rules of our model. We then go on to describe the accounting behaviour of an insurance company over a 15-year period with two scenarios for the equity and bonds markets (portfolio-ageing analysis). We conclude by commenting on how the level of equity investment affects the policy revaluation rate (the policyholder's gains) and the solvency margin (the insurer's perspective) in view of the specific features of life insurance accounting practices.

The need to develop a specific model

A number of asset allocation techniques exist, but none takes into consideration the specific accounting mechanisms of the life insurance industry. Two examples that spring to mind are the Markowitz portfolio optimisation method and the use of shortfall constraints associated with a minimal rate of return or a given level of surplus risk. Useful as they may be, these techniques cannot encompass the full range of accounting constraints. Moreover, they do not allow us to simulate the way in which portfolios change over time.

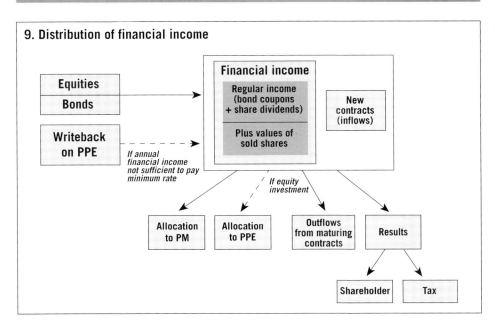

9. Distribution of financial income

For these reasons, it is necessary to develop a model that takes all these aspects into account.

Financial and accounting mechanisms
When introducing equities into a portfolio, two factors must be borne in mind: first, equities are much more volatile than bonds; and, second, insurance companies' accounting principles favour bonds over stocks insofar as provisions must be set up for capital losses on equity investments. Figure 9 shows the principal flows involved in the apportionment of financial income. The underlying mechanisms are described next.

Commercial assumptions
Commercial features of contracts The contracts in question are single-premium policies with a maturity of 10 years. We have assumed that investors do not redeem their policies before they mature and that they liquidate them after 10 years. This may seem somewhat simplistic for two reasons. First, we are dealing with one specific type of contract only; however, it would be possible to apply the model to all the contracts offered by the company and then to reconstitute a global view of the balance sheet by a linear combination of its constituent parts. Second, our simulation does not so far take into account the risk of early redemption. However, we do have the means to simulate commercial scenarios involving subscriptions and redemptions influenced by bond market trends.

Loading policy Policyholder inflows and outflows are effected at year's end and a constant loading commission (eg, 5%) is added to inflows. We ignore commissions on outstandings because they have no fundamental influence on the results generated by the model.

Financial assumptions
Type of investment We consider that the portfolio is composed solely of shares and bonds. For the bond portion, the investment universe comprises fixed-rate instruments with a 10-year maturity and annual coupons. At any given moment the portfolio will contain 10 bond issues purchased at par, each with a maturity corresponding to one of the 10 subsequent years. The equity portion of the investment will track an index such as the SBF 120. It will be simulated by a normally distributed expected return of 9% and volatility of 15%. The 10-year bond yields are simulated by means of a random variable given by a return-to-the-mean model (Orstein–Uhlenbeck) based on the French market.

It is also possible to correlate the behaviour of equities and bonds with a correlation coefficient. Lastly, we have assumed that investments and disinvestments are made at the year end.

10. Simplified balance sheet of an insurance company	
ASSETS	**LIABILITIES**
Bonds	Shareholders' equity
	Reserves
	PPE
Shares	Mathematical reserves

11. Simplified profit and loss account of an insurance company	
EXPENSES	**INCOME**
Claims	Premium
PPR	Financial income (coupons plus dividends)
MR	
Potential losses on equities	Gains from realised equities
Result	

Accounting assumptions

Global structure of the balance sheet and P&L account Shares and bonds are carried on the balance sheet at cost. It is therefore important to model the accounting portfolio and the financial portfolio simultaneously.

The balance sheet and P&L shown in Figures 10 and 11 have been simplified, but they nevertheless reflect the basic accounting mechanisms.

Our assumption for return on equity is as follows: the assets representing shareholders' equity will be invested on the basis of the same policy as those representing the MR.

Distribution policy For portfolios invested solely in bonds, we will adopt a policy of immediate and maximum payout of financial income to policyholders. In contrast, whenever a portfolio contains stocks, we will use the PPR as a cushion to smooth out any fluctuations in the equity market. To some extent we use the PPR in the same way as the *Réserve de Capitalisation* is used to smooth income streams from bond investments.

Minimum guaranteed rate Part of the financial income will be used to revalue in-force contracts (allocation to MR). Thus, the revaluation rate used for the MR can be defined as the ratio of financial income to MR. In addition to being revalued on the basis of this rate, the MR will be increased to reflect the value of new contracts signed during the year and reduced by the value of contract outflows. Note also that these outflows correspond to the inflows recorded 10 years earlier, capitalised each year at the revaluation rate over the past 10 years.

In the event that the company's financial income is not sufficient to pay the guaranteed minimum rate (set at 3.5% in the model), the amount needed to make up the difference will be drawn on the PPR. When the amount available in the PPR is zero or is insufficient to allow the desired writeback, the equity reserves will be used.

P&L income streams The P&L income streams are as follows.
❏ Financial income from bonds and equities (coupons and dividends).
❏ Capital gains and losses realised on equities to allow for portfolio readjustment. Recall that our investment strategy is to hold a constant percentage of shares in the financial portfolio or the accounting portfolio.
❏ Capital gains on equities generated on potential gains or losses that we want to realise when the equity markets perform in line with our expectations – ie, when the annual returns to the equity market are higher than the expected return parameterised in the model. We will designate the rate of realisation by K, which takes values between 0 and 1.
❏ New inflows during the course of the year.

P&L expenses P&L expenses are as follows:
❏ Outflows corresponding to inflows of contracts 10 years earlier. This corresponds to the value of the contracts revalued each year according to actual profit.

❏ Profit participation reserve. This allocation will be incremented by a portion of the capital gains realised during the period. We can define a coefficient, K′, representing those realised gains which are capitalised immediately and those capitalised at a later date. The amount [K′ times realised capital gains] will be factored into the PPR the following year and will thus form a safety cushion. If necessary, a capital loss on equities can be made up by reversing a provision from the PPR and allocating it to the MR as per the minimum guaranteed rate.

❏ Mathematical reserves. An allocation is made to the MR to increase them by the revaluation rate. That allocation represents the difference between the MR for the present year and the MR of the previous year.

In addition, we make a number of simplifications. For example, we ignore the *Réserve de Capitalisation* as well as underwriting income and charges.

FIRST SIMULATION: PORTFOLIO WITH A 10% EQUITY ELEMENT
When an equity element is introduced into a portfolio it tends to reduce the level of regular income while at the same time increasing the income related to capital gains in the equity market.

We will analyse the ageing of our accounting portfolio under two scenarios to illustrate the importance of ensuring that a company's allocation of equities is proportional to the level of its reserves (including the PPR). In our example we have invested 10% in equities. Taking a scenario based on equity-market performance over the next 15 years, we will examine the evolution of the reserves at our disposal.

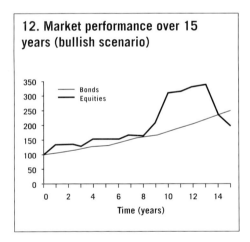

12. Market performance over 15 years (bullish scenario)

Bullish scenario
Consider a pattern over the next 15 years where the equity markets are bullish at first, and then become more volatile before moving on to a steep downtrend at the end of the period (Figure 12). We will look at the case of a company with no reserves or PPR in year 0.

Owing to the equity market run-up, the gains realised on equities and not distributed to policyholders can be capitalised in the PPR, making it possible to build substantial reserves (Figure 13). During the last

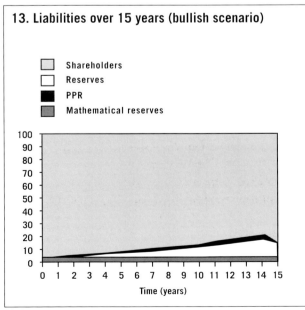

13. Liabilities over 15 years (bullish scenario)

Shareholders
Reserves
PPR
Mathematical reserves

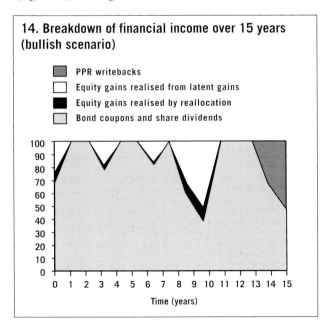

14. Breakdown of financial income over 15 years (bullish scenario)

PPR writebacks
Equity gains realised from latent gains
Equity gains realised by reallocation
Bond coupons and share dividends

two years of the downtrend, provisions must be set aside for capital losses on equities. In this case it will be necessary to draw on the PPR – and then, if necessary, on the reserves – an amount that will allow the company to pay the minimum guaranteed rate to its policyholders (see Figure 13). That same amount was used to offset the provision made for capital losses on equities in years 14 and 15!

The insurer increases the rate paid on savings because the equity element helps to increase reserves (cumulative earnings not paid out to policyholders). Further, the PPR has acted as a shock absorber in the event of capital losses on equities. Looking at the P&L, we see how the company built up a safety cushion during the bull run and then used it during the lean years.

The profit-smoothing method thus allows the company to cope with capital losses on equities. This is reflected in changes in the reserves on the balance sheet and financial income on the P&L (Figure 14).

Bearish scenario
Now consider a bleak scenario in which the equity markets perform poorly for 15 years (Figures 15 and 16).

To meet its contractual commitments, an insurer will have to draw regularly on its PPR and then on its reserves before resorting to a capital injection from shareholders. Since the PPR and the equity reserve are both nil at the beginning of the period, recapitalisation is inevitable. Consequently, the company needs an equity investment policy that is proportionate to its existing reserves. By analogy, the portfolio manager will think of the constant proportion portfolio insurance method (or CPPI, a portfolio insurance technique). Or, by transposition, the PPR can be considered as the cushion.

SIMULATION OF DIFFERENT INVESTMENT POLICIES
The results presented in this part depend heavily on the assumptions we have made. As with any model, they should be analysed with caution because they are merely a representation of a much more complex situation. Furthermore, these statistical results must in any case be accompanied by a study of how the accounts change over time – as were the previous two examples.

We now consider two investment policies. In the first the portfolio consists only of bonds. This is the less risky of the two, and its returns stem solely from regular income streams (compare our model).

The second – a riskier policy from a financial and accounting perspective – involves holding a constant proportion of equities during the period under review. This strategy

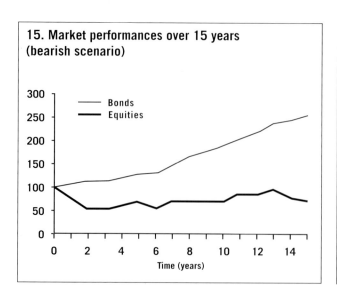

15. Market performances over 15 years (bearish scenario)

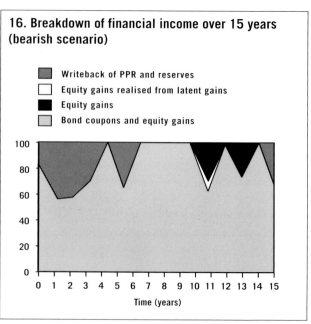

16. Breakdown of financial income over 15 years (bearish scenario)

should generate higher returns than the bond-only scenario: even though the regular income stream declines in relative terms when bonds are replaced by equities, it is nevertheless possible to realise substantial capital gains on share disposals, which in turn will easily offset the drop in regular income.

The policyholder's perspective

Figure 17 plots the changes in the average revaluation rate computed over the next 15 years. For each level of equity allocation, we analyse the results corresponding to 2,000 randomly generated scenarios (using a Monte Carlo method) for the equity and bond markets. In our model we chose to apply the market scenarios in exactly the same way to both investment strategies (viz, the all-bond and the equity-element portfolios). This choice was necessary to allow us to compare the accounting result. The horizontal axis in the figure represents the percentage of equities in the portfolio according to the chosen scenario. The vertical axis represents the average revaluation rate used for the MR over 15 years. These quantities have been computed with an expected return to equities of 9%, ie, a relatively small risk premium in view of the average level of long rates (6.7%).

The results are consistent with theory: they simply illustrate the fact that, in the long run, equities offer higher returns than bonds.

The insurer's perspective

The insurer has to weigh up the effect of asset allocation decisions on his solvency margin (ie, shareholders' equity plus unrealised capital gains as a percentage of MR). Figure 18 shows how the solvency margin changes with the percentage of equities in the portfolio.

Interestingly, once a certain proportion of equities has been reached (around 10%), unrealised capital gains no longer help to increase the solvency margin. This seems logical: on the one hand, the MR revaluation rate increases in line with the proportion of equities; and, on the other hand, the total of reserves and unrealised gains increases in non-linear fashion. This can be explained by the fact that some of the financial income goes to policyholders (through MR revaluation), some to the inland revenue (tax) and some to the insurer (dividend). As a result, reserves and unrealised gains increase rapidly at first and less quickly thereafter, which explains this local optimum.

The size of the equity investment corresponding to this optimum value is closely related to the company's payout policy. In our case, the positioning of that optimum is determined by the coefficients K and K′ (respectively, the realisation of potential gains and the apportionment of gains between the MR and the PPR). The model used by CCF Gestion allows K and K′ to be managed dynamically (depending on the percentage

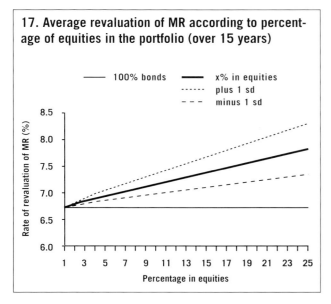

17. Average revaluation of MR according to percentage of equities in the portfolio (over 15 years)

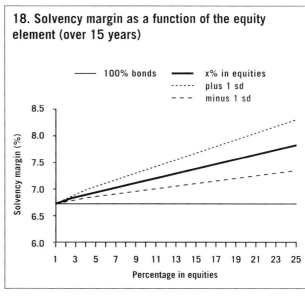

18. Solvency margin as a function of the equity element (over 15 years)

of equities) to optimise the distribution of equity gains. It is therefore possible for portfolios with an equity element of more than 10% to choose an earnings appropriation method that will be satisfactory to insurers and policyholders alike.

INVESTING IN EQUITIES

Should the proportion of equities be increased for contracts denominated in French francs? To answer that question, we need precise rules for appropriating income and managing reserves in a manner consistent with the chosen investment strategy. Based on the rules and assumptions we have adopted, our study shows that, whereas an equity allocation allows a substantial increase in earnings for both insurer and policyholder, the returns to both parties can be optimised by dynamically managing the appropriation of unrealised capital gains. Consequently, an ALM simulation tool can be used to integrate both commercial and financial scenarios with a view to defining tactical allocation choices on the basis of strategic allocation. One complementary aspect that bears examination is the transposition of the portfolio insurance method (the constant proportion method) for use by insurance companies in the field of asset allocation. The results look promising.

Conclusion

Asset liability management is fashionable, and its popularity is a good sign. Given the pressing need for many financial institutions to evolve and the importance of the ALM function for the corporate sector, it was clearly necessary to establish teams of trained professionals. Nevertheless, ALM is no panacea.

ALM practitioners generally agree on analyses and diagnostics. They also share the same arsenal of models and financial methods, which they wield with varying degrees of sophistication. In contrast, there is no such consensus on management policies. There are two basic reasons for this divergence. First, the nature of the various institutions: banks, mutual insurance companies and pension funds do not share the same goals or priorities. Second, within the banking community policies on maturity transformation, credit and capital market activities depend on strategies, investment horizons and the appetite for risk of the management and shareholders.

In this chapter we have sought to explain the attractions and risks of two basic strategies: maturity transformation and equity investment. We approached our subject primarily from a financial angle, while touching on the question of the accounting consequences. The main lessons we learned are: first, that the efficacy of transformation strategies is directly related to the slope of the yield curve and that successful implementation depends on the curve's stability; and second, that the methods used by insurance companies to account for equity holdings put a strong damper on investment. This damper exerts a downward pressure on policy returns, which are particularly sensitive to a low interest rate environment.

We also showed how, using a capital allocation method based on portfolio theory, it is possible to obtain a target return while limiting the volatility of a company's results.

A host of other questions warrant closer examination. Banks themselves have raised several issues – for example, how to evaluate and manage liquidity, how to evaluate and manage sight deposits (interest-bearing and non-interest bearing), and how credit risk interacts with ALM. Further, ALM practitioners are now faced with new problems stemming from banking innovations, such as capped adjustable-rate loans, time deposits with incremental interest pegged to maturity, new insurance products, and new open-ended, guaranteed funds generating heterogeneous liabilities. Financial solutions can be found for many of these problems. But it requires the skill and the adaptability of ALM teams for those solutions to be translated into accounting practices or to be processed through IT systems.

With the hindsight afforded by several years' practice, it seems that ALM specialists are asking an increasing number of basic questions. What management guidelines should be adopted? Should income be smoothed? What is the optimum investment horizon? (To which one tongue-in-cheek answer is: the same as the chairman's term of office). To answer these questions, more macroeconomic and financial research would be useful. For our part, we have shown how research-driven methods can be used to solve the investment management problems of financial institutions. Much remains to be done. But in the meantime, assets and liabilities have still to be managed.

Bibliography

Bellity, L., and R. Dalaud, "Focusing on Fuzzy Finance", *Quants* no. 23.

Bessis, J., 1995, *Gestion des Risques et Gestion Actif–Passif des Banques* (Paris: Dalloz).

Boulier J.-F., 1994, "Capital Allocation", EFMA Conference, Munich.

Boulier, J.-F., 1996, "Que Valent les Options Cachées?", *Revue d'Economie Financière* July, 189–201.

Boulier, J.-F., and P. Schoeffler, 1992, "Embedded Options in Commercial Banking", *JSMDA*, 137–50.

Boulier, J.-F., D. Florens and E. Trussant, 1995, "A Dynamic Model for Pension Fund Management", AFIR Conference, Brussels.

Boulier, J.-F., D. Florens and E. Trussant, "Pension Funds: Choosing an Appropriate Investment Strategy", *Quants* no. 12.

Boulier, J.-F., S. Michel and W. Wisnia, 1996, "Optimizing Investment and Contribution Policies of a Defined Benefit Pension Fund", AFFI Conference, Geneva.

D'Andria, J.-F. Boulier and L. Elie, 1991, "Modèle Analytique d'Evaluation de l'Option de Remboursement par Anticipation", *Finance*, 7–34.

Dubernet, M., 1996, *La Gestion Actif Passif* (Editions Economica).

Dyl, E.A., and M. D. Joehnk, 1981, "Riding the Yield Curve: Does It Work?", *Journal of Portfolio Management* Spring.

Fitoussi, B., and J. Sikorav, "Zero-Coupon Yield Curve – Pricing and Risk Analysis in the OAT Market", *Quants* no. 2.

Grieves, R., and A. J. Marcus, 1992, "Riding the Yield Curve: Reprise", *Journal of Portfolio Management* Summer.

Jerad, S., and J. Sikorav, 1992, "Asset Liability Management: A Dynamic Approach", AFFI Conference, Paris.

Leibowitz, M. L., N. Bader and S. Kogelman, 1995, "Global Fixed-Income Investments: The Persistence Effect", *Financial Analysts Journal*, March–April.

3

A Unified VAR Approach

Emilio Barone*

SanPaolo IMI

Until just a few years ago risk management was a "desert shore, which never yet saw navigate its waters any that afterward had known return" (Dante). Today, the "shore" is no longer so much of a desert. The first maps have been drawn and tools have been created that allow us to navigate without fear of losing our way. The sea of financial risks has been explored. Now, credit risk is all the fashion – a sea (or an ocean) that is almost all to explore. We need to create a channel that will link these two seas.

This chapter, which may be seen as a sort of "navigation diary", describes a possible approach for determining the value-at-risk (VAR) of a generic portfolio whose value changes depend on the variable conditions of financial markets. After reviewing some specific problems related to the calculation of VAR, three examples are presented: the first deals with interest rates, the second with stocks and the third with exchange rates. (A knowledge of general matters is taken for granted[1]). In the section on interest rates, I present a VAR measure that is consistent with the perfect fit of the model. In the section on stocks, the VAR is determined relative to long and short positions on highly non-linear portfolios (hedges, vertical and calendar spreads, combinations); and finally, the section on exchange rates shows how VAR changes according to the reference currency. The more technical parts of the paper are contained in the Appendix and the two panels.

A VAR checklist

THE TIME HORIZON

Q. What is the time horizon we must consider when computing VAR? What is the reference time period? Is it meaningful to consider the probabilistic distribution of the portfolio's return ten days from now?

A. If we leave the portfolio's composition unchanged in the next 10 days, the answer may be yes; if we do not, the result is evidently useless. What would be the sense of wanting to know the portfolio's riskiness in a finite time period if we continuously change the portfolio weights? In this case we would do better to concentrate on the distribution of the portfolio's returns in the next instant of time.

VAR AND BACKTESTING

Q. Can we consider as consistent a regulation that asks for the calculation of a 10-day VAR to define the capital charges for market risks and then requests the calculation of a one-day VAR in the backtesting process?

A. It is correct to base the backtesting process on the one-day VAR, in view of the arguments put forward by the Bank for International Settlements (BIS) itself,[2] but it would have been better to define a one-day VAR for the capital charges as well, increasing the adjustment factor from 3 to 9.5 (= 3×3.16). Since the 10-day VAR is equal to the one-day VAR multiplied by $\sqrt{10} = 3.16$, the adoption of a one-day VAR and an adjustment factor of 9.5 would have implied the same capital charges while making the regulation more internally consistent.

This paper was prepared for the 13th Annual General Meeting of the International Swaps and Derivatives Association, Rome, March 25–27, 1998. I am grateful to Antonio Castagna for his helpful comments.

VAR AND CAPITAL CHARGES

Q. How are VAR and capital charges connected?

A. Under the hypothesis that portfolio returns are normally distributed with a zero mean, it can be shown that the 10-day VAR (computed at a 99% confidence level) is approximately equal to $0.466\sigma W$, where σ and W are, respectively, the volatility and the current value of the portfolio. It can also be shown that a put written on the same portfolio has almost the same value ($0.4\sigma W$) if its time to maturity is one year and the exercise price is equal to the forward price of the underlying. It follows that a capital charge equal to the 10-day VAR is equal to the cost of an insurance policy (a put) guaranteeing the shareholders that after one year their net worth will not be lower than the current value of the portfolio capitalised at the riskless interest rate over the entire life of the option.

Q. Why do we need an adjustment factor of 3?

A. The normality assumption underlying the VAR calculation is not supported by the empirical evidence. Assuming a normal distribution, the probability of a four standard deviation event is about once in 130 years. In practice, however, such unusual market movements occur in most major markets on average almost every year (and this observation confutes the hypothesis of normal daily rates of return). It is the possibility of price jumps that justifies the adjustment factor.

VAR AND THE VARIANCE–COVARIANCE MATRIX

Q. The regulation proposed by the Basle Committee appears to presume that the internal models built for computing VAR necessarily use an historical matrix instead of an implied one. In other words, they are expected to use historical volatilities and historical correlations of risk factors rather than volatilities and correlations implied by market quotes. Is this a correct setting?

A. It is better to estimate volatilities and correlations implied by market quotes than to use time-series estimates.[3] The "implied" matrix should give not a simple retrospective view but a prospective view of the relationships among the risk factors. Besides, the approach based on time series may prove to be inconsistent with the methods used to determine the portfolio's value. Consider, for instance, the case of a portfolio composed of options: their value, computed on the basis of the historical rather than the implied volatility of the underlying asset, may differ significantly from the market value. It follows that the VAR computed on the basis of historical volatilities may be inconsistent with the value of the portfolio.

Q. Is it always possible to estimate an implied matrix?

A. No, because we do not always have quotes of contracts whose value depends (in a significant way) on a particular covariance. Which contracts should we consider to estimate the implied covariance between (say) the short-term interest rate in Italian lire and the S&P500 index? In such circumstances it is evidently necessary to use time-series estimates.

Q. Do we have to be particularly careful when estimating historical volatilities and correlations?

A. Yes, we must pay great attention to detail. Consider the following example. Suppose we want to compute the VAR of an arbitrage portfolio that is long on a stock index (the MIB 30 index[4]) and short on the stocks that make up its basket. The VAR should be zero because the portfolio is completely "immunised". However, if we use the MIB 30 time series to estimate the variance–covariance matrix, the VAR is not zero. Why not? Because the MIB 30 time series is based on the historical composition of the MIB 30 basket rather than on its current definition. We must consider not the actual MIB 30 but the "theoretical" index calculated on the basis of the current definition of the basket.

VAR AND REAL TIME

Q. Is it necessary to estimate VAR in real time?

A. Yes. We need real-time measures of VAR to prevent traders from taking excessive intra-day exposures. It is not sufficient for the house to be in order at the end of the day – we must be sure that it is always in order. Note that, according to the rules proposed by the

Basle Committee, value-at-risk must be computed on a daily basis but banks are nonetheless expected to "maintain strict management systems to ensure that intra-day exposures are not excessive" (Bank for International Settlements, 1996a, p. 5, paragraph 14). We need to compute the portfolio's VAR several times a day. The evidence of numerous "exceptions" in the backtesting process (symptomatic of an imperfection in the internal model) could in fact well be the result of day trades (trades set up and closed during the day), which alter the risk profiles but do not appear in the end-of-day portfolio.

Q. Is the real-time computation of VAR feasible?

A. Yes, if we avoid particularly complex models. Some examples of a possible approach are reported in the following sections.

Interest rates

Consider a portfolio made up of (long or short) positions on Euro-deposits and plain vanilla interest-rate swaps denominated in Italian lire. Suppose we are interested in computing VAR under the hypothesis of a time horizon equal to one working day ($\Delta t = 1/250 = 0.004$) and at a confidence level of $\alpha = 99.997\%$ ($\left| \varepsilon_\alpha \right| \leq 4$).

To compute the portfolio's VAR, we follow five steps (see the Appendix):

1. Identification of the risk factors;
2. Analysis, estimation and calibration of the model;
3. Estimation of the variance–covariance matrix;
4. Computation of the portfolio's elasticities with respect to the risk factors;
5. Determination of VAR.

IDENTIFICATION OF RISK FACTORS

In contrast to the more common approaches that consider m interest rates (for every term structure) as risk factors – that is, m "vertices" or "points" lying on the term structure – I prefer a parametric approach. In other words, it is preferable to describe the whole term structure of interest rates with a continuous n-parameter function instead of just concentrating on m vertices. To compute the portfolio's VAR, suppose that every term structure is determined by four risk factors, θ_1, θ_2, θ_3 and θ_4, corresponding, respectively, to: the level of the instantaneous spot zero rate, r; the level of the long-term asymptotic spot zero rate, R; the speed of adjustment of the instantaneous rate (towards its long-term level), β; and the volatility parameter (of the instantaneous rate), σ.

Given the availability of closed-form formulas that are functions of these four parameters, the valuation of contracts that depend on interest rates is easy; it does not require either mapping or interpolations and it can be implemented in real time.

ANALYSIS AND ESTIMATION OF THE MODEL

It will be assumed that the instantaneous spot zero rate follows a mean-reverting Itô process of the square-root type – the dynamics conjectured by Cox, Ingersoll and Ross (1985).

The valuation formulas for Euro-deposits and swaps are obtained under the hypothesis of constant R, σ and β (Panel 1 overleaf). This simplification is "balanced" in two ways: first, no intertemporal constraint is imposed while estimating the model parameters – the estimation of r, R, σ and β at time t is independent from that at time $t - \Delta t$; and second, the four parameters are estimated and stored on a daily basis for the computation of their historical volatilities and correlations.

By reducing the complexity of the problem, the approach that is followed also allows us to use closed-form formulas for derivative products that have a high information content (eg, futures on Treasury bonds). It follows that the model parameters can also be estimated, in real time, on the basis of these contracts' quotes.

Loss function

The model has been estimated adopting as a loss function the sum of the squared errors between the actual and theoretical contract values, instead of minimising the sum of the

VALUATION OF EURO-DEPOSITS AND INTEREST-RATE SWAPS

The current value of Euro-deposits and interest rate swaps, theoretically null at the origin, can be calculated as the algebraic sum of the value of two bonds. The first bond, which has a value of -1 at the value date (two days after entering the contract), represents initial payment in the case of Euro-deposits and the floating "leg" in the case of swaps. The second bond, which has a value of $+1$ at the value date, represents the claim on principal and interest in the case of Euro-deposits and the fixed "leg" in the case of swaps.[1]

Therefore, the value of Euro-deposits and swaps is a linear combination of zero-coupon bonds. In the Cox, Ingersoll and Ross (1985) model, the value of a zero-coupon bond is given by

$$P(t;s) \equiv Ae^{-Br} \tag{1}$$

where[2]

$$A(t;s) \equiv \left[\frac{2\gamma e^{\frac{(\gamma+\beta)}{2}\tau}}{W} \right]^{\zeta}$$

$$B(t;s) \equiv \frac{2(e^{\gamma\tau}-1)}{W}$$

$$W(t;s) \equiv (\gamma+\beta)(e^{\gamma\tau}-1)+2\gamma$$

$$\gamma \equiv \sqrt{\beta^2+2\sigma^2}$$

$$\zeta \equiv \frac{\gamma+\beta}{\sigma^2}R$$

$$\tau = s-t \tag{2}$$

The elasticities of P with respect to r, R, σ and β are as follows:

$$\mathbf{u} \equiv \begin{bmatrix} \eta_1 \\ \eta_2 \\ \eta_3 \\ \eta_4 \end{bmatrix} = \begin{bmatrix} \dfrac{\partial P}{\partial r}\dfrac{r}{P} = -Br \\[2mm] \dfrac{\partial P}{\partial R}\dfrac{R}{P} = \ln(A) \\[2mm] \dfrac{\partial P}{\partial \sigma}\dfrac{\sigma}{P} = \left(\dfrac{A_\sigma}{A} - B_\sigma r \right)\sigma \\[2mm] \dfrac{\partial P}{\partial \beta}\dfrac{\beta}{P} = \left(\dfrac{A_\beta}{A} - B_\beta r \right)\beta \end{bmatrix} \tag{3}$$

where

$$A_\sigma \equiv A\left[\zeta\gamma_\sigma\left(\frac{1}{\gamma}+\frac{\tau}{2}-\frac{W_\gamma}{W} \right)+\frac{\zeta_\sigma}{\zeta}\ln(A) \right]$$

$$B_\sigma \equiv B\left(\frac{\tau e^{\gamma\tau}}{e^{\gamma\tau}-1}-\frac{W_\gamma}{W} \right)\gamma_\sigma$$

$$A_\beta \equiv A\left[\zeta\left(\frac{\gamma_\beta}{\gamma}+\frac{\tau}{2}(\gamma_\beta+1)-\frac{W_\beta}{W} \right)+\frac{\zeta_\beta}{\zeta}\ln(A) \right]$$

$$B_\beta \equiv B\left[\frac{\gamma_\beta\tau e^{\gamma\tau}}{e^{\gamma\tau}-1}-\frac{W_\beta}{W} \right] \tag{4}$$

and

$$W_\gamma \equiv \frac{\partial W}{\partial \gamma} = e^{\gamma\tau}\left[\tau(\gamma+\beta)+1 \right]+1$$

$$W_\beta \equiv \frac{\partial W}{\partial \beta} = W_\gamma\gamma_\beta+e^{\gamma\tau}-1$$

$$\gamma_\sigma \equiv \frac{\partial \gamma}{\partial \sigma} = \frac{2\sigma}{\gamma}$$

$$\gamma_\beta \equiv \frac{\partial \gamma}{\partial \beta} = \frac{\beta}{\gamma}$$

$$\zeta_\sigma \equiv \frac{\partial \zeta}{\partial \sigma} = \zeta\left[\frac{\gamma_\sigma}{\gamma+\beta}-\frac{2}{\sigma} \right]$$

$$\zeta_\beta \equiv \frac{\partial \zeta}{\partial \beta} = \frac{\zeta}{\gamma} \tag{5}$$

[1] As a consequence, we call "long" the Euro-deposit where we make the initial payment and receive the right to principal and interest. Analogously, we term "long" the swap where we pay "variable" and receive "fixed".

[2] The formula has been changed in terms of r, R, σ and β as in Barone and Risa (1994). This notation is more similar to that used by Vasicek (1978) than by Cox, Ingersoll and Ross (1985).

squared errors between the actual and theoretical interest rates. The choice is important, as will soon be shown.

Data

Consider, for illustrative purposes, the interest rates on lira Euro-deposits and plain vanilla interest-rate swaps quoted on February 27, 1998 (Table 1). As can be seen, the Euro-deposit rates decrease as a function of maturity, whereas the swap rates increase. The instantaneous forward and spot zero rates (continuously compounded), estimated with the cubic-splines method, decrease quite rapidly and then increase (Figure 1).

Since the Cox, Ingersoll and Ross (CIR) model does not allow such a big hump, the theoretical rates will diverge (sometimes significantly) from the actual ones. The errors depend on the loss function that is used in the estimation phase. Do we want to minimise the sum of the squared errors between actual and theoretical *rates* or the sum of the squared errors between actual and theoretical *contract values*?

If the loss function is in terms of rates, the errors between actual and theoretical rates will be limited but the errors between actual contract values (null by definition) and theoretical values will be significant. *Vice versa*, if the loss function is in terms of values, the errors between actual and theoretical rates will be serious but the errors between actual and theoretical values will be limited (Figures 2 and 3).

If we want to minimise the errors between actual and theoretical rates, the life of the contracts is irrelevant. It follows that the estimated term structure will be downward sloping, because the number of Euro-deposits (13) is higher than that of swaps (nine). If we want to minimise the errors between actual and theoretical contract values, the life of the contracts is relevant and more weight will be given to swaps (mainly those with

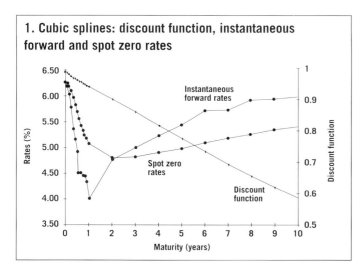

1. Cubic splines: discount function, instantaneous forward and spot zero rates

Table 1. Euro-deposits and swaps in lire (February 27, 1998)

Euro-deposits		Swaps	
Maturity	Rate	Maturity	Rate
1 week	6.199	2 years	4.855
1 month	6.191	3 years	4.865
2 months	6.125	4 years	4.955
3 months	6.062	5 years	5.025
4 months	5.937	6 years	5.125
5 months	5.812	7 years	5.205
6 months	5.687	8 years	5.275
7 months	5.562	9 years	5.345
8 months	5.437	10 years	5.395
9 months	5.348		
10 months	5.266		
11 months	5.207		
12 months	5.125		

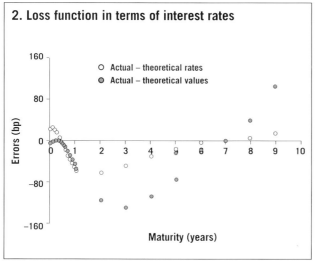

2. Loss function in terms of interest rates

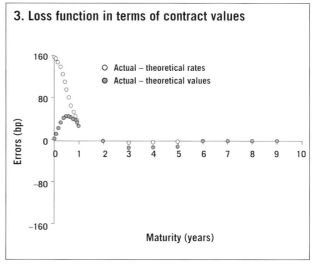

3. Loss function in terms of contract values

4. CIR model: zero curves estimated on the basis of two different loss functions

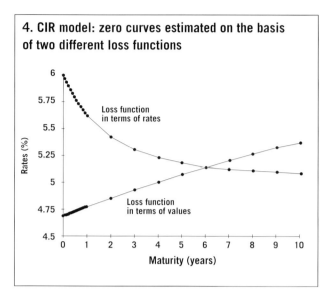

5. CIR model: discount function, instantaneous forward and spot zero rates

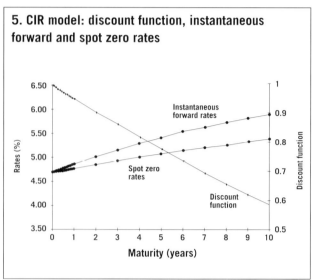

6. CIR model: rate and price volatility

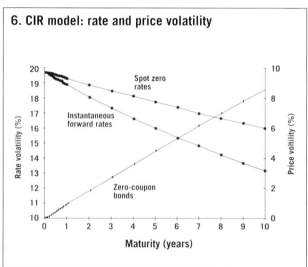

Table 2. Perfect fit: two timescales (February 27, 1998)

Maturity	Real time (t)	Process time ($\phi(t)$)	Difference (t − $\phi(t)$), (dd:hh:mm))
—	0	0	00:00:00
2 days	0.013699	0.013699	00:00:00
1 week	0.046752	0.038356	03:01:32
1 month	0.11611	0.090411	09:09:04
2 months	0.21905	0.16986	17:22:53
3 months	0.32961	0.25753	26:07:24
4 months	0.42915	0.34247	31:15:22
5 months	0.51356	0.41918	34:10:47
6 months	0.60951	0.50959	36:11:17
7 months	0.69073	0.59178	36:02:49
8 months	0.76422	0.67123	33:22:32
9 months	0.85034	0.76164	32:09:00
10 months	0.92233	0.8411	29:15:38
11 months	1.0041	0.92877	27:11:52
12 months	1.0758	1.0137	22:16:20
2 years	1.9935	2.011	−06:08:42
3 years	2.9488	3.011	−22:16:55
4 years	3.9524	4.0164	−23:09:10
5 years	4.9434	5.0164	−26:15:26
6 years	5.9779	6.0164	−14:01:31
7 years	7.0045	7.0164	−04:08:54
8 years	8.0274	8.0137	04:23:48
9 years	9.0664	9.0137	19:05:45
10 years	10.084	10.019	23:11:51

longer maturities). It follows that the estimated term structure will be upward sloping, since the swap rates increase with the contract maturity (Figure 4).

In this last case, the following parameters were estimated: r = 0.046801, R = 0.060016, σ = 0.042634, and β = 0.0095463. The term structure of instantaneous forward rates shows a rising pattern (Figure 5), while the rate volatilities decrease and the price volatilities increase as the contract maturity lengthens (Figure 6).

A loss function defined in terms of values is to be preferred to a loss function defined in terms of rates. Naturally, it is always possible to give a different weight to each contract in the estimation phase. The weight of each contract should be directly proportional to the information content of the quote determined by the market.

Model calibration (perfect fit)

In another step, called "model calibration", we can fit theoretical quotes perfectly to actual quotes. This step can be seen as corresponding to the construction of an implied volatility matrix as a function of exercise prices and option maturities in order to cope with the imperfections of the Black–Scholes model.

Following the approach proposed by Shreve (1997, pp. 315–8), we define two timescales: the market time (or process time) and the calendar time (or real time).[5] The deterministic, monotonically increasing function that links the two timescales is estimated in such a way as to fit the theoretical contract values perfectly to the actual values.

The values of this function, φ, estimated for the contracts that we have so far considered, are reported in Table 2. As can be seen, the process time is slower than the real time for maturities up to one year; it becomes faster in the interval between two and seven years and then slows again in the interval between eight and 10 years.

ESTIMATION OF VARIANCE–COVARIANCE MATRIX

On February 27, 1998, the variance–covariance matrix, **C**

Table 3. Elasticities of Euro-deposits and swaps (fixed-rate component, %, February 27, 1998)

	Euro-deposits					Swaps			
Maturity	r	R	σ	β	Maturity	r	R	σ	β
1 week	−0.219	0.000	0.000	0.000	2 years	−9.033	−0.404	−0.319	0.024
1 month	−0.543	−0.001	−0.001	0.000	3 years	−12.977	−0.852	−0.652	0.052
2 months	−1.024	−0.005	−0.004	0.000	4 years	−16.847	−1.472	−1.087	0.092
3 months	−1.540	−0.011	−0.010	0.001	5 years	−20.408	−2.214	−1.578	0.142
4 months	−2.004	−0.019	−0.016	0.001	6 years	−23.836	−3.103	−2.130	0.204
5 months	−2.397	−0.028	−0.023	0.002	7 years	−26.975	−4.084	−2.699	0.274
6 months	−2.844	−0.039	−0.032	0.002	8 years	−29.851	−5.141	−3.269	0.350
7 months	−3.222	−0.050	−0.042	0.003	9 years	−32.518	−6.276	−3.835	0.433
8 months	−3.563	−0.062	−0.051	0.003	10 years	−34.919	−7.438	−4.372	0.518
9 months	−3.963	−0.076	−0.063	0.004					
10 months	−4.297	−0.090	−0.074	0.005					
11 months	−4.675	−0.106	−0.087	0.006					
12 months	−5.008	−0.122	−0.100	0.007					

(estimated on the basis of the daily logarithmic changes of the four risk factors), was as follows:

$$
\mathbf{C} \equiv \begin{bmatrix}
8.2406\text{E}-4 & 2.8191\text{E}-4 & 6.0909\text{E}-5 & -1.2808\text{E}-4 \\
2.8191\text{E}-4 & 4.9534\text{E}-4 & 6.5174\text{E}-5 & -3.9407\text{E}-4 \\
6.0909\text{E}-5 & 6.5174\text{E}-5 & 1.0625\text{E}-5 & -4.6529\text{E}-5 \\
-1.2808\text{E}-4 & -3.9407\text{E}-4 & -4.6529\text{E}-5 & 6.9812\text{E}-4
\end{bmatrix} \tag{1}
$$

Therefore, the correlation matrix was

$$
\begin{bmatrix}
1 & 0.44124 & 0.65092 & -0.16887 \\
0.44124 & 1 & 0.89837 & -0.67012 \\
0.65092 & 0.89837 & 1 & -0.54024 \\
-0.16887 & -0.67012 & -0.54024 & 1
\end{bmatrix} \tag{2}
$$

and the four risk factor volatilities (in percentage terms and on an annual basis) were 45.39, 35.19, 5.15 and 41.78, respectively.

ELASTICITIES OF CONTRACT VALUES

The closed-form formulas reported in the Appendix allow us to determine the elasticities (with respect to r, R, σ and β) for both the components of Euro-deposits (the initial payment and the claim on principal and interests) and the swaps (the variable leg and the fixed leg). The elasticities of the contracts listed in Table 1, computed on the basis of process time, $\phi(t)$, are reported in Table 3).[6]

As can be seen, all the elasticities grow with the contract maturity. The value of Euro-deposits and swaps depends mainly on r and R, while σ and β (which do not influence the level but only the curvature of the term structure) have a much smaller effect.[7] The estimates of σ and β, based only on Euro-deposits and swaps, are not reliable: it is worth estimating the model on the basis of non-linear products as well.

VAR OF EURO-DEPOSITS AND SWAPS

At this point we have all the information needed to compute the VAR of Euro-deposits and swaps. In fact, we may apply equation (10a) (see the Appendix) to both components of the contract's value. Table 4 reports the (4σ, one working day) VAR relative to a long position on a L10 billion contract.

Table 4. VAR of Euro-deposits and swaps in lire (February 27, 1998)

Euro-deposits		Swaps	
Maturity	VAR	Maturity	VAR
1 week	1,775,569	2 years	104,376,668
1 month	5,501,905	3 years	151,291,750
2 months	11,035,103	4 years	198,051,147
3 months	16,979,931	5 years	241,787,671
4 months	22,334,266	6 years	284,658,386
5 months	26,876,137	7 years	324,670,365
6 months	32,040,606	8 years	362,055,261
7 months	36,413,864	9 years	397,472,611
8 months	40,371,279	10 years	430,037,983
9 months	45,010,699		
10 months	48,889,559		
11 months	53,295,937		
12 months	57,163,199		

CREDIT RISK

So far the analysis has ignored the problems connected with credit risks. A possible approach for computing an integrated credit and financial VAR is to estimate a further parameter, k, that measures the term-structure shift determined by the counterparty risk.[8] This parameter will be stored and used in the same way as the other parameters to estimate historical volatilities and correlations of risk factors.

Stocks

Now consider a portfolio made up of futures and European options written on the MIB 30.

IDENTIFICATION OF RISK FACTORS

In determining the portfolio's VAR, let us suppose that four risk factors, θ_1, θ_2, θ_3, θ_4, are relevant, corresponding, respectively, to: the level of the MIB 30, S; the implied volatility of the MIB 30, σ; the dividend yield of the MIB 30, q; and the three-month Rome InterBank offer rate (Ribor), r.[9]

On February 27, 1998, these four risk factors were: S = 28,964; σ = 0.18276; q = ln(1 + 0.01541) = 0.015292; and r = ln(1 + 0.06115/4) × 4 = 0.060687.

ESTIMATION OF THE VARIANCE–COVARIANCE MATRIX

On the same date the **C** matrix (estimated on the basis of the daily logarithmic changes of the four risk factors) was as follows:

$$\mathbf{C} \equiv \begin{bmatrix} 1.7439E-4 & 8.8561E-5 & -6.8695E-5 & -3.2519E-5 \\ 8.8561E-5 & 0.0045631 & -1.0165E-4 & -3.9363E-5 \\ -6.8695E-5 & -1.0165E-4 & 1.7708E-4 & 2.5465E-6 \\ -3.2519E-5 & -3.9363E-5 & 2.5465E-6 & 6.968E-5 \end{bmatrix} \tag{3}$$

Therefore, the correlation matrix was

$$\begin{bmatrix} 1 & 0.099278 & -0.39092 & -0.295 \\ 0.099278 & 1 & -0.11309 & -0.069808 \\ -0.39092 & -0.11309 & 1 & 0.022925 \\ -0.295 & -0.069808 & 0.022925 & 1 \end{bmatrix} \tag{4}$$

and the four risk factor volatilities (in percentage terms and on an annual basis) were 20.88, 106.81, 21.04 and 13.20, respectively.

VAR OF FUTURES

The theoretical value of a long position on a futures contract has been calculated on the basis of the formula

$$f = S - Ke^{-(r-q) \times (T-t)} = c - p = 0 \tag{5}$$

where $K = Se^{(r-q) \times (T-t)}$ is the theoretical futures price, c is the price of a call and p is the price of a put (both options are European, mature at time T and have the same exercise price, K).

The theoretical value of a call and a put has been calculated on the basis of Merton's proportional-dividend formula:

$$c = Se^{-q(T-t)}N(d_1) - Ke^{-r(T-t)}N\left(d_1 - \sigma\sqrt{T-t}\right)$$

$$p = -Se^{-q(T-t)}N(-d_1) + Ke^{-r(T-t)}N\left(-d_1 + \sigma\sqrt{T-t}\right) \tag{6}$$

where

$$d_1 = \frac{\ln\frac{S}{K} + \left(r - q - \frac{1}{2}\sigma^2\right)(T-t)}{\sigma\sqrt{T-t}} \qquad (7)$$

It follows that the vectors $\mathbf{u}_c$ and $\mathbf{u}_p$, containing the (long) call and the (short) put elasticities with respect to each risk factor, are given by

$$\mathbf{u}_c \equiv \begin{bmatrix} \eta_1^c \\ \eta_2^c \\ \eta_3^c \\ \eta_4^c \end{bmatrix} = \begin{bmatrix} \frac{\partial c}{\partial S}\frac{S}{c} = e^{-q(T-t)}N(d_1)\frac{S}{c} \\ \frac{\partial c}{\partial \sigma}\frac{\sigma}{c} = Se^{-q(T-t)}\sqrt{T-t}\,N'(d_1)\frac{\sigma}{c} \\ \frac{\partial c}{\partial q}\frac{q}{c} = -(T-t)Se^{-q(T-t)}N(d_1)\frac{q}{c} \\ \frac{\partial c}{\partial r}\frac{r}{c} = (T-t)Ke^{-r(T-t)}N\left(d_1 - \sigma\sqrt{T-t}\right)\frac{r}{c} \end{bmatrix} \qquad (8)$$

and

$$\mathbf{u}_p \equiv \begin{bmatrix} \eta_1^p \\ \eta_2^p \\ \eta_3^p \\ \eta_4^p \end{bmatrix} = \begin{bmatrix} \frac{\partial p}{\partial S}\frac{S}{p} = -N(-d_1)\frac{S}{p} \\ \frac{\partial p}{\partial \sigma}\frac{\sigma}{p} = Se^{-q(T-t)}\sqrt{T-t}\,N'(d_1)\frac{\sigma}{p} \\ \frac{\partial p}{\partial q}\frac{q}{p} = (T-t)Se^{-q(T-t)}N(-d_1)\frac{q}{p} \\ \frac{\partial p}{\partial r}\frac{r}{p} = -(T-t)Ke^{-r(T-t)}N\left(-d_1 + \sigma\sqrt{T-t}\right)\frac{r}{p} \end{bmatrix} \qquad (9)$$

Consider the futures contract maturing on March 20, 1998. On February 27, 1998, its time to maturity was 21 calendar days – ie, 0.057534 (= 21/365) years. The contract's current value, f, was equal to the algebraic sum of a long call (492.5) and a short put (–492.5), both having an exercise price equal to the theoretical futures price (29.004). The vector $\mathbf{u}_c$ was given by

$$\mathbf{u}_c \equiv \begin{bmatrix} \eta_1^c \\ \eta_2^c \\ \eta_3^c \\ \eta_4^c \end{bmatrix} = \begin{bmatrix} \frac{\partial c}{\partial S}\frac{S}{c} = 29.951 \\ \frac{\partial c}{\partial \sigma}\frac{\sigma}{c} = 1.0001 \\ \frac{\partial c}{\partial q}\frac{q}{c} = -0.26335 \\ \frac{\partial c}{\partial r}\frac{r}{c} = 0.10109 \end{bmatrix} \qquad (10)$$

and the vector $\mathbf{u}_p$ was given by

$$\mathbf{u}_p \equiv \begin{bmatrix} \eta_1^p \\ \eta_2^p \\ \eta_3^p \\ \eta_4^p \end{bmatrix} = \begin{bmatrix} \frac{\partial p}{\partial S}\frac{S}{p} = -28.951 \\ \frac{\partial p}{\partial \sigma}\frac{\sigma}{p} = 1.0001 \\ \frac{\partial p}{\partial q}\frac{q}{p} = 0.25456 \\ \frac{\partial p}{\partial r}\frac{r}{p} = -0.10458 \end{bmatrix} \qquad (11)$$

On the basis of equation (12a) (see the Appendix), we have

$$\sigma_c\sqrt{\Delta t} = \text{std}(\Delta c) = \sqrt{\mathbf{u}_c' \mathbf{C} \mathbf{u}_c} = 0.40770 \qquad (12)$$

and

$$\sigma_p \sqrt{\Delta t} = std(\Delta p) = \sqrt{u_p' C u_p} = 0.38146 \tag{13}$$

while $\mu = r = 0.060687$. Therefore, on the basis of (10a) and considering the contract's scale factor of 10,000, the VAR of a (long) call was

$$VAR = W\left[1 - e^{\left(\mu - \frac{\sigma^2}{2}\right)\Delta t - \sigma\varepsilon_\alpha\sqrt{\Delta t}}\right] \times 10,000 = 4,022,629 \tag{14}$$

and the VAR of a short put was

$$VAR = W\left[1 - e^{\left(\mu - \frac{\sigma^2}{2}\right)\Delta t - \sigma\varepsilon_\alpha\sqrt{\Delta t}}\right] \times 10,000 = 16,081,389 \tag{15}$$

Therefore, the VAR of a long futures, obtainable as the sum of the call VAR and the put VAR, was L20,104,018.

Analogously, we can obtain the VAR of a short call (L18,181,955) and of a long put (L3,902,070). Summing these two values, the short futures VAR is L22,078,494. As can be seen, the short futures VAR is, correctly, greater than the long futures VAR because of the asymmetric (lognormal) distribution assumed for MIB 30, which makes $+\Delta S$ more probable than $-\Delta S$.

VAR OF FUTURES AND OPTIONS PORTFOLIOS
In determining the VAR of portfolios consisting of futures and options, it is not always possible to use only extreme shocks (those equal to $-\varepsilon_\alpha$ or $+\varepsilon_\alpha$); it may be necessary to consider a whole grid of extractions from a standardised normal distribution. For instance, there are highly non-linear portfolios whose maximum potential loss occurs when the risk factors remain unchanged. In this case, the absence of shocks represents the worst scenario. This is the case for long positions on calendar spreads, butterfly spreads, straddles and strangles. Therefore, we must generally, calculate (10a) on the basis of a whole grid of ε and then set the VAR equal to the least value (changed in sign) among the ΔWs obtained in this way. In Table 5 the VAR relative to various hedges, spreads and combinations has been calculated on the basis of a grid of 101 ε, equally spaced between -4 and $+4$.

Note that, as was to be expected:
❏ The riskiness of futures spreads is much lower than the riskiness of naked positions. Besides, the March–September 1998 spread has a VAR that is almost double that of the March–June 1998 spread, consistent with a reference period that is twice as long.
❏ The naked long positions on calls and puts are much less risky than the corresponding short positions.
❏ The riskiness of hedges is similar to that of naked positions on options. A long futures, long put position is equal to a long call. A long futures, short call position is equivalent to a short put. A short futures, long call position is equal to a long put. A short futures, short put position is equal to a short call.[10]
❏ Vertical call spreads and vertical put spreads, which have similar payoffs but different values, have different VAR. Similarly, calendar call spreads and calendar put spreads, which have similar payoffs but different values, have different VAR.
❏ Long combinations are much less risky than the corresponding short positions. Note, in particular, that strangles have a VAR that is only marginally lower than that of straddles but a much lower cost (and a much lower upside potential).

Exchange rates
Finally, consider a multicurrency portfolio made up of six share baskets that refer to six countries, three in South America (Brazil, Argentina and Mexico) and three in Eastern

Table 5. VAR of futures and options on the MIB 30 (February 27, 1998)

Position	Value	VAR
Naked		
Long March 98 futures	0	20,104,018
Short March 98 futures	0	22,078,494
Long June 98 futures	0	16,754,468
Short June 98 futures	0	18,364,640
Long September 98 futures	0	17,166,630
Short September 98 futures	0	18,735,057
Spreads		
Long March–June 98 spread	0	3,349,550
Short March–June 98 spread	0	3,713,854
Long March–September 98 spread	0	2,937,388
Short March–September 98 spread	0	3,343,437
Naked		
Long L29.000 March 98 call	4,924,853	4,035,086
Short L29.000 March 98 call	–4,924,853	18,181,955
Long L29.000 March 98 put	4,888,300	3,902,070
Short L29.000 March 98 put	–4,888,300	16,061,266
Hedges		
Long March 98 futures, long L29.000 March 98 put	4,888,300	4,042,751
Long March 98 futures, short L29.000 March 98 call	–4,924,853	16,068,932
Short March 98 futures, long L29.000 March 98 call	4,924,853	3,896,539
Short March 98 futures, short L29.000 March 98 put	–4,888,300	18,176,424
Spreads		
Long L28–30.000 March 98 vertical call spread	9,864,590	6,280,919
Short L28–30.000 March 98 vertical call spread	–9,864,590	9,104,260
Long L28–30.000 March 98 vertical put spread	–10,065,700	10,183,927
Short L28–30.000 March 98 vertical put spread	10,065,700	6,259,663
Long L29.000 March–June 98 call calendar spread	8,010,498	4,828,510
Long L29.000 March–June 98 call calendar spread	–8,010,498	434,687
Long L29.000 March–June 98 put calendar spread	4,770,076	6,159,862
Short L29.000 March–June 98 put calendar spread	–4,770,076	189,838
Long L28–29–30.000 March 98 butterfly spread	3,056,120	3,194,159
Short L28–29–30.000 March 98 butterfly spread	–3,056,120	132,375
Combinations		
Long L29.000 March 98 straddle	9,813,153	737,675
Short L29.000 March 98 straddle	–9,813,153	14,279,885
Long L28–30.000 March 98 strangle	2,904,128	445,164
Short L28–30.000 March 98 strangle	–2,904,128	10,778,089
Long L29.000 March 98 strip	14,701,452	1,724,426
Short L29.000 March 98 strip	–14,701,452	28,087,447
Long L29.000 March 98 strap	14,738,005	2,044,138
Short L29.000 March 98 strap	–14,738,005	32,461,840

Source: elaborations on Borsa Italia s.p.a. data (website address, http://www.borsaitalia.it).

Table 6. Standard deviations and correlations of indexes (in US$) and L/US$ exchange rate

Standard deviations (%)		Correlation coefficients						
			Brazil	Argentina	Mexico	Czech Rep.	Poland	Hungary	L/US$
Brazil	30.550	Brazil	1						
Argentina	25.969	Argentina	0.352	1					
Mexico	27.643	Mexico	0.284	0.459	1				
Czech Rep.	20.454	Czech Rep.	–0.048	–0.007	0.059	1			
Poland	26.235	Poland	0.076	0.019	0.002	0.109	1		
Hungary	28.771	Hungary	0.075	0.050	0.040	0.114	0.169	1	
L/US$	7.274	L/US$	0.040	0.035	0.071	–0.121	0.059	–0.083	1

The estimates are based on logarithmic daily changes of historical indexes in dollar terms.

7. Stock indexes, in US$ terms, of Brazil, Argentina, Mexico, Czech Republic, Poland and Hungary

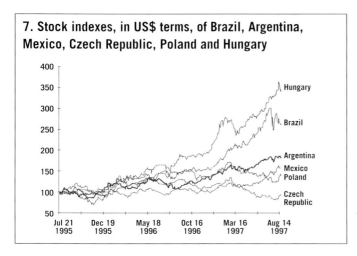

8. VAR of a multicurrency share portfolio in dollar terms

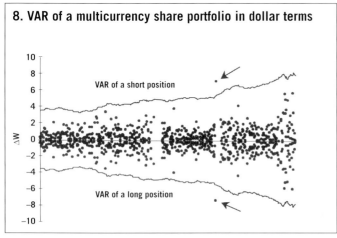

9. L/US$ exchange rate July 21, 1995 – August 14, 1997

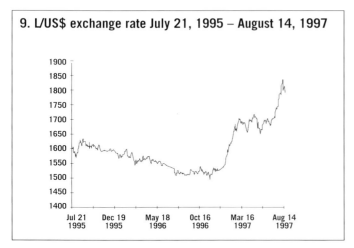

10. VAR of a multicurrency share portfolio in lira terms

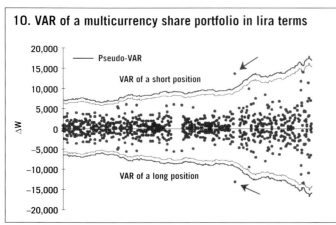

Europe (the Czech Republic, Poland and Hungary). The value of each basket is measured by the following indexes: Bovespa, Merval, Ipc, Ctx, Ptx and Htx. All the indexes have been translated into US dollars using the daily exchange rates for the reference period (Figure 7).[11] First, we estimate the variance–covariance matrix of seven risk factors: the six share indexes (in US dollar terms) and the L/US$ exchange rate. The estimates of standard deviations and correlation coefficients are reported in Table 6. Then we estimate the dividend yields of the indexes and the riskless (continuously compounded) zero rates in US dollars and in lire (Table 7). The VAR of our multicurrency portfolio in dollar terms is estimated on the basis of equation (10a). Figure 8 reports, for both long and short positions, the daily changes of the portfolio value in dollar terms and the corresponding VAR measure. As can be seen, during the reference period the limit given by the VAR is exceeded on only one day. Nevertheless, it should be remembered that the variance–covariance matrix has been estimated under the hypothesis of perfect foresight.

REFERENCE CURRENCY

The portfolio volatility is not independent of the reference currency. For instance, the volatility in dollar terms is not the same as the volatility in lira terms. It follows that the VAR of our portfolio in lira terms is not simply equal to the corresponding VAR in dollar terms multiplied by the L/US$ exchange rate (which we will call the pseudo-VAR). If we wish to consider the VAR of our portfolio in lira terms we must consider the new risk factor, the L/US$ exchange rate (Figure 9), and its relationships with the other factors, the six share indexes. In Figure 10 the actual VAR in lire is always higher than the pseudo-VAR obtained by multiplying the VAR in dollar terms by the L/US$ exchange rate.

In determining the VAR in lira terms it is not necessary to re-estimate the variance–covariance matrix, this time from a lira standpoint. The portfolio volatility in lira terms can be obtained by pre-multiplying and post-multiplying the old variance–covariance matrix

Table 7. Dividend yields of stock indexes and riskless zero rates in L and US$

Dividend yields (%)		Zero rates (%)	
Brazil	0	L	6.4
Argentina	0	US$	6.4
Mexico	0		
Czech Rep.	1.25		
Poland	1.25		
Hungary	1.25		

Since indexes of South American countries measure the total return of underlying portfolio, their dividend yields are zero.

with a new elasticities vector that only requires a small change in the original vector. In fact, it is sufficient to subtract unity from the portfolio elasticity with respect to the L/US$ exchange rate (Panel 2 overleaf). This is an elementary change, compatible with computing VAR in real time.

Conclusions

In the introductory section risk management was seen as a huge "sea" – a very interesting sea where more and more frequently we meet new exotics. Reference is made to a series of products with fascinating characteristics and names such as Asian, Bermudan, binary, chooser, cylinder, compound, barrier, flexible forwards, forward band, forward start, knock-in, knock-out, look-back, min–max, option fence, packages, rainbow, and so on. The pricing of these new products is often very complex. To determine their riskiness we need to refine our measurement tools, but we must avoid using an ad-hoc, product-by-product approach. We need measurement tools that accurately signal the possible dangers and allow us to "brake" in time. Since brakes are only useful if they are well balanced and grip immediately (otherwise it is better to know that we do not have reliable brakes), we must ask directly for risk measures that are defined in global terms and are available in real time. Such an aim can be achieved with current technology.

Appendix – VAR calculation

The portfolio's value-at-risk (VAR) represents an estimate of the maximum potential loss that the portfolio can be expected to incur in a given time period and in a certain percentage of cases.

HYPOTHESES IN CONTINUOUS TIME
In general, to determine the portfolio's VAR, we must first define the dynamics followed by the risk factors to which the portfolio is exposed. Suppose that the portfolio's value, W, is a function of n risk factors and time:

$$W \equiv W(\theta_1, \theta_2, \dots, \theta_n, t) \tag{1a}$$

and that the risk factors follow a multivariate Itô process with instantaneous drift $m_i \theta_i$ and instantaneous variance $s_i^2 \theta_i^2$:

$$d\theta_i = m_i \theta_i dt + s_i \theta_i dz_i \tag{2a}$$

where dz_i is a Wiener process ($1 \leq i \leq n$) and ρ_{ij} is the correlation coefficient between dz_i and dz_j. According to the generalised Itô's lemma, we have

$$dW = \mu W dt + \sigma W dz \tag{3a}$$

where[12]

$$\mu W = \frac{\partial W}{\partial t} + \sum_{i=1}^{n} \frac{\partial W}{\partial \theta_i} m_i \theta_i + \frac{1}{2} \sum_{i=1}^{n} \sum_{j=1}^{n} \frac{\partial^2 W}{\partial \theta_i \partial \theta_j} \rho_{ij} s_i s_j \theta_i \theta_j$$

$$\tag{4a}$$

$$\sigma W = \sum_{i=1}^{n} \sum_{j=1}^{n} \frac{\partial W}{\partial \theta_i} \theta_i \frac{\partial W}{\partial \theta_j} \theta_j \rho_{ij} s_i s_j$$

APPROXIMATIONS IN DISCRETE TIME
On the basis of (3a) we have

$$\Delta W = \mu W \Delta t + \sigma W \varepsilon \sqrt{\Delta t} \tag{5a}$$

Therefore ΔW, the change in the portfolio's value in a very short period of time, Δt, is normally distributed with average $\mu W \Delta t$ and variance $\sigma^2 W^2 \Delta t$.[13]

PANEL 2

VAR OF A MULTICURRENCY PORTFOLIO

Let W be the value of a portfolio, in lira terms, made up of m contracts:

$$W = \sum_{k=1}^{m} V_k \quad 1 \le k \le m \tag{1}$$

where V_k is the value of the kth contract.

Let us suppose that the portfolio's value, W, is a function of n risk factors and time:

$$W \equiv W(\theta_1, \theta_2, \ldots, \theta_n, t) \tag{2}$$

and that the risk factors follow a multivariate Itô process with instantaneous drift $m_i \theta_i$ and instantaneous variance $\sigma_i^2 \theta_i^2$:

$$d\theta_i = m_i \theta_i dt + s_i \theta_i dz_i \tag{3}$$

where dz_i is a Wiener process ($1 \le i \le n$) and ρ_{ij} is the correlation coefficient between dz_i and dz_j. Let us suppose that the last risk factor, θ_n, is the lira/US dollar exchange rate. The portfolio's value in dollar terms is given by

$$W_\$ = \frac{W}{\theta_n} \tag{4}$$

but the portfolio's VAR in dollars is not simply equal to the portfolio's VAR in lire (defined by (9a) or by (10a) in the Appendix) divided by the lira/dollar exchange rate. We must consider the new risk factor (the lira/dollar exchange rate) and its relationships with the other factors. Nevertheless, to calculate the portfolio's VAR in dollar terms it is not necessary to re-estimate the variance–covariance matrix from a dollar standpoint; it is sufficient to change the vector of elasticities, **u**, defined by (13a). Itô's lemma defines the dynamics followed by the portfolio's value in dollars:

$$dW_\$ = \mu_\$ W_\$ dt + \sigma_\$ W_\$ dz_\$ \tag{5}$$

where

$$\mu_\$ W_\$ = \frac{\partial W_\$}{\partial t} + \sum_{i=1}^{n} \frac{\partial W_\$}{\partial \theta_i} m_i \theta_i + \frac{1}{2} \sum_{i=1}^{n} \sum_{j=1}^{n} \frac{\partial^2 W_\$}{\partial \theta_i \partial \theta_j} \rho_{ij} s_i s_j \theta_i \theta_j$$

$$\sigma_\$ W_\$ = \sum_{i=1}^{n} \sum_{j=1}^{n} \frac{\partial W_\$}{\partial \theta_i} \theta_i \frac{\partial W_\$}{\partial \theta_j} \theta_j \rho_{ij} s_i s_j \tag{6}$$

If the portfolio's value is constrained to be positive, a more accurate approximation of ΔW can be obtained by applying Itô's lemma to $\ln(W)$.[14] In this case, on the basis of (3a), we have[15]

$$d\ln(W) = \left(\mu - \frac{\sigma^2}{2}\right) dt + \sigma dz \tag{6a}$$

It follows that

$$\Delta W = W \left[e^{\left(\mu - \frac{\sigma^2}{2}\right)\Delta t + \sigma \varepsilon \sqrt{\Delta t}} - 1 \right] \tag{7a}$$

Therefore, the portfolio volatility in dollar terms is

$$\sigma_\$ = \sqrt{\sum_{i=1}^{n}\sum_{j=1}^{n} \frac{\partial W_\$}{\partial \theta_i}\frac{\theta_i}{W_\$}\frac{\partial W_\$}{\partial \theta_j}\frac{\theta_j}{W_\$}\rho_{ij}s_i s_j}$$

$$= \sqrt{\sum_{i=1}^{n}\sum_{j=1}^{n}\eta_i^\$ \eta_j^\$ \rho_{ij}s_i s_j} \tag{7}$$

On the basis of equation (4) of this panel we have

$$\eta_k^\$ = \frac{\partial W_\$}{\partial \theta_k}\frac{\theta_k}{W_\$} = \frac{\partial W/\theta_n}{\partial \theta_k}\frac{\theta_k}{W_\$}$$

$$= \frac{W}{\theta_n}\left(\frac{\partial W}{\partial \theta_K}\frac{1}{W} - \frac{\partial \theta_n}{\partial \theta_K}\frac{1}{\theta_n}\right)\frac{\theta_k}{W_\$} = \eta_k - \frac{\partial \theta_n}{\partial \theta_k}\frac{\theta_k}{\theta_n} \tag{8}$$

where

$$\frac{\partial \theta_n}{\partial \theta_k} = \begin{cases} 1 & \text{if } k = n \\ 0 & \text{otherwise} \end{cases} \tag{9}$$

Therefore, analogously to (equation 12a), we have

$$\sigma_\$\sqrt{\Delta t} = \text{std}\left(\frac{\Delta W_\$}{W_\$}\right) = \sqrt{\mathbf{v'Cv}} \tag{10}$$

where the vector $\mathbf{v}$ contains the elasticities of the portfolio's value in dollars with respect to each risk factor:

$$\mathbf{v} \equiv \begin{bmatrix} \eta_1^\$ \\ \eta_2^\$ \\ \dots \\ \eta_n^\$ \end{bmatrix} = \begin{bmatrix} \dfrac{\partial W_\$}{\partial \theta_1}\dfrac{\theta_1}{W_\$} \\ \dfrac{\partial W_\$}{\partial \theta_2}\dfrac{\theta_2}{W_\$} \\ \dots \\ \dfrac{\partial W_\$}{\partial \theta_n}\dfrac{\theta_n}{W_\$} \end{bmatrix} = \begin{bmatrix} \eta_1 \\ \eta_2 \\ \dots \\ \eta_n - 1 \end{bmatrix} \tag{11}$$

As (10)–(11) show, $\sigma_\$$ can be obtained by changing the portfolio's elasticities but leaving the variance–covariance matrix unchanged.

The portfolio's VAR is defined by

$$\text{Prob}(-\text{VAR} \leq \Delta W) = \alpha \tag{8a}$$

where α is the confidence level.

Therefore, on the basis of (5a)

$$\text{VAR} = \sigma W \varepsilon_\alpha \sqrt{\Delta t} - \mu W \Delta t \tag{9a}$$

and, on the basis of (7a)

$$\text{VAR} = W\left[1 - e^{\left(\mu - \frac{\sigma^2}{2}\right)\Delta t - \sigma\varepsilon_\alpha\sqrt{\Delta t}}\right] \tag{10a}$$

where

$$\text{Prob}(-\varepsilon_\alpha \le \varepsilon) = \alpha \tag{11a}$$

VAR OF A PORTFOLIO

In general, when the portfolio's value is not constrained to be positive or negative, VAR can be computed by:

1. Decomposing the portfolio into a series of m contracts whose value, V_k ($k = 1,...,m$), is always positive or always negative;[16]
2. Calculating for each contract N possible ΔV_k, each of which is obtained by inserting a grid of ε, equally spaced between $-\varepsilon_\alpha$ and $+\varepsilon_\alpha$, in (7a);[17]
3. Summing the ΔV_k of the elementary contracts to obtain the ΔW for the whole portfolio;
4. Setting VAR equal to the lowest value among the ΔWs obtained in this way (and changing its sign).

This method of computing VAR is much more accurate than that based on (5a), which may determine, in the case of long positions on calls and puts, ΔWs greater than option premiums. Besides, the need to use many ε (and not only the extreme values $-\varepsilon_\alpha$ and $+\varepsilon_\alpha$) is motivated, for instance, by the possibility of the maximum potential loss occurring in the absence of shocks ($\varepsilon = 0$) – as is the case for long calendar or butterfly spreads.

The inputs for (7a) are:

❑ W, the portfolio's current value. To have a correct VAR, we need to be sure that the market value and the theoretical value coincide ("perfect fit"). For instance, if the portfolio is made up of an option, the volatility of the underlying used for the VAR calculation must coincide with the option's implied volatility.

❑ μ, the portfolio's expected rate of return. The principle of risk-neutral valuation can be applied ($\mu = r$).

❑ σ, the portfolio's volatility parameter. In matrix terms, we deduce from (4a) that

$$\sigma\sqrt{\Delta t} = \text{std}\left(\frac{\Delta W}{W}\right) = \sqrt{u'Cu} \tag{12a}$$

where the vector u contains the elasticities of the portfolio's value with respect to each risk factor, θ_i:

$$u \equiv \begin{bmatrix} \eta_1 \\ \eta_2 \\ ... \\ \eta_n \end{bmatrix} = \begin{bmatrix} \dfrac{\partial W}{\partial \theta_1} \dfrac{\theta_1}{W} \\ \dfrac{\partial W}{\partial \theta_2} \dfrac{\theta_2}{W} \\ ... \\ \dfrac{\partial W}{\partial \theta_n} \dfrac{\theta_n}{W} \end{bmatrix} \tag{13a}$$

and C is a matrix that contains the variances and covariances of the risk factors' logarithmic changes (estimated on the basis of time series with periodicity Δt):

$$C \equiv \begin{bmatrix} s_1^2 \Delta t & s_1 s_2 \rho_{12} \Delta t & \cdots & s_1 s_n \rho_{1n} \Delta t \\ s_2 s_1 \rho_{21} \Delta t & s_2^2 \Delta t & \cdots & s_2 s_n \rho_{2n} \Delta t \\ ... & ... & ... & ... \\ s_n s_1 \rho_{n1} \Delta t & s_n s_2 \rho_{n2} \Delta t & \cdots & s_n^2 \Delta t \end{bmatrix} \tag{14a}$$

❑ Δt, the reference time horizon assumed for VAR. Since the normality assumption of ΔW is only valid for a very short period of time, Δt may be set equal to one working day (out of about 250 in a year), so that $\Delta t = 1/250 = 0.004$.

❑ ε, a standardised normal random variable.

MONTE CARLO METHOD

The VAR computed on the basis of (10a) represents an approximation in discrete time based on continuous-time dynamics. To check its reliability we can use the Monte Carlo method. In order to generate shocks consistent with the estimation of the variance–covariance matrix, **C**, we can proceed as follows.

1. Fix the number, M, of simulations to be made for each of the m risk factors.
2. Fix the number, N, of smaller time intervals into which to divide the time horizon Δt (equal to one working day).
3. Generate m series of shocks, x_{ij} ($i = 1,...,N$ and $j = 1,...,m$), each made by N random extractions from m independent normal distributions.
4. To generate m series of shocks ε_{ij}, with zero mean, unit standard deviation and correlation matrix, $\prod$, consistent with **C**, we can use the following transformation:

$$\varepsilon = \mathbf{x}\alpha' \tag{15a}$$

where $\alpha = \mathbf{TZ}$, where, in turn, **T** is the matrix containing the eigenvectors of $\prod$ and **Z** is a diagonal matrix whose elements are equal to the square root of $\prod$'s eigenvalues.

Since $\mathbf{T'DT} = \mathbf{ZZ'}$, it follows that $\mathbf{Z'T'DTZ} = \mathbf{I}$, where **I** is the unit matrix containing the correlations between the independent standardised normal variables. Therefore $\varepsilon = \mathbf{x}\alpha'$.

---

1 *An excellent review is provided by Duffie and Pan (1997). A specific proposal for the calculation of VAR is made by Fong and Vasicek (1997). The "roots" of the approach followed in this paper can be found in Barone and Braghò (1995, 1996).*

2 *"... comparing the ten-day, 99th percentile risk measures from the internal models, capital requirement with actual ten-day trading outcomes would probably not be a meaningful exercise. In particular, in any given ten-day period, significant changes in portfolio composition relative to the initial positions are common at major trading institutions." (Bank for International Settlements, 1996b, p. 3).*

3 *See Fong (1996).*

4 *The Italian Stock Exchange, which issues the MIB 30, describes it as "a synthetic index calculated on the basis of a sample of shares ... as a point of reference for trading in derivatives, futures and options. The basket on which it is calculated is made up of a basket of 30 blue-chip shares (out of those with the highest capitalisation and trading volumes)..." (www.borsaitalia.it/ing/market/mib30.html).*

5 *This hypothesis is consistent with the literature on the weekend effect and with traders' practice of determining options volatility with reference to market time and interest payments with reference to calendar time. See Hull (1997, pp. 248–9).*

6 *Table 3 reports only the elasticities of the long fixed-rate component because those of the other component are almost zero in view of the very short time to value date (two working days after entering into the contract).*

7 *On the particular day we have examined the dependence on R is also very limited, but this is a singularity determined by the (almost zero) level of our estimate for β.*

8 *See the approach followed by Barone, Barone-Adesi and Castagna (1998).*

9 *From an integrated standpoint, this rate should be equal to the theoretical zero rate estimated for the specific contract's maturity.*

10 *The equivalence is not perfect because the exercise price of options (L29,000) is not exactly equal to the theoretical futures price (L29,004).*

11 *The Reuters daily time series for the period from July 21, 1995, to August 14, 1997, have been used. The indexes for the South American countries have been converted into US dollars using the dollar daily exchange rates of the local currencies in order to have indexes homogeneous with those available for the three Eastern European countries (already available in US$).*

12 *Besides, it is possible to prove that*

$$\mu = r + \sum_{j=1}^{n} \lambda_j \frac{\partial W}{\partial \theta_j} \frac{s_j \theta_j}{W}$$

where λ_i is the market price of risk associated with the ith factor. See Hull (1997, pp. 306–7).

13 *The change of W in a very short period of time follows a normal distribution but its change over longer time periods may follow a different distribution. See Hull (1997, p. 222).*

14 *It can be shown that (7a) is valid even if a short position is constrained to be negative. In this case, (10a) must be modified by changing the sign of ε_a.*

15 *See Hull (1997, pp. 221–2 and 362).*

16 *For instance, on the basis of put–call parity, the value of a long forward contract is equal to the sum of a long position on a call (whose value is always positive) and a short position on a put (whose value is always negative).*

17 *For instance, at a confidence level of $\alpha = 99.997\%$ we would choose a grid of N values equally spaced between −4 and +4 (call) and between +4 and −4 (put). In this case, using a multiplier of 4, one would follow Goldman, Sachs & Co.: "Given the non-normality of returns that we find in most financial markets, we use as a rule of thumb the assumption that four-standard-deviation events in financial markets happen approximately once per year. Given this assumption, the daily once-per-year VAR for portfolios whose pay-offs are linear is approximately four standard deviations." Litterman (1996, p. 3).*

Bibliography

Bank for International Settlements, 1996a, "Amendment to the Capital Accord to Incorporate Market Risks", Basle Committee on Banking Supervision, January.

Bank for International Settlements, 1996b, "Supervisory Framework for the Use of 'Backtesting' in Conjunction with the Internal Models Approach to Market Risk Capital Requirements", Basle Committee on Banking Supervision, January.

Barone, E., and A. Braghò, 1995, "An Integrated System for Interest-Rate Risk Management", Istituto Mobiliare Italiano, November.

Barone, E., and A. Braghò, 1996, "A Model for Measuring Financial Risks", *Rivista di Politica Economica* 86(11-12), pp. 155-93.

Barone, E., and S. Risa, 1995, "Valuation of Floaters and Options on Floaters Under Special Repo Rates", Istituto Mobiliare Italiano, October.

Barone, E., G. Barone-Adesi and A. Castagna, 1998, "Pricing Bonds and Bond Options with Default Risk", *European Financial Management* 4(3), pp. 231-82.

Cox, J. C., J. E. Ingersoll and S. A. Ross, 1985, "A Theory of the Term Structure of Interest Rates", *Econometrica* 53(2), pp. 385-407.

Duffie, D., and J. Pan, 1997, "An Overview of Value at Risk", *Journal of Derivatives* 4(3), pp. 7-49.

Fong, G., 1996, "Valuation - Multidimensional Risk", *Derivatives Strategy* 1(10).

Fong, G., and O. A. Vasicek, 1997, "A Multidimensional Framework for Risk Analysis", *Financial Analysts Journal* July-Aug, pp. 51-7.

Hull, J. C., 1997, *Options, Futures and Other Derivatives* (Englewood Cliffs, Prentice Hall).

Litterman, R., 1996, "Hot Spots and Hedges", Working paper, Goldman, Sachs & Co.

Shreve, S., 1997, "Stochastic Calculus and Finance", Mimeo.

Vasicek, O. A., 1978, "An Equilibrium Characterization of the Term Structure", *Journal of Financial Economics* 5, pp. 177-88.

4

Interest Rate Model Risk

**Rajna Gibson, François-Serge Lhabitant,
Nathalie Pistre and Denis Talay***

University of Lausanne; University of Lausanne; CERAM Group, Nice;
INRIA Research Center, Sophia-Antipolis

The concept of risk is central to players in capital markets. Risk management is the set of procedures, systems and persons used to control the potential losses of a financial institution. The explosive increase in interest rate volatility in the late 1970s and early 1980s has produced a revolution in the art and science of interest rate risk management. For instance, in the United States in 1994, interest rates rose by more than 200 basis points, and in 1995 there were important non-parallel shifts in the yield curve. Complex hedging tools and techniques were developed, and dozens of plain vanilla and exotic derivatives instruments were created to provide the ability to generate customised financial instruments to meet virtually any financial target exposure.

Recent crises in the derivatives markets have raised the question of interest rate risk management. It is important for bank managers to recognise the economic value and resultant risks related to interest rate derivative products, including loans and deposits with embedded options. It is equally important for regulators to measure interest rate risk correctly. This explains why the Basle Committee on Banking Supervision (1995, 1997) issued directives to help supervisors, shareholders, CFOs and managers to evaluate the interest rate risk of exchange-traded and over-the-counter derivative activities of banks and securities firms, including off-balance-sheet items. Under these directives banks are allowed to choose between using a standardised (building block) approach or their own risk measurement models to calculate their value-at-risk, which will then determine their capital charge. No particular type of model is prescribed as long as each model captures all the risks run by an institution.[1]

Many banks and financial institutions already base their strategic tactical decisions for valuation, market-making, arbitrage or hedging on internal models built by scientists. Extending these models to compute their value-at-risk and resulting capital requirement may seem pretty straightforward. But we all know that any model is, by definition, an imperfect simplification, a mathematical representation for the purposes of replicating the real world. In some cases a model will produce results that are sufficiently close to reality to be adopted. But in others it will not. What happens in such a situation? A large number of highly reputable banks and financial institutions have already suffered extensive losses. For instance, in 1992 JP Morgan lost US$200 million in the mortgage-backed securities market due to an inadequate modelling of the prepayments; in 1987 Merrill Lynch lost US$350 million in stripped mortgage-backed securities due to an incorrect pricing model; more recently, in March 1997 NatWest Markets announced that mispricing on sterling interest rate options due to improper volatility estimations had cost £90 million; and the Bank of Tokyo–Mitsubishi had to write off US$83 million on its US interest rate derivatives book because of the application of an inadequate pricing model, which led to systematic overvaluation of the position.

*The authors acknowledge financial support from RiskLab (Zurich). The work presented here forms part of the RiskLab project "Interest rate risk management and model risk". Correspondence should be addressed to F. S. Lhabitant, Ecole des HEC/BFSH1, Université de Lausanne, 1015 Dorigny, Switzerland. Phone/Fax: 41-79-230.40.17. Email: flhabita@hec.unil.ch.

The problem is not limited to the interest rate-contingent claims market. It also exists, for instance, in the stockmarket. In *Risk Magazine* the late Fisher Black commented: "I sometimes wonder why people still use the Black and Scholes formula, since it is based on such simple assumptions – unrealistically simple assumptions" (Black, 1990). The answer can be found in his 1986 presidential address to the American Finance Association, when he said: "In the end, a theory is accepted not because it is confirmed by conventional empirical tests, but because researchers persuade one another that the theory is correct and relevant."

Why did we focus on interest rate models rather than on stock models? First, interest rate models are more complex, since the effective underlying variable – the entire term structure of interest rates – is not observable. Second, there exists a wider set of derivative instruments. Third, interest rate-contingent claims have certainly stimulated the most abundant theoretical literature on how to price and hedge from the simplest to the most complex instrument, and the set of available models is prolific in their variety and underlying assumptions. Fourth, almost every economic agent is exposed to interest rate risk, even if he does not manage a portfolio of securities.

Despite this, as we shall see, the literature on model risk is rather sparse and often focuses on specific pricing or implied volatility fitting issues. We believe there are much more challenging issues to be explored. For instance, is model risk symmetric? Is it priced in the market? Is it the source of a larger bid–ask spread? Does it result in overfunding or underfunding of financial institutions?

In this contribution, we provide a definition of model risk, examine some of its origins and consequences and propose a methodology for its analysis and quantification. The chapter is structured as follows: the next (second) section defines model risk; the third section reviews the steps of the model-building process that are at the origin of model risk; the fourth section presents various examples of the influence of model risk in areas such as pricing, hedging and regulatory capital adequacy; and the fifth section provides conclusions.

Model risk: some definitions

As postulated by Derman (1996a, 1996b), most financial models fall into one of the following categories:

❏ Fundamental models, which are based on a set of hypotheses, postulates and data, together with a means of drawing dynamic inferences from them. They attempt to build a fundamental description of some instruments or phenomenon. Good examples are equilibrium pricing models, which rely on a set of hypotheses to provide a pricing formula or methodology for a financial instrument.

❏ Phenomenological models, which are analogies or visualisations that describe, represent or help the understanding of a phenomenon that is not directly observable. They are not necessarily true but provide a useful picture of the reality. Good examples are single-factor interest rate models, which look at reality "as if" everybody was only concerned by the short-term interest rate, whose distribution will remain normal or lognormal at any point in time.

❏ Statistical models, which generally result from a regression or best fit between different data sets. They rely on correlation rather than causation and describe tendencies rather than dynamics. They are often a useful way of reporting information on data and on their trends.

In the following we will mainly focus on models belonging to the first and second categories, but we could easily extend our framework to include statistical models. In any problem, once a fundamental model has been selected or developed there are typically three main sources of uncertainty:

❏ Uncertainty about the model structure: did we specify the right model? Even after the most diligent model selection process, we cannot be sure that the true model – if any – has been selected.

❑ Uncertainty about the estimates of the model parameters given the model structure. Did we use the right estimator?

❑ Uncertainty about applying the model in a specific situation given the model structure and the estimation of its parameters. Can we use the model extensively? Or is it restricted to specific situations, financial assets or markets?

These three sources of uncertainty constitute what we call model risk. Model risk results from the inappropriate specification of a theoretical model or the use of an appropriate model but in an inadequate framework or for the wrong purpose. How can we measure this risk? Should we use the dispersion, the worst-case loss, a percentile, or an extreme loss value function and minimise it? There is a strong need for an ability to understand and measure model risk.

The academic literature has, essentially, focused on estimation risk and uncertainty related to use of the model but not on the uncertainty related to the structure of the model. Some exceptions are:

❑ The time-series analysis literature – see for instance the collection of papers by Dijkstra (1988) – as well as some econometric problems, where a model is often selected from a large class of models using specific criteria such as the largest R^2, AIC (Akaike information criterion), BIC (Bayesian information criterion), MDL (minimum description length criterion, C_p, or C_L proposed by Akaike (1973), Mallows (1973), Schwarz (1978) and Rissanen (1978). These methods set out to select from a collection of parametric models that model which minimises an empirical loss (typically measured as a squared error or a minus log-likelihood) plus some penalty term which is proportional to the dimension of the model.

❑ The option pricing literature, such as the work by Bakshi, Cao and Chen (1997) or Buhler *et al.* (1998), where prices resulting from the application of different models and different input parameter estimations are compared to quoted market prices to determine which model is the "best" in terms of market calibration.

This sparseness of the literature is rather surprising as errors arising from uncertainty about the model structure are, *a priori*, likely to be much larger than those arising from estimation errors or misuse of a particular model.

The steps of the model-building process (or how to create model risk)

In this section we will focus on the model-building process (or, if the problem is to select a model from among a set of possible candidates, the process of adopting a model) in the particular case of interest rate models. Our problem is the following: we want to develop (or select), estimate and use a model that can explain and fit the term structure of interest rates in order to price or manage a given set of interest rate-contingent securities.

Our model-building process can be decomposed into four steps: identification of the relevant factors; specification of the dynamics for each factor; parameter estimation; and implementation.

ENVIRONMENT CHARACTERISATION AND FACTOR IDENTIFICATION
The first step in the model-building process is to characterise the environment in which we are going to operate. We ask:

❑ What does the world look like?
❑ Is the market frictionless?
❑ Is it liquid enough?
❑ Is it complete?
❑ Are all prices observable?

Answers to these questions will often result in a set of hypotheses that are fundamental for the model to be developed. But if the model world differs too much from the true

KEY STEPS IN THE MODEL-BUILDING PROCESS

1. Characterisation of the environment

2. Choice of methodological approach

3. Determination of the optimal number of factors

4. Determination of the appropriate factors

5. Specification of the dynamics of the factors

6. Estimation procedures

7. Validation of the model

world, the resulting model will be useless. Note that, on the other hand, if most economic agents adopt the model, it can become a self-fulfilling prophecy.

The next step is the identification of the factors that are driving the interest rate term structure. This step involves the identification of both the number of factors and the factors themselves.

Which methodology should be followed? Up to now, the discussion has been based on the assumption of the existence of a certain number of factors. Nothing has been said about what a factor is (nor on how many are needed). Basically, two different empirical approaches can be used. On the one hand, the explicit approach assumes that the factors are known and that their returns are observed; using time-series analysis, this allows us to estimate the factor exposures.[2] On the other hand, the implicit approach is neutral with respect to the nature of the factors and relies purely on statistical methods, such as principal components or cluster analysis, to determine a fixed number of unique factors such that the covariance matrix of their returns is diagonal and they maximise the explanation of the variance of the returns on some assets. Of course, the implicit approach is frequently followed by a second step in which the implicit factors are compared to existing macroeconomic or financial variables in order to explicitly identify them.

For instance, most empirical studies using a principal component analysis have decomposed the motion of the interest rate term structure into three independent and non-correlated factors:

❏ The first is a shift of the term structure – ie, a parallel movement of all the rates. It usually accounts for up to 80–90% of the total variance (the exact figure depending on the market and on the period of observation).

❏ The second is a twist – ie, a situation in which long rates and short-term rates move in opposite directions. It usually accounts for an additional 5–10% of the total variance.

❏ The third is called a butterfly (the intermediate rate moves in the opposite direction to the short and long-term rate). Its influence is generally small (1–2% of the total variance).

As the first component generally explains a large fraction of the yield curve movements, it may be tempting to reduce the problem to a one-factor model,[3] generally chosen to be the short-term rate. Most early interest rate models (such as Merton, 1973; Vasicek, 1977; Cox, Ingersoll and Ross, 1985; Hull and White, 1990, 1993; etc) are in fact single-factor models. These models are easy to understand, to implement and to solve. Most of them provide analytical expressions for the prices of simple interest rate-contingent claims.[4] But single-factor models suffer from various criticisms:

❏ The long-term rate is generally a deterministic function of the short rate.

❏ The prices of bonds of different maturities are perfectly correlated (or, equivalently,

IDENTIFICATION OF FACTORS: IMPLICIT AND EXPLICIT APPROACHES

Determination of factors

The goal is to summarise and/or explain the available information (for example, a large number of historical observations) with a limited set of factors (or variables) while losing as little information as possible.

Implicit method	Explicit method
Analyse the data over a specific time span to determine simultaneously the factors, their values and the exposures to the factors. Each factor is a variable with the greatest possible explanatory power	Specify a set of variables that are thought to capture systematic risk, such as macroeconomic, financial or firm characteristics. It is assumed that the factor values are observable and measurable
Endogenous specification	Exogenous specification
Factors are extracted from the data and have no economic interpretation	Factors are specified by the user and are easily interpreted
Neutral with respect to the nature of the factors	Strong bias with respect to the nature of the factors. In particular, omitting a factor is easy
Relies on pure statistical analysis (principal components/cluster analysis)	Relies on intuition and/or experience
Best possible fit within the sample of historical observations (eg, for historical analysis)	May provide a better fit out of the sample of historical observations (eg, for forecasting)

there is a perfect correlation between movements in rates of different maturities).

❏ Some securities are sensitive to both the shape and the level of the term structure. Pricing or hedging them will require at least a two-factor model.

Furthermore, empirical evidence suggests that multifactor models do significantly better than single-factor models in explaining the whole shape of the term structure. This explains the early development of two-factor models (see Table 1), which are much more complex than the single-factor models. As demonstrated by Rebonato (1997), a multifactor model will often give a better fit to the term structure but makes it necessary to solve partial differential equations in a higher dimension to obtain prices for interest rate-contingent claims.

What is the optimal number of factors to be considered? The answer generally depends on the interest rate product that is examined and on the profile (concave, convex or linear) of its terminal payoff. One-factor models are more comprehensible and relevant to a wide range of products or circumstances, but they also have their limits. As an example, a one-factor model is a reasonable assumption to value a treasury bill, but it is much less reasonable for valuing options written on the slope of the yield curve. Securities whose payoffs are primarily dependent on the shape of the yield curve and/or its volatility term structure rather than its overall level will not be modelled well using single-factor approaches. The same remark applies to derivative instruments that marry foreign

Table 1. Examples of various two- and three-factor models

Model	Factors
Richard (1978)	Real short-term rate, expected instantaneous inflation rate
Brennan and Schwartz (1979)	Short-term rate, long-term rate
Schaefer and Schwartz (1984)	Long-term rate, spread between long-term and short-term rates
Cox, Ingersoll and Ross (1985)	Short-term rate, inflation
Schaefer and Schwartz (1987)	Short-term rate, spread between long-term and short-term rates
Longstaff and Schwartz (1992)	Short-term rate, short-term rate volatility
Das and Foresi (1996)	Short-term rate, mean of short-term rate
Chen (1996)	Short-term rate, mean and volatility of short-term rate

exchange with the term structures of interest rates risk exposures – such as differential swaps for which floating rates in one currency are used to calculate payments in another currency. Furthermore, for some variables the uncertainty in their future value has little influence on the value given by the model, while for others uncertainty is critical. For instance, interest rate volatility is of little importance for short-term stock options, whereas it is fundamental for interest rate options. But the answer will also depend on the particular use of the model.

What are the relevant factors? Here again there is no clear evidence. As an example, Table 1 lists some of the most common factor specifications to be found in the literature.[5] It appears that no single technique clearly dominates another when it comes to the joint identification of the number and identity of the relevant factors. Imposing factors by a pre-specification of some macroeconomic or financial variables is tempting, but we do not know how many factors are required. Deriving them using a non-parametric technique such as a principal component analysis will generally provide some information about the relevant number of factors – but not about their identity. When selecting a model one has to verify that all the important parameters and relevant variables have been included. Oversimplification and failure to select the right risk factors may have serious consequences.

SPECIFICATION OF FACTOR DYNAMICS

Once the factors have been determined, their individual dynamics have to be specified. Recall that specification of the dynamics has distribution assumptions built in.

Should we allow for jumps or restrict ourselves to diffusions? And in the case of diffusions, should we allow for constant parameters or time-varying ones? Should we place restrictions on the drift coefficient, such as linearity or mean-reversion? Should we think in discrete or in continuous time? What specification of the diffusion term is more suitable, and what are the resulting consequences for the distribution properties of interest rates? Can we allow for negative nominal interest rate values, if with a low probability? Should we prefer normality to lognormality? Should the interest rate dynamics be Markovian? Should we have a linear or a non-linear specification of the drift? Should we estimate the dynamics using non-parametric techniques rather than impose a parametric diffusion?

The problem is not simple because some models are often nested into other models. We will focus on single-factor diffusions for the short-term rate. For instance, let us consider the general Broze, Scaillet and Zakoian (1995) specification for the dynamics of the short-term rate:

$$dr(t) = \left(\alpha + \beta r(t)\right)dt + \sigma_0 \left(r^\gamma(t) + \sigma_1\right)dW(t) \qquad (1)$$

where $W(t)$ is a standard Brownian motion and $r(0)$ is a fixed positive (known) initial value. This model encompasses some of the most common specifications found in the literature (Table 2). Should we then automatically adopt the most general specification and let the estimation procedure decide on the value of some parameters – or, rather, specify and justify some restrictions?

CONSIDERATIONS/COMPARISONS OF USING JUMP AND DIFFUSION MODELS

Diffusions	Jumps	Jump–diffusion
Smooth and continuous changes from one price to the next	Prices are fixed but subject to instantaneous jumps from time to time	Smooth and continuous changes from one price to the next, but prices are subject to instantaneous jumps from time to time
Continuous price process	Discontinuous price process	Discontinuous price process with "rare" events
Convenient approximation, but clearly inexact representation of the real world	Purely theoretical	Good approximation of the real world
Simpler mathematics	Complex methodology	Complex methodology
The drift and volatility parameters must be estimated	The average jump size and the frequency with which jumps are likely to occur must be estimated	Calibration is difficult as both diffusion parameters and jump parameters must be estimated
Closed-form solutions are frequent	Closed-form solutions are rare	Closed-form solutions are rare
Leads to model inconsistencies such as volatility smiles or smirks, fat tails in the distribution, etc	Can explain phenomena such as "fat tails" in the distribution, or skewness and kurtosis effects	Can explain phenomena such as "fat tails" in the distribution, or skewness and kurtosis effects

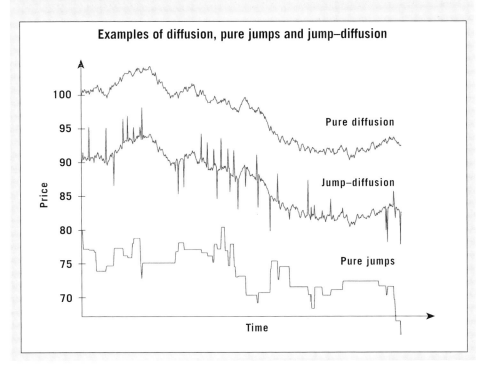

Examples of diffusion, pure jumps and jump–diffusion

Table 2. Parameters for various interest rate models

	α	β	σ_0	σ_1	γ
Merton (1973)		0		0	0
Vasicek (1977)				0	0
Cox, Ingersoll and Ross (1985)				0	0.5
Dothan (1978)	0	0		0	1
Geometric Brownian motion	0			0	1
Brennan and Schwartz (1980)				0	1
Cox, Ingersoll and Ross (1980)	0	0		0	1.5
Constant elasticity of variance	0			0	
Chan et al. (1992)				0	
Broze, Scaillet and Zakoian (1995)	◄		Totally unrestricted		►

Of course, assumptions about the dynamics of the short-term rate can be verified by reference to past data.[6] But, on the one hand, this involves undertaking estimation procedures before the right model can be selected. On the other hand, a misspecified model will not necessarily provide a bad fit to the data. For instance, duration-based models could provide better replication of results than multifactor models in the presence of parallel jumps in the term structure. Models with more parameters will generally give a better fit to the data but may give worse out-of-sample predictions. Models with time-varying parameters can be used to calibrate the model exactly to current market prices, but the error terms might be reported as unstable parameters and/or non-stationary volatility term structures (Carverhill, 1995).

PARAMETER ESTIMATION
The final step – which comes only after the two previous steps have been completed – is the parameter estimation procedure. Most people generally confuse model risk with estimation risk. Whereas estimation risk is an essential part of the process, it remains only a nested part of the model-production chain.

The theory of parameter estimation generally assumes that the true model is known. Once the factors have been selected and their dynamics specified, the model parameters must be estimated using a given set of data. Nowadays, using appropriate computer software, fitting a time-series model is usually straightforward. However, in the context of model risk, some important issues should be considered.

Is the set of data representative of what we want to model? A model may be correct, but the data fed into it may be incorrect. If we lengthen the data set, we might include some elements that are too old and insignificant; if we shorten it, we might end up with non-representative data. Of course, one can always use higher-frequency data, but is this really appropriate to solve a given problem?

Is the data set adequate for asymptotic and convergence properties to be fulfilled? For instance, in the case of the Vasicek (1977) or Cox, Ingersoll and Ross (1985) models Fournie and Talay (1991) have shown that natural estimators (such as maximum likelihood and a generalised method of moments) applied to daily interest rate observations required such a lengthy observation period – 110 years, over which model parameters were assumed to be constant – that the corresponding model was totally unrealistic.

Is the set of data subject to measurement errors (for instance, non-simultaneous recording of options and underlying quotes, bid–ask bouncing effects or other liquidity effects)?

How can we estimate parameters that may not be observable? The factors of our model have to correspond to observable variables to be estimated. But, in finance, some of the quantities we are dealing with are pure abstractions. For instance, even if we assume that the volatility of an asset is constant, how can we estimate it? How about future volatility? Some of the variables are directly measurable, while others are human expectations and, therefore, are indirectly measurable.

What if the result of the estimation procedure is one that does not make sense? For instance, the Hull and White (1993) extended model

$$dr(t) = \big(\alpha(t) + \beta(t)r(t)\big)dt + \sigma r^{\gamma}(t)dW(t) \qquad (2)$$

specified with $0 < \gamma < 0.5$ does not necessarily provide a unique solution (see Arnold (1973, p. 124)). What should one do if the result of the estimation is 0.4? As another example, Chan *et al.* (1992) empirically tested the following model:

$$dr(t) = \big(\alpha + \beta r(t)\big)dt + \sigma r^{\gamma}(t)dW(t) \qquad (3)$$

They found that there was no mean-reversion and that $\gamma = 1.5$, which implies non-stationarity – in contradiction to most popular one-factor models.

Another important problem arises with the use of a continuous-time modelling framework: approximations. Continuous-time stochastic processes provide a very elegant abstraction for describing market situations. But real market data are more of a discrete form, whether sampled at a regular time interval or at random time intervals (tick-by-tick). Thus, to estimate a continuous-time model we must discretise it – that is, we must replace the continuous-time model by a discrete-time approximation. We then can estimate the parameters of the discrete-time model using our discrete-time data and, later on, use these parameters as estimators of our continuous-time model parameters. But it is important to appreciate that the discretised process is only an approximation of the continuous-time specification.

Furthermore, the econometric estimation of continuous-time financial models using discrete-time observations is still unexplored despite important developments in the recent literature (see, for instance, Fournie and Talay, 1991; Chan *et al.*, 1992; Chen and Scott, 1993; or Broze, Scaillet and Zakoian, 1995). Which estimation methodology should one use? There are a large number of econometric techniques for the estimation of parameters, including non-parametric methods.[7] Examples of these are: maximum likelihood (MLE) and its different adaptations, which focus on the probability of having the most likely path between those generated by a model; the generalised method of moments (GMM), which relies on finding different functions – called "moments" – which should be zero if the model is perfect, and attempts to set them to zero to find correct values of the model parameters; and filtering techniques, which require an initial guess and continually improve it as more data become available.

Which technique is best? It depends. For instance, compare GMM with MLE. The former is reasonably fast, easy to implement and does not require knowledge of the distribution of a noise term, but it does not make use of all the information we may have regarding a specific model. If we have a complete specification of the joint distribution for interest rates in a multifactor model,[8] MLE is more efficient than GMM but may introduce additional specification errors by specifying arbitrary structures for the measurement errors.

In addition to these problems, there is the structural incompleteness of the market. If we take the example of the estimation of the term structure, in a complete market the required term structure would be directly observable. But in practice this is not the case: zero-coupon bonds are not available for all maturities and suffer from liquidity and tax effects (Daves and Ehrhardt, 1993; Jordan, 1984), and the term structure must be estimated using coupon bonds. Even if correct bond data are available, which methodology should be selected? In 1990 a survey of software vendors (Mitsubishi, 1990) indicated that 12 out of 13 used linear interpolation to derive yield curves, a methodology that is still recommended by RiskMetrics (1995). But spline techniques are also a recommended technique when smoothness is an issue (Adams and van Deventer, 1994). Barnhill *et al.* (1996) have compared four methodologies for estimation of the yield curve: linear interpolation along the par-yield curve followed by bootstrap calculation of spot rates; cubic spline interpolation along the par-yield curve followed by bootstrap calculation of spot rates; cubic spline regression estimation of a continuous discount function using all treasury bonds; and the Coleman–Fisher–Ibbotson method of regression estimation of a piecewise-constant forward rate function for all treasury bonds. The resulting spot rates were then

PANEL 4

COMPARISON OF GMM AND MLE

Let $X_1, \ldots, X_n$ be a random sample from a distribution, denoted f(x, q), that depends on a parameter θ. Let $x_1, \ldots, x_n$ be a set of observed values.

Maximum likelihood estimation (MLE)

The basic idea starts with the joint distribution of $X_1, \ldots, X_n$. The likelihood of the sample is the joint probability density function evaluated at $x_1, \ldots, x_n$ and is denoted by $L(\theta, x_1, \ldots, x_n)$, where θ denotes a given set of parameters, or $L(\theta)$ in brief notation. $L(\theta)$ is a statistic that depends on the observed sample.

For a fixed θ, probability statements can be made about $X_1, \ldots, X_n$. If we have the observations $x_1, \ldots, x_n$, but θ is unknown, we regard information about θ as being contained in the likelihood. Therefore, the statistical inference or procedure should be consistent with the assumption that the best explanation of a set of data is provided by θ^*, a value of θ that maximises the likelihood function. This value of θ is called the maximum likelihood estimate.

Roughly speaking, the MLE method yields values for the unknown parameters that maximise the probability of obtaining as a result the observed set of data. It is convenient when the likelihood (ie, the joint distribution) is known analytically – for example in the Vasicek (1977) or Merton (1973) models, where interest rate changes are normal.

Generalised method of moments (GMM)

The generalised method of moments consists in finding different functions – called "moments" – which should be zero if the model is perfect. For example, the Chan, Karolyi, Longstaff and Sanders (1992) model specified by equation (3) in the main text can be expressed in discretised form as

$$r(t + 1) - r(t) = \alpha + \beta r(t) + \varepsilon(t + 1)$$

with moments conditions

$$E[\varepsilon(t + 1)] = 0$$

and

$$E[\varepsilon^2(t + 1)] = \sigma^2 r^{2\gamma}(t)$$

The problem is now to find the model parameters σ and γ so that these two expectations are as close as possible to zero for the set of observed interest rate values.

Roughly speaking, the GMM yields values for the unknown parameters that verify a set of necessary intuitive and logical conditions. It is convenient when we do not have the likelihood function or when it is too complicated – for instance in the Cox, Ingersoll and Ross (1985) model, where interest rate changes are proportional to a non-central chi-squared variate.

fed into a Hull and White extended Vasicek model to compute estimates of European calls on zero-coupon bonds, American calls on coupon bonds, and swaptions. The estimated prices of all the instruments were then compared to the effective market prices based on the known term structure of spot rates. For some of the estimation techniques it appeared that option pricing errors were, on average, between 18% and 80%, depending on the estimation procedure.

In addition, one should always be cautious about over-parameterisation or under-parameterisation of a problem. Calibration can always be achieved by using more parameters or by introducing time-varying parameters. But heavily fluctuating values of the estimated parameters can often point to a misspecified or a mis-estimated model. For instance, Hull and White (1995) themselves wrote: "It is always dangerous to use time-varying model parameters so that the initial volatility curve is fitted exactly. Using all the degrees of freedom in a model to fit the volatility exactly constitutes an over-parameterisation of the model. It is our opinion that there should be no more than one time-varying parameter used in Markov models of the term structure evolution, and this should be used to fit the initial term structure." This explains why, in practice, the Hull and White (1993) model specified in equation (2) is often implemented with β and σ constant and α as time-varying. This also explains why, when comparing the fit of different models, the Bayesian information criterion is generally preferred to the Akaike information criterion so as to penalise adequately the introduction of additional parameters.

A PARTICULAR PARAMETER: THE MARKET PRICE OF RISK
A particular parameter in interest rate-contingent claim pricing models is the market price of risk. Most valuation models based on the martingale pricing technique require as an input the market price of risk,[9] which is usually denoted by λ. This parameter is generally not visible in the specification of the factor dynamics but appears in the partial differential equation that must be fulfilled by the price of an interest rate-contingent claim.

The market price of risk is defined as the risk premium demanded by investors for holding an asset divided by the risk incurred (volatility):

$$\lambda = \frac{\mu - r_F}{\sigma} \qquad (4)$$

where μ is the instantaneous return on the asset, σ is its volatility and r_F is the risk-free rate. The ratio can change over time (as μ and σ change), but it should be the same for all traded assets to avoid arbitrage opportunities.

When the underlying variable is a traded asset, as in the Black and Scholes (1973) framework, the replicating portfolio idea eliminates the need for the market price of risk as choosing adequate portfolio weights eliminates uncertain returns and, thus, risk itself. But when the underlying variable is not a traded asset the risk premium has to be specified or estimated from market data. Which methodology is better? Unfortunately, there is no definite answer. Various specifications can be found in the literature: for instance, Vasicek (1977) exogenously assumed a constant risk premium. Cox, Ingersoll and Ross (1985) showed that the endogenous risk premium at equilibrium in their model is $\sqrt{\pi(t)}$, a result from their very specific representative investor (which has a logarithmic utility function). But the same risk premium specification was adopted exogenously by Hull and White (1990).

On the other hand, inferring the value of the risk premium from market data is not an easier task. In theory, the market price of risk is the same across all derivatives that are contingent on the same stochastic variable. This should allow one to extract information from one traded security and to use it to value other securities – providing relative valuation as everything becomes dependent on the correct pricing of one initial security. But, in practice, the inferred market price of risk may differ across instruments.

As shown by Bollen (1997), an incorrect specification of the risk premium can have dramatic consequences on the valuation of interest rate derivatives – causing variations of more than 42% of the price. It seems that there is still important work to be performed in the field of the estimation of the market price of risk.

MODEL RISK AND IMPLEMENTATION ISSUES
Finally, model risk may arise even if all of the previous steps have been performed correctly. For instance, the model may produce numerically unstable or incorrect solutions. As an example, most of the time-invariant models listed in Table 2 suffer from the shortcoming that the short-term rate dynamics implies an endogenous term structure, which is not necessarily consistent with the observed structure. Furthermore, these models cannot be calibrated to effective yield curves, and they cannot at the same time fit the initial term structure and a predefined future behaviour for the short-term rate volatility. As a

consequence, practitioners are very reluctant to use them; they often make the parameters time-varying and use this degree of freedom to calibrate the model exactly to current market prices. Model risk, therefore, results in unstable parameters. But this instability can also result from numerical problems (such as the inversion of a near-singular matrix) or from problems of implementation: the model may require a large number of iterations to converge (a typical problem in Monte Carlo simulations or in solving partial differential equations), may require a higher precision (for floating point numbers) or may use inappropriate approximations.

It should also be noted that some of the hypotheses on which the model is based may simply not hold in the real world, resulting in a model that performs poorly. For instance, the model may assume that there exist zero-coupon bonds for all required maturities although, in practice, the set of available maturity dates is restricted.

Major consequences of model risk

In this section we will examine the major consequences of model risk in three different domains – namely, those of pricing, hedging, and the definition of rules for regulatory capital adequacy. When do they arise? Can we measure them, with or without assuming an objective function?

MODEL RISK IN PRICING

The importance of model risk in pricing should be clear. In the presence of model risk theoretical prices will diverge from observed prices. If we remain in the framework proposed by Harrison and Kreps (1979), under which we can compute the price of a contingent claim as the discounted expected value of its future price, the pricing model for an option (say, a call option $C(t)$) depends on a pricing function, f, a set of observable parameters, $\Omega(t)$, and a set of non-observable parameters, $\theta(t)$:

$$C(t) = f\big(\Omega(t), \theta(t)\big) \tag{5}$$

But one can add mutually independent, zero-mean homoscedastic error terms to the basic model:

$$\hat{C}(t) = f\big(\Omega(t), \theta(t)\big) + \varepsilon(t) \tag{6}$$

or, as suggested by Jacquier and Jarrow (1996), a multiplicative error specification:

$$\hat{C}(t) = f\big(\Omega(t), \theta(t)\big)e^{\varepsilon(t)} \tag{7}$$

which has a zero expected value. This implies that even if we use the true pricing function, f, the true parameters, $\Omega(t)$, and appropriate estimations of the non-observable parameters, $\theta(t)$, our theoretical prices, $C(t)$, will differ from the market prices $\hat{C}(t)$.

How do we distinguish "noise" from model error? A market error can be the basis of an arbitrage opportunity, whereas a model error cannot. Once we have cleared the observed market prices of these errors, use of the true model should provide us with the true price. But, in practice, we often have to use the observed price as the true price as there is no procedure for clearing these errors or for exhaustive definition of the effect of market frictions.

In addition, there still remain some problems relating to the performance of theoretical models for pricing purposes:

❏ First, the pricing models are often derived under the paradigm of a market that is perfect and complete. In practice, they are applied in markets which are incomplete and imperfect. The resulting price is not unique any more, and one can only derive bounds for the no-arbitrage price.

❏ Second, when comparing model and market prices one generally uses a quadratic criterion such as the mean and standard deviation of the pricing errors at a given point in time or the root mean squared error. But such a criterion is only valid if the errors are normally distributed or if the user has a quadratic utility function. The first condition is generally not fulfilled, and the second is a very specific preference description that has very undesirable properties.

❏ Third, if all traders use an incorrect model, the model becomes a self-fulfilling prophecy and comparing theoretical prices to observed ones will result in low average errors. As an example, in the context of stock index options pricing Chesney, Gibson and Louberge (1995) show that one can artificially improve the performance of a pricing model by using an implied volatility estimate, while at the same time the basic assumptions of the model are not verified.

MODEL RISK IN HEDGING (AND PRICING AGAIN!)

The presence of model risk will affect any hedging strategy. As a very simple illustration, let us consider the Black and Scholes (1973) framework: in a complete, perfect market the asset price follows a geometric Brownian motion with constant parameters and constant interest rates:[10]

$$\frac{dS(t)}{S(t)} = \mu\, dt + \sigma\, dW(t) \tag{8}$$

This defines our true model. We denote by $C(t)$ the value at time t of a European call option with maturity T on the asset $S(t)$. By Itô's lemma

$$dC(t) = \left(\frac{\partial C(t)}{\partial S(t)}\mu S(t) + \frac{\partial C(t)}{\partial t} + \frac{1}{2}\frac{\partial^2 C(t)}{\partial S^2(t)}\sigma^2 S^2(t) \right) dt + \frac{\partial C(t)}{\partial S(t)}\sigma S(t)\, dW(t) \tag{9}$$

Furthermore, we know that the call price, $C(t)$, must satisfy the partial differential equation

$$\frac{\partial C(t)}{\partial S(t)}rS(t) + \frac{\partial C(t)}{\partial t} + \frac{1}{2}\frac{\partial^2 C(t)}{\partial S^2(t)}\sigma^2 S^2(t) - rC(t) = 0 \tag{10}$$

with boundary condition $C(T) = \max(S(T) - K, 0)$.

An investor is short one call option and wants to hedge by creating a replicating portfolio. When hedging in continuous time using the true model in a frictionless market, a delta-hedging strategy should eliminate the option writer's risk completely. At time t, to hedge the short position in the option $(-C(t))$, the investor will hold $\partial C(t)/\partial S(t)$ units of the underlying asset and $\left(C(t) - [\partial C(t)/\partial S(t)]S(t)\right)$ units of cash. The value of his total portfolio, $\Pi(t)$, will be equal to zero if there are no arbitrage opportunities. The instantaneous variations of the portfolio are defined by

$$d\Pi(t) = -dC(t) + \frac{\partial C(t)}{\partial S(t)}dS(t) + \left(C(t) - \frac{\partial C(t)}{\partial S(t)}S(t) \right)r\, dt \tag{11}$$

which can be shown to be equal to zero. Any other return would give an arbitrage opportunity.

What happens when the hedger uses a misspecified and/or mis-estimated model? For simplicity, let us assume that he still uses a single-factor model. By misspecified, we mean that the hedger uses an alternative option pricing model. For instance, the hedger could use an arithmetic Brownian motion with time-varying parameters or a mean-reverting diffusion process. By mis-estimated, we mean that the hedger uses the Black and Scholes model but mis-estimates the parameters μ and/or σ. In both cases, the option pricing model will give a price $\hat{C}(t)$ for the option that differ from the true (market) price $C(t)$ and provide an incorrect hedge ratio $\partial\hat{C}(t)/\partial S(t)$. Consequently, the hedger's replicating portfolio value will be defined as

$$\Pi(t) = -C(t) + \frac{\partial \hat{C}(t)}{\partial S(t)} S(t) + \left(\hat{C}(t) - \frac{\partial \hat{C}(t)}{\partial S(t)} S(t) \right) \tag{12}$$

Note that $\Pi(t)$ is not necessarily any longer equal to zero. The variation on his portfolio will be

$$d\Pi(t) = -dC(t) + \frac{\partial \hat{C}(t)}{\partial S(t)} dS(t) + \left(\hat{C}(t) - \frac{\partial \hat{C}(t)}{\partial S(t)} S(t) \right) rdt \tag{13}$$

Using (8) and (9) and rearranging terms yields

$$d\Pi(t) = \left[\frac{\partial \hat{C}(t)}{\partial S(t)} - \frac{\partial C(t)}{\partial S(t)} \right] (\mu - r) S(t) dt + \left(\hat{C}(t) - C(t) \right) rdt$$

$$+ \left[\frac{\partial \hat{C}(t)}{\partial S(t)} - \frac{\partial C(t)}{\partial S(t)} \right] \sigma S(t) dW(t) \tag{14}$$

This equation summarises the problems of hedging in the presence of model risk. The instantaneous variation of the portfolio depends on three terms:

❏ The first results from a difference between the true delta parameter and the delta given by the model. It also depends on the difference between the drift of the underlying asset and the risk-free rate.[11] Depending on these differences, at maturity the hedging strategy will create a terminal profit or a terminal loss, and the hedger may end up with a replicating portfolio that is far from what he needs to fulfill his liabilities. For some exotic options, delta hedging can in fact even increase the risk of the option writer (see, for instance, Gallus, 1996a).

❏ The second is a consequence of the difference between the true option price and the price given by the model. The initial investment to set up the replicating portfolio is incorrect and the difference is carried through time at the risk-free rate. As a consequence, the delta-hedging strategy may cease to be self-financing. In other words, at some point in time the hedger may have to borrow and infuse external funds into the strategy to maintain the delta hedge. As the borrowed amount may be larger than the total value of his portfolio, delta hedging with model risk can imply bankruptcy.

❏ The third results, again, from a difference between the "true" delta parameter and the delta given by the model. In addition, it depends on a stochastic term, making the hedging strategy result stochastic and path-dependent, and it depends also on the "true" volatility.

To summarise, in the presence of model risk – even if we assume frictionless markets – the delta-hedging strategy is no longer replicating or self-financing and, even worse, is path-dependent. The hedger undertakes risk, and should be compensated for it.

How, in practice, can we take into account model risk in hedging? Rebalancing the hedge more frequently does not help as there will still be a difference between the true hedging parameters and those given by the model. In some specific cases a possible solution consists in looking for a super-hedging strategy – ie, a strategy such that the hedging result is guaranteed whatever the true model.[12] Another solution can be to specify a loss function to be minimised by the hedging strategy.[13] Thus, perfect hedging is transformed into minimum "residual risk" hedging. As a consequence, pricing is not uniquely determined: the risk-neutrality argument cannot be invoked any more, and there is no self-financing strategy for trading a portfolio of the underlying asset and a risk-free bond such that the payoff of the contingent claim equals the value of the self-financing portfolio strategy.

Another important issue in hedging is the aggregation procedure. Using ad hoc models for each product can provide a better pricing or a better hedging strategy for each individual position. But if these models make distinct, idiosyncratic assumptions that are mutually inconsistent, can we simply add them up when examining the aggregated portfolio of various instruments? Certainly not. Nevertheless, this is widely done in practice, particularly with exotic products.

MODEL RISK IN A CAPITAL CHARGE REGULATORY FRAMEWORK

The regulators seek to ensure that the banks and other financial institutions have sufficient capital to meet large losses with an acceptable margin. Consequently, as we mentioned already, the managements of financial institutions must have the ability to identify, monitor and control their global exposure to interest rate risk. When an institution's assets and liabilities are contingent on the term structure and its evolution, any change in interest rates may cause a decline in the net economic value of the bank's equity and in its capital-to-asset ratio. Proposition 6 of the Basle Committee (1997) proposal states: "It is essential that banks have interest rate risk measurement systems that capture all material sources of interest rate risk and that assess the effect of interest rates changes in ways which are consistent with the scope of their activities. The assumptions underlying the system should be clearly understood by risk managers and bank management."

This proposition provides banks with a large degree of freedom to choose from a large class of ad hoc interest rate term structure models. Using their own internal models, banks may calculate their capital requirement as a function of their forecast 10-days-ahead value-at-risk. The aim is to estimate the potential loss that would not, with 99% certainty, be exceeded over the next 10 trading days.

To ensure that banks use adequate internal models, regulators have introduced the idea of backtesting and multipliers: the market risk capital charge is computed using the bank's own estimate of the value-at-risk times a multiplier that depends on the number of exceptions[14] over the last 250 days. For instance, in the US, the market risk capital charge at time $t+1$ is defined by[15]

$$MRC_{t+1} = \max\left[VAR_t(10,1); \frac{M_t}{60}\sum_{i=1}^{60} VAR_{t-i}(10,1)\right] \qquad (15)$$

where $VaR_t(10, 1)$ denotes the value-at-risk on day t using a 10-day holding period and a 99% coverage. As noted by the Basle Committee on Banking Supervision (1996), the multiplier M_t must be equal to at least 3; furthermore, it should increase with the magnitude and the number of exceptions, as both are a matter of concern for the regulators. If there are four or fewer exceptions, M_t remains at 3. Between five and nine exceptions, M_t increases with the number of exceptions. For 10 and more exceptions, M_t is set to 4 and the bank's model is deemed to be inaccurate and must be improved. Alternative model-evaluation methods include the binomial distribution and interval forecast evaluation. In the first method banks report their one-day value-at-risk estimate and their actual portfolio losses; the latter are then modelled as a random variable drawn from an independent binomial distribution with a probability of occurrence specified as 1%; the test consists in computing a likelihood ratio and comparing it to a one-degree of freedom chi-square critical value.[16] In the second method, adapted from Christoffersen (1997), the test consists of a conditional or unconditional forecast of the lower 1% interval of the one-step-ahead return distribution.

The newly proposed pre-commitment approach is more flexible: banks choose and report a level of capital that they consider adequate to back their trading books. This level of capital can be computed by any procedure, including the use of an internal model. But if the cumulative losses of the trading book exceed the chosen capital charge, the bank will be penalised (in a way that remains to be specified – eg, by disclosure) by the regulators.

Whatever these penalties or value-at-risk adjustments, they result in overfunding and are nothing other than simple "ad hoc" safety procedures to anticipate the impact of model risk. A bank might use an inadequate or inappropriate model, but the resulting impact is mitigated by adjusting the capital charge. As a consequence, banks that attempt to use "better-quality" models are penalised if model risk analysis is poorly assessed.

In addition, these penalties or value-at-risk adjustments also reduce the moral hazard problem that is introduced by the freedom to select an internal model. For instance, as Aussenegg and Pichler (1997) have shown, when estimating the value-at-risk of a bond portfolio models of the spot rate based on the normality assumption perform very poorly – even when they are extended with time-dependent means and volatilities – while historical simulation performs better. But the value-at-risk estimated from normality-based models is less than that given by models involving historical simulation. Knowing that its charge in capital will depend on its value-at-risk, will a bank select the most adequate model or the one that gives the lowest value-at-risk?

Clearly, whatever method the Bank of International Settlements selects to measure and take into account model risk, it will create an opportunity for regulatory-induced model arbitrage.

NECESSITY OF A MODEL RISK LOSS FUNCTION

In all the above-cited cases the objectives of the model user were clearly different. This shows that we need to specify a loss function to measure how precise a model proves to be. The objective will be to select the model that minimises the value of this loss function for a specific agent or institution.

Of course, the loss function will depend on the specific applications associated with the model. For instance, when pricing, we may select as a loss function the root mean squared error, the average error, or the maximum error compared to effectively quoted prices; when hedging, the loss function may depend on the statistical properties of the terminal value of the total position (such as the average terminal profit or loss,[17] its variance, etc) or be defined in terms of intertemporal behaviour (eg, in terms of average error over time, maximal loss, first passage time below zero, etc); in a regulatory context, the loss function can be defined in terms of the magnitude and number of value-at-risk exceptions, as proposed by Lopez (1998), or any alternative function that captures certain aspects of regulators' concerns (for instance, minimising the systemic risk of large losses).

In addition, such a loss function will often depend on a specific time-horizon that varies with the type of positions considered, the division and/or the responsibility levels involved (trading desk versus management), the motivation (private versus regulatory), the asset class (equity, fixed income, derivatives), the activity (trading, pricing, hedging, etc), the risk aversion, the relative size of the position, or the industry (bank versus insurance). It can also differ between a marginal position and the aggregate portfolio if diversification allows a reduction of model risk. And for a given model and a specific instrument, the loss function will also depend on whether the model user's net position is on the short or the long side.

This clearly shows that the model risk loss function will depend on the specific application and that it should be decided on an application-by-application basis under the constraints faced by and objectives of the financial institution.

Conclusion

This chapter has shown that the reliance on models to handle interest rate risk carries its own risks because the use of mathematical models requires simplifications and hypotheses which may cause the models to diverge from reality. Furthermore, developing or selecting a model is always a trade-off between realism and accuracy and computability.

Whatever the model used in interest rate risk management, three key issues should always be addressed. First, have all important variables and relevant parameters been included in the model? Second, have all the assumptions about the dynamics of these variables been verified? And third, are the results obtained from simulation compatible with similar observed market situations? Once these points have been verified, it is important to be aware of the presence of model uncertainty, even if one has to accept that there is no simple way of overcoming the problem.[18]

What should the properties of a "desirable" and ideal term structure model be? First of all, the model should be applicable in the market considered, parsimonious in the number of factors, quick to operate, and easy to calibrate and use. The results it gives should be easily interpretable and comprehensible by every user (in particular, they should not be counter-intuitive or esoteric or the model might be rejected because lack of understanding by users will lead to an erosion of confidence and trust in the model). The model should also be internally consistent and accurate against the market and it should be arbitrage-free; this is another essential point in building the confidence required if the model is to be used. Its parameters should be robust and stable from one fitting to another; under normal conditions unstable parameters are often an indication of a poorly specified model. Finally, the model should be exhaustive across products and perform equally well under differing economic conditions or strategies.

In practice, a "good" model will simply provide a useful and applicable approximation for the task at hand. Model risk should be assessed with a loss function and a time horizon that are adequate and relevant on the basis of the institution's current objectives; in particular, users of the model (traders, regulators, senior managers, etc) should be made aware of the model's limits and the loss function should be made consistent with the objectives of the users.

Measuring model risk is challenging – particularly in the domain of interest rates, where simultaneously there exist a large number of products and of incompatible models. Model risk should not be considered a tool to find *the* perfect model but rather as an instrument and/or a methodology that helps in understanding the weaknesses and in exploiting the strengths of the alternatives at hand. Progressive dynamic learning has already been proved effective in the enhancement of model performance.

Last, but not least, another essential issue is related to the diversification of model risk. If model risk cannot be fully diversified, the residual risk should be priced by the agents in the market. An important consequence for the banking industry is to determine who bears the costs – the clients, the shareholders, the bondholders or the government – if there is a systemic, model-driven failure in the financial market.

1 *Since supervisory authorities are aware of model risk associated with the use of internal models, as a precautionary device they have imposed adjustment factors: the internal model value-at-risk should be multiplied by an adjustment factor subject to an absolute minimum of 3, and a plus factor – ranging from 0 to 1 – will be added to the multiplication factor if backtesting reveals failures in the internal model. This overfunding solution is nothing but an insurance or an ad hoc safety factor against model risk.*

2 *An alternative is to assume that the exposures are known, which allows the factor returns for each period to be recovered cross-sectionally.*

3 *It must be stressed at this point that this does not necessarily imply that the whole term structure is forced to move in parallel but simply that a single source of uncertainty is sufficient to explain the movements of the term structure (or the price of a particular interest rate-contingent claim).*

4 *See Gibson, Lhabitant and Talay (1997) for an exhaustive survey of existing term structure model specifications.*

5 *For a detailed discussion of the considerations involved in choosing the number and type of factors and the empirical evidence, see Nelson and Schaefer (1983) or Litterman and Scheinkman (1991).*

6 *Or rejected! Ait-Sahalia (1996) rejected all the existing linear drift specifications for the dynamics of the short-term rate using non-parametric tests.*

7 *See, for instance, Chen and Scott (1993) for MLE, Gibbons and Ramaswamy (1993) or Longstaff and Schwartz (1992) for GMM, and Chen and Scott (1995) for the Kalman filter.*

8 *Otherwise we have to use an approximate likelihood function, but this may lead to inconsistent estimators (see Going, 1997).*

9 *Multifactor models require the input of multiple prices of risk – in fact, one for each factor!*

10 *Working in the Black and Scholes framework leads to an important analytic simplification without any loss of generality. The equivalent derivation in the case of a more general interest rate model can be found in Bossy et al. (1998).*

11 *Note that if the hedger uses the Black and Scholes model, but with a mis-estimated drift coefficient, this first term vanishes as the true delta parameter and the delta given by the model are the same.*

12 *See, for instance, Lhabitant, Martini and Reghai (1998) for options on a zero-coupon bond.*

13 *See, for instance, Bouchaud, Iori and Sornette (1996).*

14 *An exception occurs when the loss exceeds the model-calculated value-at-risk.*

15 *In fact, there is an additional capital charge for the portfolio-specific credit risk.*

16 *The methodology is subject to various criticisms, as shown by Kupiec (1995), including poor properties in finite samples and a low power in medium-size samples.*

17 *This is often referred to as building a risk-neutral strategy "on average", as the hedged portfolio grows at the risk-free rate on average for multiple realisations of the underlying but not necessarily for one given realisation.*

18 *An alternative approach to reducing model risk is to assume that more than one model may provide a sufficiently close approximation to the given data for the required objective. This notion of using more than one model and weighting them is a key element of the Bayesian model averaging proposed by West and Harrison (1989, chapter 12).*

Bibliography

Adams, K. J., and D. van Deventer, 1994, "Fitting Yield Curves and Forward Rate Curves with Maximum Smoothness", *Journal of Fixed Income* 4 (June), pp. 52–62.

Ait-Sahalia, Y., 1996, "Testing Continuous-Time Models of the Spot Interest Rate", *Review of Financial Studies* 9, pp. 385–426.

Akaike, H., 1973, "Information Theory and an Extension to the Maximum Likelihood Principle", in P. N. Petrov and F. Csaki (eds), *Proceedings of the Second International Symposium on Information Theory*, (Budapest: Akademia Kiado), pp. 267–81.

Arnold, L., 1973, *Stochastic Differential Equations* (New York: John Wiley and Sons).

Aussenegg, W., and S. Pichler, 1997, "Empirical Evaluation of Simple Models to Calculate Value-at-Risk of Fixed Income Instruments", Working paper, Vienna University of Technology.

Bakshi, G., C. Cao and Z. Chen, 1997, "Empirical Performance of Alternative Option Pricing Models", Working paper, University of Maryland.

Barnhill, T., Jr, J. Jordan, T. Barnhill and S. Mackey, 1996, "The Effects of Term Structure Estimation on the Valuation of Interest-Rate Derivatives", Working paper, FRB – Atlanta.

Basle Committee On Banking Supervision, 1995, "Framework for Supervisory Information About Derivatives Activities of Banks and Securities Firms".

Basle Committee On Banking Supervision, 1996, "Supervisory Framework for the Use of Backtesting in Conjunction with the Internal Models Approach to Market Risk Capital Requirements", Manuscript, Bank for International Settlements.

Basle Committee On Banking Supervision, 1997, "Principles for the Management of Interest Rate Risk".

Black, F., 1986, "Noise", *Journal of Finance* 41, pp. 529–43.

Black, F., 1990, "Living Up to the Model", *From Black–Scholes to Black Holes* (London: Risk Publications), pp. 17–22.

Black, F., and M. Scholes, 1973, "The Pricing of Options and Corporate Liabilities", *Journal of Political Economy* 81, pp. 637–59.

Bollen, N. P. B., 1997, "Derivatives and the Market Price of Risk", *Journal of Futures Markets* 17(7), pp. 839–54.

Bossy, M., R. Gibson, F. S. Lhabitant, C. Martini, N. Pistre and D. Talay, 1998, "Model Risk Analysis for Discount Bond Options", RiskLab Report.

Bouchaud, J. P., G. Iori and D. Sornette, 1996, "Real World Options", *Risk Magazine* 9(3), pp. 61–5.

Brennan, M. J., and E. S. Schwartz, 1979, "A Continuous-Time Approach to the Pricing of Bonds", *Journal of Banking and Finance* 3, pp. 135–55.

Brennan, M. J., and E. S. Schwartz, 1980, "Analysing Convertible Bonds", *Journal of Financial and Quantitative Analysis* 15, pp. 907-29.

Broze, L., O. Scaillet and J.-M. Zakoian, 1995, "Testing for Continuous-Time Models of the Short Term Interest Rate", *Journal of Empirical Finance* 2, pp. 199-223.

Buhler, W., M. Uhrig-Homburg, U. Walter and T. Weber, 1998, "An Empirical Comparison of Forward and Spot Rate Models for Valuing Interest Rate Options", *Journal of Finance,* forthcoming.

Carverhill, A., 1995, "A Note on the Models of Hull and White for Pricing Options on the Term Structure", *Journal of Fixed Income* September, pp. 89-96.

Chan, K. C., A. Karolyi, F. Longstaff and A. Sanders, 1992, "An Empirical Comparison of Alternative Models of the Short Term Interest Rate", *Journal of Finance* 47, pp. 1209-27.

Chatfield, C., 1996, "Model Uncertainty and Forecast Accuracy", *Journal of Forecasting* 15, pp. 495-508.

Chen, L., 1996, *Stochastic Mean and Stochastic Volatility: A Three Factor Model of the Term Structure of Interest Rates and its Application to the Pricing of Interest Rate Derivatives* (Oxford: Blackwell).

Chen, R., and L. Scott, 1993, "Maximum Likelihood Estimation of a Multi-Factor Equilibrium Model of the Term Structure of Interest Rates", *Journal of Fixed Income* December, pp. 14-32.

Chen, R., and L. Scott, 1995, "Multi-factor Cox-Ingersoll-Ross Models of the Term Structure: Estimates and Tests from a Kalman Filter Model", Working paper, Rutgers University and University of Georgia.

Chesney, M., R. Gibson and H. Louberge, 1995, "Arbitrage Trading and Index Option Pricing At the SOFFEX: An Empirical Study Using Daily and Intra-Daily Data", *Finanzmarkt und Portfolio Management* no. 1, pp. 35-61.

Christoffersen, P. F., 1997, "Evaluating Interval Forecasts", Manuscript, Research Department, International Monetary Fund.

Cox, J. C., J. E. Ingersoll and S. A. Ross, 1980, "An Analysis of Variable Rate Loan Contracts", *Journal of Finance* 35, pp. 389-403.

Cox, J. C., J. E. Ingersoll and S. A. Ross, 1985, "A Theory of the Term Structure of Interest Rates", *Econometrica* 53, pp. 385-407.

Das, S. R., and S. Foresi, 1996, "Exact Solution for Bond and Option Prices with Systematic Jump Risk", *Review of Derivatives Research* 1, pp. 7-24.

Daves, P. R., and M. C. Ehrhardt, 1993, "Liquidity, Reconstitution and the Value of U.S. Treasury Strips", *Journal of Finance* 48 (March), pp. 315-29.

Derman, E., 1996a, "Valuing Models and Modeling Value: A Physicist's Perspective on Modeling on Wall Street", *Journal of Portfolio Management* Spring, pp. 106-14.

Derman, E., 1996b, "Model Risk", *Risk Magazine* 9(5), pp. 34-7.

Dijkstra, T. K., 1988, *On Model Uncertainty and Its Statistical Implications* (Berlin: Springer Verlag).

Dothan, U. L., 1978, "On the Term Structure of Interest Rates", *Journal of Financial Economics* 6, pp. 59-69.

Duarte, A. M., 1997, "Model Risk and Risk Management", *Derivatives Quarterly* Spring, pp. 60-72.

El Karoui, N., and M. Jeanblanc-Picque, 1994, "Robustness of the Black and Scholes Formula", Prepublication no. 3, Equipe d'Analyse et de Probabilité, Université d'Evry.

Fournie, E., and D. Talay, 1991, "Application de la statistique des diffusions à un modèle de taux d'intérêt", *Finance* 12(2), pp. 79-111.

Gallus, C., 1996a, "Exploding Hedging Errors for Digital Options", Working paper, Deutsche Morgan Grenfell, October.

Gallus, C., 1996b, "Robustness of Hedging Strategies for European Options", Working paper, University of Erlanger.

Gibbons, R. M., and K. Ramaswamy, 1993, "A Test of the Cox, Ingersoll and Ross Model of the Term Structure", *Review of Financial Studies* 6, pp. 619-58.

Gibson, R., F. S. Lhabitant and D. Talay, 1997, "Modeling the Term Structure of Interest Rates: A Review of the Literature", RiskLab Report.

Going, A., 1997, "Estimation in Financial Models", RiskLab Report.

Harrison, M. J., and D. M. Kreps, 1979, "Martingales and Arbitrage in Multiperiod Securities Markets", *Journal of Economic Theory* 20, pp. 381–408.

Hull, J., and A. White, 1990, "Pricing Interest Rate Derivative Securities", *Review of Financial Studies* 3, pp. 573–92.

Hull, J., and A. White, 1993, "One Factor Interest Rate Models and the Valuation of Interest Rate Derivative Securities", *Journal of Financial and Quantitative Analysis* 28(2), pp. 235–54.

Hull, J., and A. White, 1995, "A Note on the Models of Hull and White for Pricing Options on the Term Structure. Response", *Journal of Fixed Income* September, pp. 97–102.

Jacquier, E., and R. Jarrow, 1996, "Model Error in Contingent Claim Models Dynamic Evaluation", Cirano Working paper 96s–12.

James, J., 1998, "Calibration Issues for Interest Rate Models", Mimeo, First National Bank of Chicago.

Jordan, J. V., 1984, "Tax Effects in Term Structure Estimation", *Journal of Finance* 39, June, pp. 393–406.

Kupiec, P., 1995, "Techniques for Verifying the Accuracy of Risk Measurement Models", *Journal of Derivatives* 3, pp. 73–84.

Lhabitant, F. S., C. Martini and A. Reghai, 1998, "Volatility Risk for Options on a Zero-Coupon Bond", RiskLab Report.

Litterman, R., and J. Scheinkman, 1991, "Common Factors Affecting Bond Returns", *Journal of Fixed Income* 1, pp. 54–62.

Longstaff, F., and E. Schwartz, 1992, "Interest Rate Volatility and the Term Structure: A Two Factor General Equilibrium Model", *Journal of Finance* 47, pp. 1259–82.

Lopez, J. A., 1998, "Methods for Evaluating Value-at-Risk Estimates", Working paper, Federal Reserve Bank of New-York.

Mallows, C. L., 1973, "Some Comments on C_p", *Technometrics* 15, pp. 661–75.

Merton, R. C., 1973, "Theory of Rational Option Pricing", *Bell Journal of Economics and Management Science* 4, pp. 141–83.

Merton, R. C., 1976, "The Impact on Option Pricing of Specification Error in the Underlying Stock Price Returns", *Journal of Finance* 31, no 2, pp. 333–50.

Mitsubishi, 1990, *Mitsubishi Finance Risk Directory, Risk Magazine,* London.

Nelson, C. R., and S. Schaefer, 1983, "The Dynamics of the Term Structure and Alternative Portfolio Immunization Strategies", in G. G. Kaufman and G. O. Bierwag (eds), *Innovations in Bond Portfolio Management* (Greenwhich, Conn.: JAI Press).

Rebonato, R., 1997, *Interest Rate Option Models* (New York: John Wiley).

Rebonato, R., and I. Cooper, 1996, "The Limitations of Simple Two Factor Interest Rate Models", *Journal of Financial Engineering* 5(1), pp. 1–16.

Renault, E., 1996, "Econometric Models of Option Pricing Errors", Working paper, World Congress of Econometrics Society, Tokyo.

Richard, S., 1978, "An Arbitrage Model of the Term Structure of Interest Rates", *Journal of Financial Economics* 6, pp. 33–57.

RiskMetrics, 1995, *RiskMetrics Technical Document* (New York: JP Morgan), May 26.

Rissanen, J., 1978, "Modeling by Shortest Data Description", *Automatica* 14, pp. 465–71.

Schaefer, S. M., and E. S. Schwartz, 1984, "A Two Factor Model of the Term Structure: An Approximate Analytical Solution", *Journal of Financial and Quantitative Analysis* 19(4), pp. 413–24.

Schaefer, S. M., and E. S. Schwartz, 1987, "Time Dependent Variance and the Pricing of Bonds", *Journal of Finance* 42, pp. 1113–28.

Schwarz, G., 1978, "Estimating the Dimension of a Model", *Annals of Statistics* 6, pp. 461–4.

Vasicek, O., 1977, "An Equilibrium Characterization of the Term Structure", *Journal of Financial Economics* 5, pp. 177–88.

West, M., and P. J. Harrison, 1989, *Bayesian Forecasting and Dynamic Linear Models* (New York: Springer Verlag).

5

Integrating Interest Rate Risk and Credit Risk in ALM

Robert A. Jarrow and Donald R. van Deventer

Cornell University and Kamakura Corporation, Honolulu;
Kamakura Corporation, Honolulu

A recent study by the Federal Reserve Board (Cole, Cornyn and Gunther, 1995) came to the startling conclusion that no interest rate risk variables were statistically significant in predicting bank failures in the United States. The new FIMS monitoring system discussed in this study predicts failure on the basis of 11 key variables collected from the Report of Condition submitted to bank regulators in the United States. Five of the eleven variables are related to the riskiness of commercial lending, and none of the others are related to interest rate risk.

The demise of much of the savings and loan industry in the early and mid-1980s when interest rates were high and volatile certainly suggests that interest rates should be a significant risk factor. A cynic might argue that the regulators did not collect a meaningful measure of interest rate risk from reporting banks until very recently.[1] Nonetheless, the FIMS research is an indication that many market participants, including various software vendors,[2] seem to believe that credit risk can be analysed without the consideration of interest rate risk.

In stark contrast, the traditional approach to fixed-income analysis (see Fabozzi and Fabozzi, 1989) assumes that only interest rate risk, and not credit risk, is the important factor in pricing corporate debt. This approach utilises the standard techniques of duration and convexity hedging to risk-manage a portfolio of corporate debt. These techniques are in common use by the industry.[3]

The purpose of this chapter is to analyse critically these two contrasting approaches to pricing credit risk. Using a unique data set, we provide an empirical analysis (a case study) of which risk – interest rate or credit (or perhaps both) – is most important in the pricing of risky debt. The data set is unique because it consists of weekly quotes on a bank's (primary) debt offerings, for various maturities, over an eight-year observation period. Two standard models are compared in terms of their hedging performance. One is Merton's risky debt model, which assumes that interest rate risk is non-existent. The second is the traditional fixed-income duration/convexity approach, which assumes that credit risk is non-existent.

The hedging results are quite intriguing. The traditional fixed-income approach dominates Merton's model, indicating that interest rate risk is significantly more important than credit risk in the pricing of corporate debt. The implication, of course, is that for pricing and hedging purposes, if one risk needs to be ignored, it should be credit risk. But, this is not the final conclusion.

The results also indicate that the traditional fixed-income approach to valuation still leaves a significant component of the bank's debt unhedged. We attribute the remaining hedging error to the omission of credit risk. The punch line is that the newer models, those that include both interest rate (market) and credit risk, are needed for more accurate pricing and hedging (see Jarrow and Turnbull, 1995; and Jarrow, Lando and Turnbull, 1997).

This chapter is divided into four sections. The first presents an overview of the credit risk problem and how it relates to valuation, pricing, and hedging. The second section provides an introduction to Merton's risky debt model, which is tested against the traditional fixed-income approach in the section that follows. The fourth section concludes by discussing the need to integrate both interest rate (market) and credit risk for enterprise-wide risk management.

An overview of the credit risk problem

The objectives of the credit risk process in asset and liability management are varied but closely related to each other. The objective is not just to know whether to make a particular loan or not. Nor is it merely to estimate the probability of default of a particular borrower over a particular time period. These are just two of many important questions, all of which should be answered by a comprehensive approach to credit and interest rate risk management. The questions are:

❏ Should I make this loan or not?
❏ What is the probability of default by company XYZ?
❏ What are the major risk factors driving the value of my loan portfolio?
❏ Am I as diversified as I could be?
❏ What is the market value of my portfolio?
❏ How can I hedge the risks of the portfolio?
❏ How should this loan be priced?
❏ How much value-added does the loan business create for the firm?
❏ From a credit policy perspective, how should I view the risk of the bank's loan portfolio given that economic conditions have recently changed?
❏ What should my loan loss reserve be?
❏ Do I have enough capital in the bank?
❏ Do I have enough capital in this business unit?

As emphasised above, in looking at various models of credit analytics we have to recognise that the objective is not just to avoid bad loans or to measure credit quality. Asset and liability management also relates to minimising the loss when a good loan turns bad through hedging the price shocks. It relates to accurate pricing and continued marking-to-market so that capital is allocated efficiently. Finally, it relates to the correct measurement of risks so that the proper capital reserves can be determined (the ultimate protection) to conserve scarce capital resources.

A good risk management model provides answers to all of these questions. The key ingredient of any solution is a valuation model that accurately prices and hedges corporate debt. Indeed, if the model accurately prices and hedges corporate debt, the model has accurately assessed the relevant risks, including the likelihood of default and the credit quality of the loan. The purpose of this chapter is, thus, to analyse critically the two leading credit risk models along the indicated dimension of accurate pricing and hedging.

An introduction to Merton's risky debt model

Robert Merton won the Nobel Prize in 1997 in part for his insights in recognising that the pricing of corporate debt is related to the options model introduced in 1973 by Black and Scholes (see Merton, 1974). Merton's model of risky debt rests upon a number of assumptions:

1. Interest rates are constant.
2. The firm issues only one type of debt and that is a zero-coupon bond.
3. The usual perfect market assumptions apply (frictionless and competitive markets).
4. The assets of the company are perfectly liquid.

Under these conditions, if, on the maturity date of the debt, the firm's assets are worth less than the amount due on the debt, the equity is worthless. Equity has a positive value only if the corporate assets are worth more than the maturing debt. In this case, the value of equity is the residual firm value after paying off the debt.

Equity has the same cashflow as a "call option" (an option to buy) on the assets of the firm at a strike price equal to the amount due on the debt and with a time to exercise equal to the maturity of the debt. Therefore, the value of debt equals the value of the firm assets less the value of a call.

Because of the constant interest rate assumption, the value of the firm's debt has zero correlation with interest rates. Furthermore, since interest rates are not random, this debt-pricing model has no interest rate risk.

This model depends on two parameters – the firm's asset value and its volatility. These two parameters can be calibrated to fit market observables; in particular, they can be calibrated to fit historical default frequencies; and to fit an observable yield curve for risky debt.

This simple model is elegant from a theoretical perspective. Does it work in practice? That is the subject of the following sections.

Testing the hedging performance of various credit models

As argued in the first section, the proper way to evaluate a credit model is to analyse its pricing and hedging performance. In practice, however, calibration of a model's parameters to market observables, such as the historical default frequency or the initial zero-coupon price curve, always guarantees accurate pricing.[4] For example, in the traditional approach to fixed-income analysis, the bond's price can always be calibrated to market quotes by choosing the parameters of the model to match the initial zero-coupon price curve. As mentioned earlier, Merton's model can also be calibrated to match historical default frequencies and market prices. Hence, in practice, the only dimension that one can use to differentiate these models (in fact, any model) is their hedging performance. Panel 1 (overleaf) summarises the major characteristics of the leading credit model alternatives.

To compare the two models we test their hedging performance on a unique data set. The best possible data set would cover a long period of time and relate to one or more issuers whose credit quality has been volatile over the observation period. The frequency and quality of the debt prices is crucial. One source for these data is secondary market bond prices reported by large securities companies (eg, the Wisconsin Fixed Income Data Base provided by Lehman Brothers). The problems with secondary market prices (none of which should rule out their use) are that: the data are often collected infrequently (eg, monthly); there is little economic incentive for dealers to quote realistic levels or bid-offered prices; and insufficient debt issues are available to give accurate yield curves.

For hedging purposes, the frequency of the data is important as hedging theory is based on the notion of "continuous" trading. Monthly observation intervals are too long to approximate "continuous trading". Weekly or daily price observations are best. Finally, it is obvious that accurate price quotes are necessary to provide a reasonable assessment of a model's hedging ability. Because of liquidity considerations, secondary market prices often fall short on this dimension. The data set we employ was constructed to avoid these problems.

THE FIRST INTERSTATE DATA SET
Our data set is a collection of weekly quotes on primary issuance spreads over US Treasuries for First Interstate Bancorp, a major debt issuer, whose credit quality varied considerably over the observation period of January 1986 to August 1993.

First Interstate Bancorp, which was recently acquired by Wells Fargo & Co., collected these data for risk management purposes. First Interstate, where one of the authors served as treasurer from 1984 to 1987, was one of the 10 largest bank holding companies in the United States in the mid-1980s. In spite of the large number of bank failures at the time,

BRIEF DEFINITIONS OF CREDIT MODELS

The traditional duration approach

The traditional duration approach implicitly assumes that all interest rates move in a parallel fashion. When dealing with bonds of different credit risk, this assumption implies that credit spreads are constant. The model assumes that the risk of any bond can be hedged by selling short US Treasuries. The hedge ratio is calculated by using the parallel shift assumption to calculate the relative change in the prices of both bonds for small changes in interest rates. The hedge ratio is that ratio where the price changes of both bonds are equal in magnitude and opposite in sign. It depends on the coupon, payment frequency and maturity of the two bonds involved.

The Merton approach

The Merton approach assumes that the value of a company's equity is determined solely by the value of the firm's assets and its debt outstanding. Since the model assumes that there is only one debt issue outstanding (or, in generalised form, many debt issues whose amounts and maturities are known), the model implies that the firm's liability structure remains unchanged as the value of assets rises and falls. In contrast, most firms attempt to maintain a fairly constant debt-to-equity ratio – borrowing more against assets as they rise in value and reducing debt when they decline. The model also assumes that interest rates are constant and therefore uncorrelated with asset values and the probability of default. The hedge ratios for the Merton model reflect the fact that, under these assumptions, equity is a simple option on the assets of the firm. The credit risk of the firm's debt can be hedged by selling short either the assets of the firm or the firm's equity. To add realism to the model, we calculate a hedge ratio for interest rate movements even though the model assumes that they are constant (this is analogous to the standard practice of vega-hedging volatility in the constant-volatility Black–Scholes option model).

A better approach

A better approach needs to be consistent with the following market observations, which affect both debt and equity prices. First, corporations appear to maintain a more constant debt-to-equity ratio. Indeed, corporate capital structures are not essentially "all equity" when asset values are high nor "all debt" when asset values are low (as the Merton model implies). A better model needs to be consistent with this fact. Second, random interest rates influence credit-risky bond prices. This is a key variable that needs to be incorporated explicitly into the dynamics of a better model. Third, changing liquidity conditions in debt markets also affect bond prices – as the recent collapse of Long Term Capital Management confirms. Liquidity differences between Treasury bonds, equity and credit risky debt need to be recognised in a better model's structure. Finally, in the parameter estimation and calibration of the default probabilities and recovery rates, a better model needs to utilise all available information. This means that in addition to equity prices, balance-sheet data and historical occurrences of default, a better model needs to incorporate the "rich" information contained in the market prices of credit risky debt.

First Interstate was an AA issuer of debt and one of the most frequent issuers of debt in both the United States and the Euro markets. First Interstate was the world's first issuer of Euro medium-term notes and the first issuer of bank medium-term notes. It was also one of the most active early dealers in interest rate swaps and fixed-income options, ranking at one time in the top 10 dealers in the United States. As such, First Interstate represents exactly the type of institution for which the measurement of credit risk would be necessary and desirable.

In 1984 First Interstate's treasury department began polling leading investment banking firms regarding spreads to US Treasury bonds for a new issue of $100 million of non-callable bonds at the "on-the-run" maturities of two, three, five, seven, and 10 years.

The data series collected by First Interstate consists of quotations taken each Friday from six investment banking firms. The high and low estimates were eliminated and the remaining four quotes averaged. Because the spreads represent the on-the-run maturities, there is no need to engage in yield curve smoothing to extract the on-the-run spreads to Treasuries from odd dates, a practice that is often necessary when using secondary market quotes for corporate debt issues.

There was considerable economic pressure on the investment banks to provide accurate quotations in that a spread that was too high could have resulted in a bond underwriting being missed by the investment banker. Conversely, a quoted spread that was too low might lead to a "prove it" request by First Interstate to underwrite the issue at the level. Finally, consistently inaccurate quotes relative to the mean spread of all the underwriters polled had an adverse effect on the relationship of the investment banking firm with First Interstate.

First Interstate provides a challenging test for any credit model since its credit rating fell from AA to BBB+ in January 1990 and to BBB in January 1991, but rose back to A- by January 1993. Furthermore, First Interstate's stock price also showed considerable variation over the sample period – from below $20 per share to almost $70 per share (Figure 1).

In what follows we will concentrate on the First Interstate two-year spread over Treasuries. Two years is close to the average maturity of the typical financial institution's liabilities, thereby providing a useful comparison. The two-year zero-coupon bond yield for First Interstate showed a 93.6% correlation with US Treasury zero-coupon bond yields (Figure 2).

Figure 3 shows that the spreads for the two-year zeros over Treasuries exhibited tremendous variation over the sample period. This was partly due to the fact that during this period First Interstate went through a failed attempt to acquire BankAmerica Corporation, was the subject of numerous merger rumours itself and suffered from serious credit quality problems.

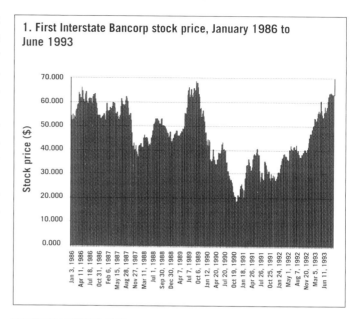

1. First Interstate Bancorp stock price, January 1986 to June 1993

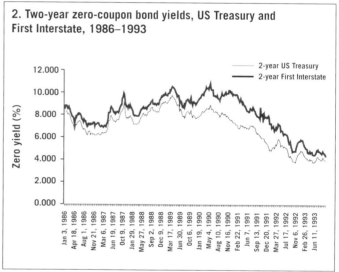

2. Two-year zero-coupon bond yields, US Treasury and First Interstate, 1986–1993

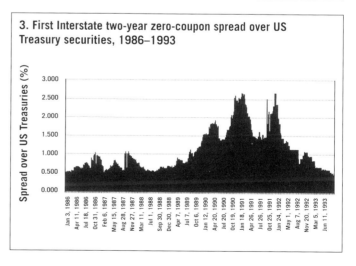

3. First Interstate two-year zero-coupon spread over US Treasury securities, 1986–1993

Only two weeks of data (two out of 377 observations) were omitted as outliers. The outliers were determined by screening the data for unusual values. On August 14, 1992, the First Interstate two-year spread over Treasuries exhibited such a value. It jumped from 90 basis points in the previous week to 350 basis points, and then back to 88 basis points on August 21. In contrast, over the same period, the stock price did not exhibit the same unusual movements – the three relevant values being $38.125 to $37.75 and then to

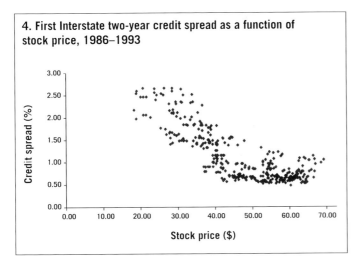

4. First Interstate two-year credit spread as a function of stock price, 1986–1993

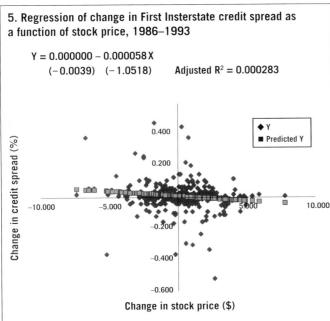

5. Regression of change in First Insterstate credit spread as a function of stock price, 1986–1993

$Y = 0.000000 - 0.000058 X$

(-0.0039) (-1.0518) Adjusted $R^2 = 0.000283$

$37.25. So, the week of August 14 was omitted from the data, and because much of the subsequent analysis concerns weekly changes in prices, the August 21 observation was necessarily omitted as well.

RELATIONSHIP BETWEEN STOCK PRICE AND CREDIT SPREAD

Before testing hedging performance, it is instructive to perform some preliminary data analysis to get a sense of the relationships involved between interest rates, credit risk and stock prices.

Figure 4 plots First Interstate's two-year credit spread against the stock price over the observation period. The graph produces a downward sloping pattern that bends as the stock price increases – something that seems, at least at first glance, to be consistent with the Merton model of risky debt. Merton's model implies that the debt's value is negatively related to the stock price and, hence, that the credit spread is non-linearly and negatively related to the stock price as well.

As a result, one would expect to see only three possible combinations of stock price and credit spread movements:
❏ stock prices rise when credit spreads fall;
❏ stock prices fall when credit spreads rise; and
❏ the stock price remains unchanged when credit spreads are constant.

Accordingly, a graph of changes in credit spreads versus changes in the stock price will provide a quick check on this relation. Figure 5 gives this comparison, showing weekly changes in the credit spread against changes in stock price pairs.

If Merton's model is valid, we would expect to see all the data points clustered either in the upper left-hand quadrant (lower stock prices and higher credit spreads) or lower right-hand quadrant (higher stock prices and lower credit spreads). Casual observation indicates that this is not the case. Only 42% of the data points in the 375 weeks of the First Interstate data are consistent with this relationship. More importantly, 58% of the data points are not. A regression analysis of the change in credit spreads on changes in the stock price is downward sloping, as the Merton model predicts, but the explanatory power is very, very low. T-scores are given in parentheses below the coefficients in Figure 5.

CONSTRUCTING THE HEDGE

The hedging test was constructed as follows.
❏ At the start of the observation period we simulate the purchase of $1 million principal amount of First Interstate two-year zero-coupon bonds.
❏ Simultaneously, we construct the appropriate hedge with US Treasury two-year bonds, First Interstate common stock, or both. The exact hedge ratios (discussed below) differ for each of the models tested.
❏ After one week the position is liquidated. The First Interstate bonds are "sold" and all hedging positions closed out. The sale price of the First Interstate bonds and the US Treasury bonds correctly recognises the fact that they now have one year and 358 days to maturity. The yields used for pricing the First Interstate bonds, however, are

the prevailing two-year zero-coupon yields quoted at the end of the one-week holding period.

❑ The net profit or loss from this one-week strategy is calculated and stored, and then the process is repeated 375 times.

Since the net investment in the hedged portfolio is non-zero, if the model is correct, the hedged portfolio will be riskless and therefore earn the weekly Treasury rate (for a week). We examined changes in the value of the hedged portfolio (profits or losses) over the week. For purposes of comparison, this change should be nearly constant across time and approximately zero.[5]

To avoid computing the return on the net investment, we computed the standard deviation of the hedged position's weekly profits. For all practical purposes, computing the standard deviation of the profits across time eliminates this expected (riskless) profit on the net investment from the analysis. This is because the expected profit is approximately constant (and small); therefore, its value is incorporated into the computation of the standard deviation.

Thus, the "best" credit model using this hedge is the one with weekly profit numbers with the lowest standard deviation over the sample period. The following models were tested:

❑ Do nothing (no hedge)

❑ One-to-one US Treasury hedge

❑ (Macauley) duration hedge

❑ Constant hedge ratio

❑ Merton's risky debt model hedge

The first hedge is to do nothing. This provides an upper bound on the standard deviation that is useful for comparison purposes.

The next three hedges relate to the traditional fixed-income approach to bond pricing. The one-to-one US Treasury hedge is the most naive, ignoring duration considerations. The duration hedge is the one proposed by the traditional theory. But, because the duration of a two-year US Treasury note is close to two years, the one-to-one Treasury and the duration hedge will give similar results. The constant-ratio hedge is a modification of the traditional approach to take advantage of "in sample" estimation. By this we mean that the constant hedge ratio was selected to minimise the standard deviation of the profit. This hedge, therefore, provides the "best" possible performance for the traditional approach.

The final hedge is based on Merton's model. This is the most complex of the five hedges, and the technique we employ is discussed next.

IMPLEMENTING THE MERTON MODEL HEDGE

To implement the hedge based on Merton's model we need to estimate the strike price of the single zero-coupon bond issued by the firm, the value of the firm's assets, and the volatility of the firm's assets.

Estimating the strike price for the assumed zero-coupon bond liability structure is the most problematic of the three. This needs to be done from balance-sheet data. First, First Interstate's quarterly financial statements were used to measure the "book value" of all its liabilities.[6] Second, two years of interest expense, calculated by compounding the quarterly average cost of liabilities for two years, was added to this to take into account the interest appreciation. The combined result is the estimate used.

The firm's asset values and the volatility of the assets were estimated implicitly. The Merton model's parameters were calibrated weekly to fit the observable credit spread and stock price at the initiation of the trading position.

Figure 6 (overleaf) presents the estimates for the asset values. These values appear reasonable. Their values jump quarterly based on new financial information.

The values for the firm's implied asset volatility are contained in Figure 7 (overleaf). Except for the outliers, these estimates also appear reasonable.

6. Implied asset values for First Insterstate are reasonable, subject to normal jumps due to new financial information

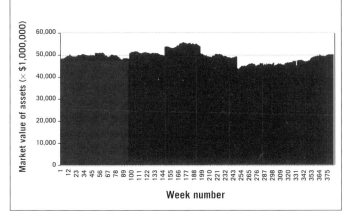

7. Implied asset volatility, except for the outlying data point, is also reasonable

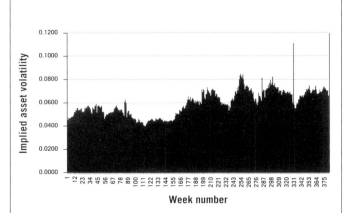

Table 1. Reduction in risk by hedging strategy

	Standard deviation	Reduction in hedge error (%)
Optimal constant hedge ratio	1837.73	41.07
Macauley duration hedge	1848.22	40.73
One-to-one principal amount hedge	1850.52	40.66
Merton hedge	2488.41	20.20
Unhedged position	3118.28	0.00

8. Number of shares sold short under Merton hedging strategy

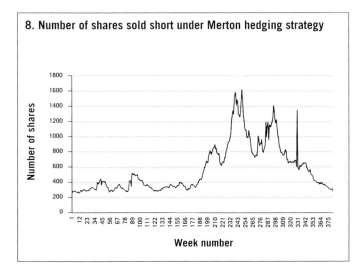

The Merton risky debt model hedge consists of two securities, both stock and the US Treasury note.[7] For the stock position, hedge ratios were calculated using the well-known "deltas" from the Black–Scholes model (see Jarrow and Turnbull, 1995, for this calculation).[8] The US Treasury hedge implied by the model was calculated by computing "rho", the derivative of risky debt with respect to changes in the riskless interest rate, and then neutralising this derivative with a position in US Treasury bonds.

RESULTS

The hedging performance of the two credit models can be judged from the data given in Table 1. As expected, for the traditional approach to fixed-income security valuation, the optimal constant hedge ratio provides the lower bound and the one-to-one hedge the upper bound, with the duration hedge in the middle. The differences between the three hedging techniques are slight. They all reduce the standard deviation, relative to an unhedged position, by about 40–41%. The ranking of the models produces the surprising result that Merton's risky debt model gives the poorest performance. In contrast to the traditional approach to fixed-income analysis, it reduces the standard deviation, from that of an unhedged position, by only about 20%.

These hedging results indicate that, for the pricing of First Interstate's two-year bond, interest rate risk is a more important component than is credit risk. The traditional approach provides a more accurate hedging model.

This, however, is not the only implication of the results in Table 1. Although interest rate risk is the most important factor, a significant portion – between 59 and 60% – of the portfolio's standard deviation was unhedged. The percentage that is unexplained is greater than the percentage explained. Together with the fact that credit risk is ignored in this approach (and that the Merton hedge reduced the standard deviation), this is strong evidence that a model which combines both interest rate and credit risk is needed for more accurate pricing and hedging.

REASONS FOR THE POOR PERFORMANCE OF THE MERTON MODEL HEDGE

The poor performance of the Merton model compared to the traditional approach to fixed-income analysis is surprising. It is useful to investigate further the reasons for this poor hedging performance.

Figure 8 plots the number of shares sold short under the Merton model. These hedge ratios look reasonable at first glance, the number of shares sold increasing as credit quality deteriorates. However, looking at hedging errors as a function of credit quality, one can see that the magnitudes of the hedging errors increased substantially as the credit quality deteriorates. So, the more "risky" the debt, the less well the hedge performed, as shown in Figure 9.

We then did an optimisation, "in sample", on the hedge ratios prescribed by the Merton model to see whether hedging performance could be improved by scaling the Merton hedges up or down. The results were unexpected:

❏ The debt hedges should be reduced to 95% of the hedge ratio implied by the Merton model; and

❏ the equity hedges should be reduced to 21% of the Merton equity hedge ratio, and the hedge should be executed by *buying the common stock instead of selling it*!

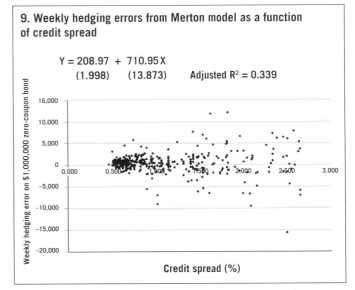

9. Weekly hedging errors from Merton model as a function of credit spread

$$Y = 208.97 + 710.95\,X$$
$$(1.998) \quad (13.873) \quad \text{Adjusted } R^2 = 0.339$$

The second adjustment is noteworthy. On average, the direction of the Merton hedge appears to be incorrect. This is a result of the fact that 58% of the weekly data points in the sample had stock price and credit spreads moving in a direction opposite to that predicted by the model.

Regression analysis on the hedging errors of the Merton model shows that the change in stock price is a statistically significant explanatory variable. T-scores are given below the coefficient in Figure 9. This result is certainly not a recommendation to buy common stock to hedge risky debt. Selling stock short, as recommended by the Merton risky debt model, is almost certainly the correct strategy. The implication of the above analysis is that risk factors not included in the Merton model have caused the large hedging errors and that the stock hedge ratio was compensating for the fact that other hedging instruments were necessary but missing from the hedge.

Conclusion

This chapter has compared two common modelling approaches to pricing and hedging credit risk. The first is the traditional approach to pricing fixed-income securities, and the second is Merton's risky debt model. The traditional approach ignores credit risk and only prices interest rate risk. Merton's risky debt model ignores interest rate risk and only prices credit risk. Both approaches are implemented in professional software and both approaches are used in practice.

A comparison of the hedging performance of the two models was performed using a unique data set. This consisted of weekly quotes on First Interstate Bancorp's two-year bonds from January 1986 to August 1993. First Interstate experienced significant changes in its credit rating over this period, providing a good case study for analysis.

The results are intriguing. The traditional approach to hedging fixed-income securities outperforms Merton's risky debt approach. So, if only one risk is to be included, interest rate risk appears to be the most important. But the hedge based on the traditional fixed-income approach eliminates less than half of the portfolio's standard deviation, indicating that significant risk – the credit risk – remains unhedged.

The conclusion of our investigation is that the newer models (see Jarrow and Turnbull, 1995; Jarrow, Lando and Turnbull, 1997) are needed to price and hedge corporate debt more accurately. The existing approaches, although of some use, leave most of the risk of corporate debt unexplained and unhedged. This model misspecification is too large to be ignored, especially as these models become more relevant in the determination of capital requirements.

1 *Historically, regulators have collected interest rate sensitivity gap information with various assets and liabilities assigned maturities in a fairly arbitrary way.*

2 *An example is JP Morgan's CreditMetrics.*

3 *An example is the rich set of traditional fixed-income analytics displayed by the Bloomberg financial information service.*

4 *In theory, pricing and hedging are equivalent characteristics of an options model. This is due to the fact that arbitrage pricing theory values by synthetic replication. Synthetic replication is equivalent to hedging. So, to test accurate pricing and hedging one only needs to test accurate hedging.*

5 *To see this, let I be the net investment. The theoretical change in the value of the hedged position is* Ir(1/52), *where r is the weekly rate on a per-year basis. This change is less than* (0.07)(1/52) = 0.0013 *times the net investment. For a net investment of $500,000, this change is $673. Since the net investment is approximately constant across time, so will be this expected profit.*

6 *Merton's model was treated more favourably than would be possible in practice. It was assumed that financial statements for a given quarter were instantly known to the trader on the last day of the quarter, but in reality there would be a lag of some weeks before detailed balance sheets were publicly available.*

7 *Although the model implies that an interest rate hedge is unnecessary, we use a simple Taylor-series expansion to extend the model to include an interest rate hedge. The expansion is* DD = (∂D/∂E)DE + (∂D/∂r)Dr. *To use the Black–Scholes deltas, note that* ∂D/∂E = (∂D/∂V)/(∂E/∂V). *The ratios in the last expression can be obtained using the Black–Scholes formula.*

8 *See footnote 7.*

Bibliography

Black, F., and M. Scholes, 1973, "The Pricing of Options and Corporate Liabilities", *Journal of Political Economics* May, pp. 637–59.

Cole, R., B. Cornyn and J. Gunther, 1995, "FIMS: A New Monitoring System for Financial Institutions", *Federal Reserve Bulletin* January, pp. 1–15.

Fabozzi, F., and T. Fabozzi, 1989, *Bond Markets, Analysis and Strategies* (New York: Prentice Hall).

Jarrow, R., and S. Turnbull, 1995, *Derivative Securities* (Cincinnati, Ohio: Southwestern Publishers).

Jarrow, R., and S. Turnbull, 1995, "Pricing Derivatives on Financial Securities Subject to Credit Risk", *Journal of Finance* 50(1), pp. 53–85.

Jarrow, R., D. Lando and S. Turnbull, 1997, "A Markov Model for the Term Structure of Credit Risk Spreads", *The Review of Financial Studies* 10(2), pp. 481–523.

Levin, J., and D. van Deventer, 1997, "The Simultaneous Analysis of Interest Rate Risk and Credit Risk", Chapter 27 in A. Cornyn, R. Klein and J. Lederman (eds), *Controlling and Managing Interest Rate Risk* (New York: New York Institute of Finance).

Merton, R. C., 1974, "On the Pricing of Corporate Debt: The Risk Structure of Interest Rates", *Journal of Finance* 29, pp. 449–70.

Shimko, D., N. Tejima and D. van Deventer, 1993, "The Pricing of Risky Debt When Interest Rates are Stochastic", *Journal of Fixed Income* September, pp. 58–66.

van Deventer, D., and K. Imai, 1997 *Financial Risk Analytics: A Term Structure Model Approach for Banking, Insurance, and Investment Management* (Burr Ridge, Illinois: Irwin Professional Publishing).

6

Modelling and Managing Credit Risk

Derek H. Chen, Harry H. Huang, Rui Kan,
Ashok Varikooty and Henry N. Wang

Credit Suisse First Boston; Credit Suisse First Boston; Credit Suisse First Boston;
Flatiron Capital Management; Credit Suisse First Boston

Over the past decade credit markets have seen tremendous growth in both geographical reach and range of new products. The extraordinary growth of the derivatives market has increased both the number of counterparties and the size of the positions held with individual counterparties by financial institutions. Market innovation has also enabled more and more firms and sovereign states with low credit qualities to enter markets that traditionally have been dominated by issuers with the highest credit qualities. As a result, it becomes imperative for market participants to understand credit risk and how to monitor and properly manage it.

Unfortunately, history seems to have a way of repeating itself. Credit eventually expands excessively, which inevitably leads to abrupt credit crunches. In today's market this is also accompanied by costly financial de-leveraging. Although there were ample examples of the danger of improperly managed credit in the eighties and early nineties, the current financial difficulties experienced by many once highly regarded financial institutions in the face of the crisis in emerging markets can no doubt be partially attributed to poor credit management policies. What is more, these firms' severe credit exposure is decapitalising and weakening the financial health of more banks, investment firms and finance companies, and, if left improperly managed, may someday pose a severe threat to the global financial system.

What is credit risk? Generally speaking, credit risk, as considered in this chapter, is the risk that one party to a financial transaction who is under contractual obligation to make a scheduled payment to another party fails to do so. When this party is the issuer of a fixed-income instrument who defaults on either interest or principle or both of its debt obligations, the risk is an issuer credit risk; if the party is the counterparty in a derivative transaction, such as swaps, it is a counterparty credit risk. Certain transactions involve both issuer risk and counterparty risk.

Credit risk is usually measured by credit ratings assigned by commercial rating agencies such as Moody's Investor Service, Standard & Poor's Corporation, Duff & Phelps Credit Rating Co. or Fitch Investors Service. Many major financial institutions maintain their own credit rating systems based on internally developed methodologies either because commercially available ratings fail to meet the institution's needs exactly or simply because many potential debtors and counterparties are not rated by these rating agencies.

As the risk of default exists in almost every financial contract, the pricing of default risk is essential to the valuation and hedging of these contracts. It has therefore received much attention from practitioners, who need to quantify such risks accurately in the market, from academics and from regulators with a strong interest in whether and how credit-sensitive transactions should be regulated in light of the credit risk-related debacles of recent years. Recent developments in the credit derivative market, while providing more flexibility in the management of credit risk, also demand more rigorous ways of modelling credit risk.

Review of credit risk studies

Two approaches to modelling default risk are generally found in the literature. The first, pioneered by Merton (1974), models the firm's liabilities as contingent claims issued against the firm's underlying assets, with the payoffs to all the firm's liabilities in bankruptcy completely specified. Bankruptcy occurs when the firm's assets fall below certain levels specified in the debt covenants. In Merton's model, for example, default can only occur at bond maturity when the value of the firm's assets falls below the face value of the debt, liquidation is costless and the absolute priority rule holds. Furthermore, the value of the firm's assets follows a geometric Brownian motion. The equity holders have a call option on the value of the firm with strike price the face value of the debt. Using the contingent claims argument of Black and Scholes (1973) and Merton (1973), Merton derived the value of the equity in closed form, and the value of the risky debt is simply the difference between the value of the firm and the value of the equity. Among authors who have used this approach are Black and Cox (1976), Hull and White (1995), Longstaff and Schwartz (1995) and Shimko, Tejima and van Deventer (1993). Although the term structure of the yield spread derived from Merton's model exhibits some useful qualitative results, the yield spreads are significantly lower than those implied by empirical evidence (see, for example, Jones, Mason and Rosenfeld, 1984), and it has been less successful in practical applications. In addition, Merton-type models are difficult to implement in practice since not all of the firm's assets are either tradable or observable, so the contingent claims approach may not apply. Furthermore, empirical evidence has shown that liquidation and reorganisation are costly and the absolute priority rule is often violated, so the frictionless market assumption on which many Merton-type models are based is no longer valid. On the other hand, it is very difficult to model realistic boundary conditions for the default process because of the complexity of the debt covenants and the firm's capital structure. Finally, since this approach does not explicitly model the default time and any possible change in credit ratings, it cannot be used to price credit derivatives whose payoffs depend directly on the credit rating (eg, credit-sensitive notes and spread-adjusted notes; see Das and Tufano, 1996, for additional elaboration).

In response to these difficulties with the contingent claims method, an alternative approach to modelling the risk of default has been developed in recent years. In the event of default the risky debt pays off a fraction of each promised face value. The time of default as a measure of the default probability is given by an exogenous process. Both the recovery rate and the default probability can be stochastic, and together they determine the price of the credit risk. In fact, the default-adjusted short-rate process is given by $R = r + hL$, where r is the default-free short rate, h is the hazard rate or the default probability and L is the recovery rate in the event of default. Although these processes governing default are not formally linked to the firm's asset value, there is presumably some underlying relation; thus Duffie and Singleton (1998) describe this approach as a reduced-form model. In a risk-neutral world the price of any defaultable contingent claim can be obtained by taking the expectation of future cashflows discounted by a default-adjusted short rate, R. Pioneering work using such a methodology is that by Fons (1994), Jarrow and Turnbull (1995), Jarrow, Lando and Turnbull (1997) and Duffie and Singleton (1998). Among the advantages of this approach are that: it allows exogenous assumptions imposed only on observable factors; with certain assumptions concerning the default probability and the recovery rate, many results stemming from the available literature on the term structure of interest rates are readily applicable to the pricing of default risk; it can be used to price credit derivatives whose payoff depends on changes in credit ratings; and it is much more tractable mathematically than Merton-type models.

The much greater analytical tractability of reduced-form models than the contingent claims approach pioneered by Merton (1974) makes them more useful in practical applications. With multifactor specification of the underlying process for the risk-free rate, hazard rate and recovery rate, one can utilise the flexibility of affine models to capture some basic empirical features of historical yields and yield spreads. Potentially this type of model will allow one to value defaultable bonds correctly in closed form and offers sufficient tractability and flexibility to price more complex credit derivatives. However, as the implementation of reduced-form models is still in its infancy, the success of the approach remains to be seen. Preliminary findings using a two-factor square-root process for riskier interest rates and a single-factor square-root process for the mean loss rate by Duffee (1996) point to a strong possibility of misspecification, though the estimated models are moderately successful at pricing the defaultable bond. In particular, Duffee's (1996) estimated reduced-form models cannot generate both relatively flat yield spreads for lower-rated firms and steeper spreads for higher-rated firms, as documented empirically by Duffee (1998).

Some authors (for example, Altman, Handleman and Narayanan, 1977; Altman and Kishore, 1995) have focused primarily on the empirical study of different credit ratings assigned to corporate bonds. Using state-of-the-art statistical tools – such as the probability transition matrix, discriminant analysis and probit analysis – on historical data, these authors attempt to establish which variables and processes determine the credit ratings of a corporate bond and which trigger a rating upgrade or downgrade.

Selected studies of credit risk published in the past three decades are summarised in Table 1 (overleaf).

Identifying credit risks

The recent turmoil in emerging markets provided painful lessons to many corporations and investors about the importance of risk management and how much can go wrong if one does not have a sensitive and reliable way of measuring and managing risks.

The first step in any risk management methodology is to identify correctly and separate risks from different sources. For credit-related products, it is important to distinguish credit-related risks from other risks.

Example
Consider a one-year zero-coupon bond issued by some corporate. The bond is traded off the US Treasury. Suppose that the treasury rate is r and the spread of the bond is s; the bond price is then given by $P = 100/(1 + r + s)$. Two risks are involved in this simple example: treasury interest risk and spread risk.

In many credit-related markets (eg, emerging markets) credit risk can manifest itself in two different ways: small market fluctuations caused by normal market movements; and big jumps caused by certain events that result in real credit concerns. The latter is sometimes called the credit gap risk. These two different forms can have totally different effects and should be treated differently. Conventional risk management models based on a value-at-risk type of approach may be acceptable for small market fluctuations but may fail badly for the gap risk. More sophisticated models which can deal with credit risks (such as default risk) explicitly should be used.

Sometimes there may be more than one source of credit risk. In this case it is important to distinguish not only the effects from the different sources but also the interactions among them. Especially when market conditions are deteriorating, there tends to be very high correlation between different sectors of the market – and even between different markets. It is very important to understand how the different sectors and different markets are related to each other and how the relationships change with market conditions.

Example
Consider a repo contract. Party A lends some money to Party B, while Party B puts up some securities as collateral. In this case Party A faces credit risks from two sources: Party B and the issuer of the collateral. It is not a trivial task to measure and manage both risks, especially when they are correlated.

Table 1. Approaches to credit risk

Key studies	Comments
Contingent claims approach (CCA)	
Merton (1974)	Pioneering work applying CCA to model credit risk of defaultable bond in frictionless economy. Unable to generate credit spreads consistent with empirical evidence.
Black and Cox (1976)	Extends Merton (1974) to model risky debt under specific bond indentures and finds that they may have significant impact on price of risky debt.
Jones, Mason and Rosenfeld (1984)	Empirical study of predictive power of CCA model. Finds that, for investment-grade bonds, CCA model is not an improvement on naive model that assumes no risk of default. Also finds that introduction of stochastic interest rates may improve performance of CCA model.
Kim, Ramaswamy and Sunderesan (1993)	Stochastic short rates. Explicit assumptions on bankruptcy process and bond indenture. Finds that stochastic interest rates have significant impact on yields but not on yield spreads.
Shimko, Tejima and van Deventer (1993)	Stochastic short rates. In addition to results similar to Merton (1974), finds credit spread increasing with risk-free term-structure volatility.
Reduced-form approach	
Litterman and Iben (1991)	Stochastic short rates. Zero recovery rate. Default probability described by hazard rate and is specified exogenously.
Longstaff and Schwartz (1995); Nielsen, Saa-Requejo and Santa-Clara (1993)	Stochastic short rates. Bankruptcy occurs when firm's asset value hits exogenous (possibly stochastic) boundary and debt pays off fixed fractional face amount upon default. Finds that correlation between short rate and default risk has significant effect on credit spreads.
Fons (1994)	Discrete-time setting. Models default probability and survival rate explicitly using historical default rates. Constant recovery rate.
Jarrow and Turnbull (1995)	Arbitrage-free pricing of defaultable bond under independent and exogenous processes for short rate and bankruptcy.
Jarrow, Lando and Turnbull (1997)	Extends Jarrow and Turnbull (1995) to model credit risk under bankruptcy process characterised by finite-state Markov credit ratings process. Estimation can be made using observable variables.
Duffie and Singleton (1996)	Price of defaultable security is expected value of promised cashflows discounted at default-adjusted short rate in risk-neutral world. Default-adjusted short rate can be modelled directly or as sum of default-free short rate and risk-neutral mean loss rate. Estimation can be made using observable data.
Duffie and Singleton (1998); Dai and Singleton (1998)	Apply Duffie and Singleton (1996) to model interest swap yields econometrically. Default-adjusted short rate is sum of two independent square-root diffusions.
Duffee (1996)	Applies an earlier version of Duffie and Singleton (1996) with mean loss rate following single-factor square-root process. Finds that single-factor model fares poorly in matching term structure of credit spreads.
Statistical approach	
Altman and Kishore (1995)	Transition matrix of default probabilities approach. Uses transition rates from one rating category (eg, AAA) to another (eg, AA). Specifically, looks into fact that these transition probabilities are not fixed for life of bond.
Altman, Handleman and Narayanan (1977)	Uses discriminant analysis. Assumes that independent variables are multivariate normal. Uses these independent variables to categorise firms into different rating categories.
Carty and Fons (1994)	Models hazard (or default) rate as Weibull distribution. If hazard rate increases with time it is said to have positive duration-dependence, and if it decreases with time it is said to have negative duration-dependence. Authors show that there was positive duration-dependence for AAA-rated and negative duration-dependence for B- and CAA-rated bonds.
Blume, Lim and MacKinley (1998)	Qualitative dependent variables are often used when dependent variables are not from real domain (eg, rating categories). The independent variables can be of type used in simple regressions. Two common ways of modelling this are probit and logit models. Authors use ordered probit models (where dependent variable pertains to rating categories). They find that 'constants' in qualitative model regressions change through time, indicating that standards used in assigning ratings are becoming more stringent through time.

Here is another example where two credit risks are involved.

Example

Consider emerging market corporate bonds. The direct credit risk one is dealing with is the corporate credit. However, it would be a mistake not to consider the sovereign risk of the country where the corporate resides, especially in periods when the sovereign risk is large.

MEASUREMENT OF CREDIT RISK

Value-at-risk (VAR) has become increasingly popular as a measurement of the risk to which a portfolio of securities is exposed. The simplest VAR framework is based on the portfolio variance approach. It is intuitively obvious that the portfolio risk should be associated with the observed dispersion of the portfolio's return around its average value. The basic VAR approach assumes that the dispersion of the return can be captured by a single quantity, the variance of the return. Risk, therefore, is a simple, quantifiable entity. This approach has the advantage of being simple and it does work reasonably well for many markets. But it also has some serious shortcomings, as the next example illustrates.

Example

Consider two portfolios, A and B. Portfolio A's return can take one of two values: 30% with 99% probability and – 100% (which can be regarded as a default) with 1% probability. Portfolio B's return can also take one of two values: 28% with 99.9% probability or 728% with 0.1% probability. Both portfolios have the same expected return (28.7%), but portfolio A appears to be much riskier than portfolio B. Their standard deviations, however, are 12.93% and 22.12%, respectively. Hence, if VAR is used, one will draw the incorrect conclusion that B is riskier than A.

An important application of VAR is calculating a confidence level for any estimate of maximum loss. In order to do so, it is necessary to make assumptions regarding the statistical distribution of the changes in the underlying asset prices in the portfolio. Common wisdom in the market decides that a normal distribution is the natural choice. Not only is it the easiest distribution to deal with but it also has the following attractive properties: once the mean and variance are known, the whole distribution is known – no higher moments are needed; and if the return on each individual asset is normal, the return on the whole portfolio is also normal.

A casual look at the histogram of the weekly returns on Argentina par bonds for the last three years shows that it is obviously not normal (Figure 1): the distribution is asymmetric and has large tails. The extended tail on the left-hand side corresponds to the credit gap risk discussed earlier. It is extremely important to measure and manage this risk because it is more likely than is normal market fluctuation to land one in deep trouble.

PORTFOLIOS AND THE CONTAGIOUS EFFECT

In this section we will discuss how the correlations between different assets affect the risk associated with a portfolio of assets.

It is well known that one can mitigate risk by holding a portfolio instead of a single asset. How much risk one can mitigate by doing so, however, is dependent on how diversified the portfolio is. The simplest way of quantifying the degree of diversification is to use the correlation between different assets. The lower the correlation, the better the diversification. Unfortunately, for some markets the correlation is so high that very limited diversification can be achieved.

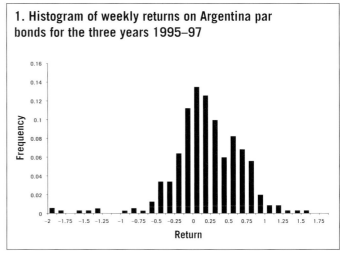

1. Histogram of weekly returns on Argentina par bonds for the three years 1995–97

For example, using half a year of stripped spread data, the estimated correlation between the Argentina par bond and the Brazil par bond is 0.97 and that between the Mexico par bond and the Venezuela par bond is 0.99. With such high correlations one can hardly diversify any risk.[1]

If the returns are normally distributed, it is sufficient to know the correlation. But when the distribution has large, fat tails, the higher-order moments are needed to determine the joint distribution of the portfolio. A very important phenomenon is that a crisis in one country can spread to several others very rapidly – this is the "contagious effect". The following simple model illustrates this effect.

Example

Consider two countries, A and B. Suppose that the default risk of each country can be modelled as a Poisson process. To be precise, suppose that the probability that country A does not default before time t is given by $\exp(-\lambda_A t)$, and that the probability that country B does not default before time t is given by $\exp(-\lambda_B t)$. Furthermore, suppose that after country i defaults, the probability that country j does not default before time t is given by $\exp[-\lambda_{j,i}(t - \tau)]$, where τ is the time at which country i defaults and $i, j = A, B$. Suppose that $\lambda_a = \lambda_B = 0.1$ and $\lambda_{a,B} = \lambda_{B,A} = 0.8$, then some simple algebra shows that the probability that A or B will default alone before t = 1 is 6.2%, while the probability that both A and B default is 5.9% – which is almost as large as the probability of individual default.

In general, when the markets are relatively quiet correlation can describe the diversification achieved by a portfolio reasonably well. However, when there are big movements in the markets we need to go beyond simple correlation. That is, when we need to deal with credit gap risks simple correlation is not sufficient. Unfortunately, it is these gap risks which will bankrupt a bank.

Modelling credit risk

The starting point in modelling credit risk is to understand that a defaultable security is usually sold at a discount relative to a similarly structured security, which carries no default risk. In the corporate bond markets this premium is normally expressed as a credit spread over treasury bond yields at comparable maturity. While the value of credit spreads reflects the perception of a firm's future probability of default and loss rate after default, modelling credit risk is equivalent to quantifying these unknown values from available market information. Traditional credit analysis for an issue is a combination of both industrial and financial analyses. Industrial analysis focuses on economic cyclicality, growth prospects, R&D expenses, competition, source of supply, degree of regulation, labour, and company accounting factors, whereas financial analysis looks closely at various financial ratios, equity returns, foreign exposure, management quality and other factors. Analysts compare these factors with their historical values as well as for competing companies in the same industry when drawing conclusions about the creditworthiness of a company. A more objective variant of the approach employs statistical tools, such as linear regression or discriminant analysis, when studying these factors. For example, one may assign numerical values of 1, 2, 3, 4, … to ratings of AAA, AA, A, BBB, etc, and write

$$R_i = a_0 + a_1 \cdot x_{1i} + a_2 \cdot x_{2i} + a_3 \cdot x_{3i} + \dots$$

where R_i is a numerical representation of the credit rating of company i, $a_0, a_1, \dots$ are regression coefficients, and $x_{1i}, x_{2i}, \dots$ are factors determining the company's credit risk, such as financial leverage, interest coverage ratio, asset turnover, government bond yield, swap spread and so on.

This approach, which borrows much from equity analysis, is highly important in establishing risk management guidelines such as counterparty position limits. But the expansion of the credit market and new market innovations sometimes call for more sophisticated methodologies. The pricing of credit derivatives, for example, requires modelling of the timing and correlation of possible default events under different probabilistic scenarios. Relative value trading among credits by the same issuers or highly correlated issuers is another example where the fair market level of the credit spread – possibly at different maturities – must be established.

More recent approaches have been based on the application of stochastic differential equations. In the remainder of this section we will illustrate the basic components and procedures employed in modelling credit risk and pricing credit derivatives.

Credit derivatives consist of, but are not limited to, credit swaps, total return swaps, collateralised loan obligations (CLO), credit spread options, credit default options and credit-linked notes (CLN), etc, of which the credit default swap or option is one of the most common. In its simplest form a credit default swap requires the payment of an annuity at a predetermined fixed rate until one or other of the following conditions holds, whichever comes first: prespecified credit default events;[2] or the maturity of the swap.

If a default event occurs ahead of the swap maturity, the annuity receiver is usually required to pay the annuity payer the difference between the face value and the recovery value of the referenced asset.[3] The annuity can be regarded as a credit spread which the investor demands for taking on the default risk of the underlying asset. In case of default a credit default option is similar in its payment schedule to a credit default swap, except that the annuity is replaced by an upfront payment. It is usually written for a short-dated agreement. The introduction of credit derivatives increases the means available to diversify credit risk.

The remainder of the section, then, is divided into three parts: the characteristics and basic components of credit risk models; stochastic and empirical approaches to modelling default rates; and the estimation of loss rates.

CHARACTERISTICS AND BASIC COMPONENTS OF CREDIT RISK MODELS
It is desirable that credit risk models possess the following attributes.

First, they should be be arbitrage-free and they should reflect current market information (Harrison and Kreps, 1979). This is akin to fitting an interest rate model to the current term structure of interest rates. We fit a credit risk model to the current term structure of credit spreads. Allowing for multifactor movements in spreads adds to the richness of the model but tends to be more complex.

Second, the models should produce default rates (sometimes called hazard rates) that are plausible.

Third, they should cater to the requirements of the application. For example, a simple credit risk model may suffice to obtain relative values as between US investment-grade corporates, but a multifactor model may be required to model default rates for emerging market derivatives.

Fourth, models should be computationally tractable where the inputs to the model are readily estimable.

The basic components of a credit risk model consist of, although they are not limited to, the following.
❏ The cashflows and maturity of the instrument, and its characteristics in terms of seniority, embedded options (eg, prepayments), convertibility, etc.
❏ The credit quality of the credit-protection buyer and seller.[4]
❏ The correlation between the protection buyer and seller.
❏ The correlation between the protection seller and the referenced asset.
❏ The probabilities of default at any point in time up to the maturity of the instrument.
❏ Recovery rates (which is one less the loss rate) in the event of a default.
❏ The spreads (or market prices) of the instrument. This may be slightly tautological as the spreads are related to the default probabilities and loss rates.

❏ An underlying pricing model (eg, a Heath–Jarrow–Morton model) to value the instrument. This is required because the pricing of a credit-risky instrument requires a valuation not only of the credit risk component but also of the interest rate component. For example, to value an IBM corporate issuance we typically need to model US interest rates and the IBM credit curve.

We now look at different ways of modelling default rates. To simplify our analysis we will only emphasise the fifth and sixth factors listed above (default probability and recovery rate upon default) in the pricing of defaultable instruments and their derivatives. Broadly, there are two approaches to modelling default rates: stochastic and empirical.

MODELLING THE DEFAULT PROCESS – THE STOCHASTIC APPROACH

An increasingly large number of authors have attempted to model the default process, mainly using stochastic diffusion processes and jump–diffusion processes (Merton, 1974; Duffie and Singleton, 1998; Duffie, 1998b; and Li, 1998). In addition to the short rate process, a *hazard rate* process and a *recovery rate* process are introduced for modelling the default process, where the hazard rate represents the probability of default and the recovery rate depicts the proportion of the face value recovered after default. The multiplication of these two processes is viewed as a premium over the risk-free rate to account for the default risk. It is shown that, under certain technical assumptions, explicit solutions can be derived for pricing defaultable instruments and their derivatives.

We model the default process as a combination of Markov diffusion and Poisson jump processes. As mentioned earlier, two of the key factors in determining the value of defaultable instruments and their derivatives are the default probability and the recovery rate upon default. Historical data for these factors are available at major credit agencies and from most financial databases. However, we tend to believe that, if the market is efficient, this information can also be extracted in function form from market prices[5] – see the empirical approach described later in this section.

To give the reader some flavour of this type of model, we now describe one model in more detail.

Duffie and Singleton (1998) model the default process as joint processes of risk-free interest, r, the hazard rate, h, and the recovery rate, L. Formally, the risk-adjusted interest is given by $R = r + hL$ and the initial price of a defaultable contingent claim that promises a payment of X at maturity is given by

$$V_0 = E^Q\left[\exp\left(-\int_0^T R_t dt\right)X\right] \qquad (1)$$

where the expectation is taken over the risk-neutral probability measure, Q. The authors describe this approach as a reduced-form model. To make this approach more analytically tractable, most reduced-form models further assume that default hazard rates and recovery rate do not depend on the value, V_t, of the contingent claim. A key feature of (1) is that the familiar formula for the default-free term structure is readily applicable to defaultable claims after replacing the risk-free rate with a risk-adjusted rate that depends on the hazard rate, h, and the recovery rate, L. The first approach was followed by Duffie and Singleton (1996) and by Dai and Singleton (1998) in modelling the term structure of interest rate swap yields. By parameterising R directly, one combines the effects of changes in the riskless rate, r_t, and mean loss rate, $h_t L_t$, on bond prices. The second parameterising approach was taken by Duffee (1996), who specified the processes for r_t and $h_t L_t$ separately. In doing so, he was able to recover information about the mean loss rate from historical information on the yield of defaultable bonds. All of these models are special cases of the affine family of term structure models developed by Duffie and Kan (1996).

Markov diffusion process

The value of a firm can be modelled as a stochastic diffusion process. Default occurs when the firm value falls below a certain threshold value[6] and the firm declares bankruptcy. The basic stochastic differential equation is

$$\frac{dV}{V} = \mu\,dt + \delta\,dW \tag{2}$$

where $V(t)$ is the value of the firm at time t, μ is the drift, δ is the volatility of the firm value and $W(t)$ is the standard Brownian motion. Notice that the drift rate and volatility can also be functions of time or can even be stochastic processes. However, to keep the model simple they are treated as constants. The first passage time, τ, is defined to be the first time at which V becomes equal to or less than the default threshold, $V_{default}$. We can obtain the probability density distribution of the first passage time by solving equation (2).

Jump–diffusion process

Even though it can capture the slow drift in the credit quality of a defaultable instrument, the continuous diffusion process alone is not sufficient to characterise the behaviour of a typical default process. This is supported by the evidence that the short-term credit spread of corporate bonds is not zero. To overcome this shortcoming, an independent jump process is introduced in addition to the Markov diffusion process. This process is intended to accommodate an abrupt change in the credit quality of a firm – a sudden default. A Poisson process with event arrival intensity λ is used to model the occurrence of such a change. By specifying the value of λ, the probability of default between $(t, t + \Delta t)$ conditional on no default occurring prior to t is $\lambda\Delta t$. Again, we assume that λ is constant. In general it can be modelled to be a function of time or even as a stochastic variable.

Probability of default

We must point out that the independence of the default process from the interest rate process is assumed. This assumption is critical to obtaining an analytical solution for the price of a defaultable instrument. There are, however, cases such that this assumption is not valid. In these circumstances a less stringent set of assumptions has to be made, discussion of which is beyond the scope of this survey.

   Knowing the probability distribution of τ and the intensity of the Poisson jump–diffusion process, we can then compute the probability $\pi(t, T)$, where $\pi(t, T)$ denotes the probability of a firm's default in time interval $[t, T]$. This probability, along with knowledge of the recovery rate,[7] is then sufficient to price most defaultable instruments and their contingent claims. In the calibration procedure the bond prices (or par spread curve) are usually parameterised using μ, δ and λ[8] and are fitted to the market prices. The parameters are then used to evaluate the default probability across time.

   A simple but useful relationship between short-term spread, recovery rate and Poisson arrival intensity rate can be deduced from the model:

Short-term yield spread =
(1 − Recovery rate) × Poisson arrival intensity rate

This equation can give us a quick estimation of the jump default probability based on the current level of short-term yield spread and historical recovery rate for the credit rating of a credit-risky instrument.

   The above model can easily be extended to the default process for multiple firms by introducing the proper correlation matrix between the Brownian and Poisson processes across different firms. However, the number of factors in the model needs to be carefully selected when calibrating to market prices.

Pricing credit default swaps and options

Although many factors contribute to the recovery rate after default, it is not completely unreasonable to assume that it remains a constant throughout the maturity of the credit swap. This should save a lot of time by removing the need to model the recovery rate process. The recovery scheme to which traders usually refer is *recovery of par*, whereby a constant portion of the par value is recovered after the default regardless of the underlying bond's maturity and coupon. It is worth pointing out that, due to seniority, debts issued by the same issuer may have different recovery rates. Thus, we need to screen the bonds selected for calibration carefully. Other common types of market default payment are recovery of market value, digital cash payment, initial price minus after-default price, normalised initial price minus after-default price, and recovery of treasury.

Recall that a plain vanilla swap is to pay an annuity until either default occurs or the term of the swap is reached. The value of a swap can be established from the equation

$$S(t) = (1 - R)B(t, T) - A(t, T)C$$

where R is the constant recovery rate, C is the amount of the annuity, $B(t, T)$ is the present value of the claim which pays \$1 upon default and $A(t, T)$ is the price of the annuity which pays \$1 until either the end of the swap or the time of default, whichever is first. Knowing the probability of default across time along with an interest rate diffusion process, both $B(t, T)$ and $A(t, T)$ can be calculated. Setting the initial value of the swap to be zero gives us the amount of the annuity:

$$C = \frac{(1-R)B(t,T)}{A(t,T)} \qquad (3)$$

The reader should notice immediately that the valuation of the credit default option resembles equation (3) very closely since the annuity is replaced by a one-time upfront payment called the "option premium" by the protection buyer. The valuation for the default option is therefore given by

$$O(t, T) = (1 - R)B(t, T)$$

In practice, the default probability can be extracted by calibrating to the market prices of the traded bonds or the par yield spread curve of a firm. Figures 2 and 3 show a typical cumulative default probability and marginal default probability calibrated to a synthetic par spread curve.

MODELLING THE DEFAULT PROCESS – EMPIRICAL APPROACHES

We next look at empirical approaches to modelling default rates. Within this category there are four broad approaches. The first tries to model transition probabilities among different rating categories. The second is the use of duration models. The third is the use of qualitative dependent variable techniques. Finally, we describe a new non-parametric approach to modelling disasters called CART.

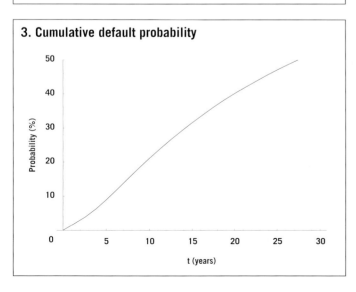

2. Marginal default probability curve

$\beta = -5.0$, $\theta = 0.06$, and $\lambda = 0.0150$, where $\beta = \ln(V(o)/V_{default})/\sigma$ and $\theta = \mu/\sigma - \sigma/2$

3. Cumulative default probability

In the first case, Markov chain techniques are used to model the transition matrix of firms from one rating category to another. The problem with this technique is that firm ratings often lag behind changes in their spreads and that rating categories lose some firm-specific information as not all firms within a rating category are alike.

In analysing default rates, the dependent variable is binary (ie, default or no default). One way to measure the probabilities of this binary variable is through the use of duration modelling (which is our second approach). Duration models allow the modelling of conditional defaults – ie, of having a default in time period $[t, t+\Delta]$ conditional on no default in time period $[0, t]$.

The third approach to deriving these probabilities is through qualitative dependent variable techniques. The basic idea is to identify a set of independent variables to classify firms into two potential categories: default or no default. For example, we can use a developing country's balance of payments, local interest rates, etc, as variables to determine whether it is likely to default or not. The analysis assumes that the independent variables are conditionally normally distributed. This, however, may not be a tenable assumption. The approach provides unconditional probabilities of default. This is a disadvantage compared to duration modelling techniques, which derive a conditional probability of default.

The last approach is a non-parametric, heuristic-based method and is called CART ("classification and regression trees" – see Huang, Ketkar and Varikooty, 1998). This derives unconditional probabilities of default. It looks at a large set of variables and derives a decision tree, which indicates whether a firm or a country is likely to default, along with the probabilities of default.

ESTIMATING THE LOSS RATE

We look at different ways of evaluating the loss rate (or, equivalently, the recovery rate) in the event of default. There are two ways of doing this. The loss rate can be exogenously specified. Typically, this is done by obtaining the historical loss rate from sources such as Moody's for a given rating and industry category. For instance, from Moody's 1996 data the average defaulted bond prices for senior unsecured issues is \$51, which implies a loss rate of 49% assuming recovery of par. However, since the negotiation of bond prices between creditors and shareholders after default is an extremely complex process, the historical loss rate typically exhibits a large standard deviation. Any attempts to estimate the loss rate from historical data need to take this into account.

Moreover, Moody's only provides historical loss rates for corporate bond issuers. The situation with sovereign debt or corporate debt issued by many emerging economies is even more complicated. Because in general it is extremely difficult, if not entirely impossible, for creditors to enforce legal claims once the issuer goes into default, all post-default recovery must be obtained through lengthy negotiation. In this situation, the only recourse creditors have to persuade the defaulter to repay is through threats to withhold future capital investment by all creditors involved, which, depending on the arrangements between the various creditors, may be difficult to enforce. Incidentally, for various political and diplomatic reasons creditors' home governments are often unwilling to step in to support their cause in cross-border default disputes. Courts in both London and New York have also historically been reluctant to enforce default claims in foreign territories because of the limitation of jurisdiction. Ultimately, how much can be recovered hinges on the relative bargaining positions of creditors and debtors. This makes it even more difficult to estimate the recovery rate.

Another more elegant way would be to infer the loss or recovery rate from market information about the credit-risky security that is being evaluated. To obtain separate information about the default and the loss rates we also need options on the credit-risky security in addition to the prices (Duffie and Singleton, 1998). In general, if we only have information on the prices of credit-risky securities but not their option prices, we could only infer joint information about the default rates and loss rates.

In this section we consider several issues fundamental to the modelling of credit derivatives. Whereas the pricing of credit derivative products is computationally tractable, the hedging of credit-risky instruments is notoriously difficult. After origination derivatives usually have non-zero values when marked to markets. Because of the jump default feature they possess it is almost impossible to find a security that is highly correlated with credit derivative products except for one of their own type. Traders are usually reluctant to expose themselves to this kind of small-event, big-loss product because of the lack of reliable hedging schemes. Since single-instrument perfect hedging often proves to be elusive, the widely accepted approach in managing credit risk is through diversification. In other words, credit risk can often be diversified away by aggregating poorly or negatively correlated instruments into a portfolio. The next section presents more details on the issue of properly managing and hedging credit risk.

Mitigating and managing credit risk

Managing credit risk requires an approach quite different to that needed for market risk. An investor with a large portfolio of default-free domestic and foreign bonds, for example, faces market risk (interest rate and currency rate risk) but no credit risk. In this case it is generally possible to identify a relatively low number of underlying market-wide factors that are highly correlated with individual bonds in the portfolio. The effect of each underlying factor on the value of the entire portfolio can be calculated by netting its effect on each bond. Consequently, investors can hedge their market risk exposure effectively by taking appropriate positions in, for example, interest rate swap, futures and currency swap contracts. Credit risks, on the other hand, often are not highly correlated with any market index or benchmark. This indicates that diversification, rather than taking positions in market indices, may be the preferred approach to mitigate credit risk. Another major difference between managing market risk and credit risk is that companies usually have small probabilities of default, but such events often have catastrophic consequences for investors. This makes it crucial to model comprehensively the tail of the probability distribution and give careful study to extreme outlier events, both of which are generally ignored by conventional financial models.

Three approaches are commonly employed to manage credit risk: collateralisation; diversification; and hedging through credit derivatives. Before we turn to describe these approaches, however, a few words of caution are warranted. In the end, no methodology can completely replace prudent human judgement. Economic, political and natural news can change credit risk exposure rapidly and unexpectedly and no risk management system can claim to be exhaustive in every possible scenario. Also, it is important to recognise that there is always the possibility that a human- or model-produced error may more than cancel out the benefits of a sophisticated risk management system in the event of adverse market developments. It is vital that all these concerns be addressed when designing a sound risk management system.

COLLATERALISATION

Managing credit risk through collateralisation is nothing new. In fact, it is as old as the practice of borrowing and lending itself. Pawn, mortgage loan, secured bond and home equity loan are examples that immediately come to mind. In principle, the borrower or a third party pledges an asset to the lender in exchange for a loan so that, should the borrower fail to repay his debt obligation, the lender can take possession of the pledged collateral to cover or reduce his loss.

Collateralisation is commonly used in the credit market to mitigate both issuer and counterparty default risk. A firm with low credit quality can enhance its credit by obtaining a third-party guarantee, such as a standby line of credit from a commercial bank, and thus gain access to capital markets that traditionally are restricted to firms with high credit qualities. In this instance, the standby line of credit serves as collateral. The government of a developing country can borrow from the global capital market by issuing bonds that have part of the future cashflows collateralised by default-free assets. Under the Brady plan, many Latin American countries and, subsequently, non-Latin American developing countries have issued Brady bonds, such as par bonds and discount bonds, whose principals are collateralised by US Treasury zero-coupon bonds and interests partially by rolling interest rate guarantees. Another example is the repo contract, which is essentially a short-term loan collateralised by the securities which the borrower uses the loan to purchase. In the term repo market, securities with low credit quality and long borrowing term can only collateralise a loan at a fraction of the market value of the securities – a situation referred to as a "haircut". This is similar to the way a margin account works, to ensure that the lender does not suffer huge losses should the value of the securities drop unexpectedly. Major players in the term repo market have developed sophisticated tools to determine the amount of haircut that should be applied to different types of collateral. An interesting situation arises when two counterparties enter into a swap contract. Depending on how the market moves, either party may face counterparty default risk over time. In this case both parties normally need to put up collateral to hedge their credit exposures, although the amount of such collateral can often be substantially reduced through netting.

How does one determine the proper amount of capital to be set aside as collateral? The precise amount is a function of at least the following factors:

❏ The timing and probability of default of the counterparty or issuer.

❏ The correlation between the default probabilities of the counterparty and issuers, if applicable.

❏ The expected loss in the event of a default.

❏ Whether the asset is guaranteed by a high-credit third party.

❏ Whether the asset's default exposure is hedged by taking a position in some other instrument.

❏ Major economic and market factors that affect the performance and financial position of the firm and the tail distribution of these factors.

❏ The liquidity of the asset.

❏ The Bank for International Settlements (BIS) risk weighting of the asset if the investor is a bank.

Elsewhere in this chapter detailed examples are given of how to calculate credit exposures. In any estimation of collateral requirements it is important to incorporate stress testing under extreme scenarios. In addition to margin requirements and haircuts, there are also some regulatory guidelines. In 1988 the Bank for International Settlements issued a framework for setting minimum capital requirements for international banks. According to the framework, each type of asset is assigned a risk-based weight ranging from 0% for the sovereign debt issued by OECD member countries, to 20% for senior debt obligations of OECD banks, to 100% for corporate debt and non-OECD sovereign debt. Then all banks are expected to set aside a minimum of 8% of the risk-weighted asset. So, for example, an investment of $20 million in the senior debt of an OECD bank requires $0.20 \times 0.08 \times \$20,000,000 = \$320,000$ in capital to be set aside against this asset.

The sovereign debt of OECD countries is assigned a 0% risk weight because it is perceived to be virtually default-free. A bank may try to hedge its positions by taking offset positions. Whether the bank is able to reduce its BIS capital requirement depends on how perfect the hedge is and whether the positions are held on the trading book or the bank book. In fact, it is entirely possible that a bank may reduce its credit risk exposure substantially using hedging techniques but that, according to current BIS rules, it actually ends up with a greater capital charge. As a result, banks sometimes take positions for the sole purpose of circumventing the BIS capital requirement rather than to maximise returns and minimise the actual risk that they face. Another problem with the current BIS framework is that, in practice, individual countries have considerable freedom in the interpretation of BIS guidelines and have set up their own capital requirement guidelines, which are often at odds with the BIS guidelines.

In recent years regulators have been considering a new capital adequacy policy. Instead of relying on the somewhat arbitrary risk weights assigned to different categories of assets, the new regulation will be based on risk management models developed by international banks, provided that these models meet certain requirements. This will take advantage of the banks' sophisticated hedging policies and make risk capital work more efficiently. A recent speech by the chairman of the BIS committee, Mr William McDonough, who is also President of the Federal Reserve Bank in New York, indicates that the process of switching to the new regime may be accelerated in view of the problems with the current BIS framework. The risk modelling-based approach to capital adequacy also has drawbacks. No model is perfect, and most of these models rely on certain empirical inputs, such as correlation and volatility, which have to be estimated from historical data.[9] In a rapidly changing financial environment historical data may offer little guidance as to how the market will evolve. To counter these deficiencies it is imperative that model users design extreme benchmark scenarios to stress-test their model and set aside additional capital for the unexpected situations.

Ultimately, neither hedging nor diversification can guard against catastrophic market movements, and no amount of sophistication in risk management modelling can prevent losses arising from from human errors and model errors. In this regard, capital set aside can guard not only against credit risk but also against other unforeseeable risks, such as execution risk and model risk.

DIVERSIFICATION

As noted above, credit risks are specific to particular counterparties or issuers and may have very low correlation with each other. In these circumstances an investor's exposure to credit risk can be substantially reduced through diversification by taking a portfolio that consists of many such risks.

According to modern portfolio theory, if assets are highly correlated with each other, they tend to move together under various market conditions. In this situation a portfolio consisting of such assets is still exposed to the same risk that the underlying assets are exposed to, and diversification does not help to reduce risk. On the other hand, if the assets have low, or even negative, correlation with each other, then, when one asset performs badly, on average other assets do not perform badly at the same time or may even perform better. In a portfolio that includes a large number of these assets the overall exposure to each individual risk is thus diversified away.

Do credits have high correlation with each other? The answer, as with most things in life, is not a simple one. In general, it depends on the quality of the credits, the type of market and, as amply demonstrated recently, the overall health of the financial market.

In a normal market, high credit-rated issues historically have very low correlation with each other because the default risk of a company is closely tied to its own performance and not to that of other companies. By some estimates the average one-year default correlation between two investment-grade credits is as low as 0.01, even for companies in quite closely related businesses. This implies tremendous benefits in lowering credit risk through diversification in a portfolio. Also, by combining assets of different industries, markets and countries, theory suggests that one can further reduce the overall exposure of the portfolio to credit risk since the default risks in this case would be even less correlated.

The potential benefits of diversification decrease as one moves from very high grade credits to lower-quality credits. Companies with lower credit quality are financially weaker and more vulnerable, and are more likely to succumb to adverse movements in general market conditions. For example, Indonesian banks and companies may all be susceptible to the flow of foreign funds. As a result, lower credits tend to be more closely correlated with each other. This suggests that, to hedge credit risk exposure when investing in a portfolio of lower credits, one may employ diversification to mitigate the non-systematic portion and use hedging to reduce the systematic portion of the credit risk. One problem is that it is not always possible to find suitable market index contracts to hedge the systematic risk.

A much more serious problem is amply demonstrated by the recent turmoil in the global financial market, which started in 1997 when the Thai baht was devalued and subsequently spread to other emerging markets. Only a short time ago it was threatening to bring down the global economy. Characteristic of the current crisis is the "contagion" effect – that is, financial crisis in one country spilling over into neighbouring countries, affecting trading partners or even spreading to other emerging markets that seemingly do not have a great deal in common with the country in crisis. As the crisis worsens, the global credit crunch caused by investors' loss of appetite for risk begins to drive up the yield spreads of all credit markets – investment-grade and speculative grade alike – to historic levels. Liquidity dries up in all but the safest havens of the fixed-income universe, namely the treasury markets of the strongest economies. This seemingly "grand unification"[10] of credit spread widenings is illustrated in Figure 4.

When all credit spreads widen in time like this diversification becomes less effective. It is important to combine collateralisation and/or credit derivative hedging with the diversification approach, and the collateral amount required can be computed from a simulation-based extreme scenario stress test, a value-at-risk approach or an extreme event theory (EVT) methodology.

HEDGING WITH CREDIT DERIVATIVES

Credit derivatives are one of the fastest growing areas in financial engineering. They have been used by securities firms, global banks, mutual funds, corporations, insurance companies and hedge funds in credit risk management, portfolio management, arbitrage trading and the creation of new synthetic assets. To quote the Bank for International Settlements' (1998) report, "International Banking and Financial Market Developments":

> ... the growing use of credit derivatives (default swaps in particular) provided greater scope for adjusting credit exposures. Such techniques are increasingly used as an alternative to secondary market sales, allowing the preservation of customer relations (since the consent of original borrowers is not required) and the offering of ancillary services.

According to an estimate by the British Bankers' Association, the total outstanding stock of credit derivatives amounted to $US170 billion at the end of 1997, compared to only $40 to $50 billion at the end of 1996. The US Office of the Comptroller of the Currency reports that credit derivatives held by US banks alone amounted to $91 billion at the end of March 1998, compared with $55 billion at the end of 1997 and $19 billion in the first quarter of that year. Much of the growth has resulted from transactions on emerging market paper and structured securities. As the importance of the credit market continues to grow in the global financial market, credit derivatives will undoubtedly see wider application and be increasingly accepted as an essential part of investors' strategies.

Although credit derivatives products have found many important applications among market practitioners, we are primarily concerned with the application of these instruments to credit risk management. Below we present two examples to

4. "Grand unification" of credit spread widenings

Global financial crisis

↑

All credit products, high- or low-risk, move together. Only risk-free OECD government bonds considered safe now.

Credit risks highly correlated across many low credit rating segments through contagion; but good-quality credits still uncorrelated.

Credits in high-risk market segments are correlated within the segment (eg, a Korean corporate and a Korean bank); but across segments and in high grades the correlations are still low.

Credit risks issuer-specific, largely uncorrelated with each other.

Normal market

give an indication of how they can be used effectively for this purpose. Bear in mind, though, that credit derivatives are often tailor-made to suit the particular needs of a transaction and can be quite complicated in structure. Also, the credit derivatives market is currently undergoing rapid development and new structures constantly emerge. At best, these examples only serve to scratch the surface of the tremendous versatility of credit derivatives.

Example – credit default swap or option

A credit default swap or option can be used to effectively hedge the default risk of the asset. The option seller receives a fee (the premium) – either upfront (a default option) or paid over time (a default swap) – from the seller of the default risk, the investor. The investor receives a prespecified amount from the option seller when a credit event occurs, and nothing otherwise. The default option differs from an American option in that a payment is made to the option buyer only if a credit event, as carefully defined in the contract, occurs. The premium can be thought of as the credit spread required for the option seller to take the default risk of a given asset. Default options can be purchased on a bond, a loan, sovereign risk due to international trade, or counterparty risk in an interest rate or currency swap. They can be linked to an individual credit or to a basket of credits. In fact, the credit event that triggers the payment does not have to be a default event. It is negotiable between the two parties in the default option transaction and can be a spread widening, a rating agency downgrade or even an event in a foreign country that adversely affects the price of the asset.

A simplified example of a default swap might run as follows:

The protection buyer owns risky bond A, and receives interest and possible principal payments regularly, as long as bond A does not default. By purchasing a default swap from a third party the investor can recoup his loss through payment made by the protection seller, thus reducing the credit exposure. Naturally, this protection is not free.

When an investor intends to buy a credit default option, it is advisable that the option seller has low correlation with the issuer of the asset. For example, it makes no sense to buy default protection from Merrill Lynch on a bond issued by Merrill Lynch.

Example – total return swap

A total return swap is a financial contract between two counterparties. The total return payer pays the total return of an asset, including all the cashflows generated by the asset and any appreciation in price during the life of the swap; in return, he receives from the total return receiver a form of payment, such as Libor plus a spread. If the price declines over the term, the receiver must pay the difference to the payer. The underlying asset can be corporate bonds, sovereign debt, mortgage-backed securities, term loans, equities, indices, commodities, and so on. Total return swaps are off-balance-sheet transactions. They are among the most popular and most widespread of all the credit derivatives.

The basic structure of a total return swap is shown below.

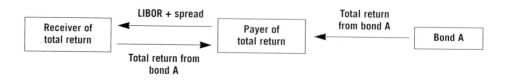

Often the term of the swap contract is shorter than underlying asset. The total return receiver receives all the cashflows of a security during this period without actually owning it. In most cases, however, if the underlying asset defaults prior to the maturity of the total return swap, the swap contract terminates and the total return receiver bears the credit risk. From the total return payer's point of view, he originally owns the credit risk of bond A. By entering the total return swap he transfers this exposure to the receiver. In the meantime, he is exposed to the credit risk that the total return receiver may default on his floating-rate payment obligation. But, in reality, the total return payer is at risk only when *both* the total return receiver *and* the issuer of bond A default. This joint probability of default is in general substantially lower than the original risk of default by the issuer of bond A alone as long as the bond issuer and his swap counterparty are not highly correlated. When the correlation condition is met, the investor in the underlying asset has successfully managed to reduce his credit risk through a total return swap.

Conclusion

It should be clear from the foregoing discussion that credit-related markets are growing rapidly into extremely dynamic and complicated entities. As a result, modelling and managing credit risk become a vitally important task that every practitioner in the credit markets needs to understand. This task, however, requires a thorough understanding of the market and the risks associated with it, as well as the quantitative skills to quantify and analyse them. Due to the complexity and constant change of the market environment, the concepts and the methodology for credit risk management are also undergoing rapid development. Many new issues have been raised, and many new products and theories have been created.

The recent meltdown in the emerging markets, for example, has taught us some valuable lessons. First, the globalisation of economies has made it possible for a crisis in one corner of the globe to spread at unprecedented speed. This makes the securities in different markets move with an extremely high correlation. As a result, a portfolio may have very little diversification. Second, liquidity movements in the market can, if accompanied by suitable market sentiment, make a huge wave from a small ripple that has little to do with economic fundamentals. Third, when there is a crisis liquidity can evaporate in a matter of hours. This is a matter of considerable concern to the designers of hedging strategies. And, in a market meltdown, liquidity issues become one of the most important factors in determining the value of a portfolio as well as the validity of any hedging strategy. Fourth, in the case of a default the recovery value can be very different from what people or the market expect. For example, the Russian Prins has been traded at $US5 lately – much less than expected by market consensus before the crisis.

Some of the models discussed in this chapter have to some extent addressed the above issues, but none of them is satisfactory. It is an important and challenging task to build a model or a methodology for risk management that not only solves the issues discussed in earlier sections but which also correctly describes, first, how the liquidity of the market may change and its effects on the portfolio risk, and second, how the correlation among different assets may change with the market environment and how this will affect the diversification achieved by the portfolio.

---

1 *The data used are from March to August 1998. The correlation varies from time to time and, typically, is higher when there are big movements in the markets. Also see the discussions below.*

2 *It is important to separate default from a drop in market price, which could be caused solely by market conditions. Default derivative does not cover market risk.*

3 *The annuity payer and receiver may negotiate other types of payment schedules.*

4 *For simplicity, we assume that the credit derivative seller is also the issuer.*

5 *It is generally believed that hazard rate and recovery rate cannot usually be identified separately from the market prices.*

6 *A good proxy is the outstanding debt level. This value is endogenously determined by some authors.*

7 *The value of the recovery rate is usually exogenously specified on the basis of historical data.*

8 *In fact, function forms of* μ, δ *and* λ.

9 *Many techniques have been developed to forecast future volatility and correlation, with mixed results. For a survey, see Varikooty, Liu and Huang (1997).*

10 *To shamelessly borrow a term from theoretical physics.*

Bibliography

Altman, E., and J. Bencivenga, 1995, "A Yield Premium Model for the High-Yield Debt Market", *Financial Analysts Journal* September, pp. 49–56.

Altman, E., and V. Kishore, 1995, "Report on Defaults and Returns on High Yield Bonds: Analysis Through 1994", New York University, Salomon Brothers Working paper S/95/3.

Altman, E., R. Handleman and P. Narayanan, 1997, "ZETA Analysis – A New Model to Identify Bankruptcy Risk of Corporations", *Journal of Banking and Finance*, pp. 29–54.

Bank for International Settlements, Monetary and Economic Department, 1998, "International Banking and Financial Market Developments", August.

Black, F., and J. Cox, 1976, "Valuing Corporate Securities: Some Effects of Bond Indenture Provisions", *Journal of Finance* 31, pp. 351–67.

Black, F., and M. Scholes, 1973, "The Pricing of Options and Corporate Liabilities", *Journal of Political Economy* 81, pp. 637–54.

Blume, M. E., F. Lim and A. C. MacKinley, 1998, "The Declining Credit Quality of U.S. Corporate Debt: Myth or Reality?", *Journal of Finance* 53, pp. 1389–413.

Carty, L., and J. Fons, 1994, "Measuring Changes in Corporate Credit Quality", *Journal of Fixed Income* 4, pp. 27–41.

Dai, Q., and K. Singleton, 1998, "Specification Analysis of Affine Term Structure Models", Working paper, Stanford University.

Das, S., and P. Tufano, 1996, "Pricing Credit Sensitive Debt When Interest Rates, Credit Ratings and Credit Spreads are Stochastic", *Journal of Financial Engineering* 5, pp. 161–98.

Duffee, D., 1996, "Estimating the Price of Default Risk", Research paper, Federal Reserve Board, Washington D.C.

Duffee, D., 1998, "The Relation Between Treasury Yields and Corporate Bond Yield Spreads", Forthcoming, *Journal of Finance*.

Duffie, D., 1998a, "Credit Swap Valuation", *Journal of Finance* 51, pp. 921–49.

Duffie, D., 1998b, "Defaultable Term Structure Models with Fractional Recovery of Par", Working paper, Stanford University.

Duffie, D., and M. Huang, 1996, "Swap Rates and Credit Quality", *Journal of Finance* 51, pp. 921–49.

Duffie, D., and R. Kan, 1996, "A Yield Factor Model of Interest Rates", *Mathematical Finance* 6, pp. 379–406.

Duffie, D., and K. Singleton, 1996, "An Econometric Model of the Term Structure of Interest Rate Swap Yields", *Journal of Finance* 44, pp. 19–40.

Duffie, D., and K. Singleton, 1998, "Modelling Term Structures of Defaultable Bonds", Working paper, Stanford University.

Fabozzi, F. J., 1997, *The Handbook of Fixed Income Securities*, Fifth edition (Chicago: Irwin Professional Publishing).

Fons, J., 1994, "Using Default Rates to Model the Term Structure of Credit Risk", *Financial Analysts Journal* September/October, pp. 25–32.

Harrison, M., and D. Kreps, 1979, "Martingales and Arbitrage in Multiperiod Securities Markets", *Journal of Economic Theory* 20, pp. 381–408.

Huang, H., S. Ketkar and A. Varikooty, 1998, "Predicting Large Peso Devaluations: The 'CART' Approach", Research paper, Credit Suisse First Boston.

Hull, J., and A. White, 1995, "The Impact of Default Risk on the Prices of Options and Other Derivative Securities", *Journal of Banking and Finance* 19, pp. 299-322.

Jarrow, R., and S. Turnbull, 1995, "Pricing Options on Financial Securities Subject to Default Risk", *Journal of Finance* 50, pp. 53-86.

Jarrow, R., D. Lando and S. Turnbull, 1997, "A Markov Model for the Term Structure of Credit Spreads", *Review of Financial Studies* 10, pp. 481-523.

Jones, E. P., S. P. Mason and E. Rosenfeld, 1984, "Contingent Claims Analysis of Corporate Capital Structure: An Empirical Investigation", *Journal of Finance* 39, pp. 611-25.

Kim, I. J., K. Ramaswamy and S. Sunderesan, 1993, "Does Default Risk in Coupons Affect the Valuation of Corporate Bonds: A Contingent Claims Approach Model", *Financial Management* 20, pp. 117-31.

Li, T., 1998, "A Model of Pricing Defaultable Bonds And Credit Ratings", Working paper, Washington University.

Litterman, R., and T. Iben, 1991, "Corporate Bond Valuation and the Term Structure of Credit Spreads", *Journal of Portfolio Management* 17, pp. 52-64.

Longstaff, F., and E. Schwartz, 1995, "A Simple Approach to Valuing Risky Fixed and Floating Rate Debt", *Journal of Finance* 50, pp. 789-820.

Merton, R., 1973, "Rational Theory of Option Pricing", *Bell Journal of Economics and Management Science* 4, pp. 141-83.

Merton, R., 1974, "On the Pricing of Corporate Debt: The Risk Structure of Interest Rates", *Journal of Finance* 29, pp. 449-70.

Nielsen, L. T., J. Saa-Requejo and P. Santa-Clara, 1993, "Default Risk and Interest Rate Risk: The Term Structure of Default Spreads", Working paper, INSEAD, Fontainebleau, France.

Shimko, D., N. Tejima and D. van Deventer, 1993, "The Pricing of Risky Debt When Interest Rates are Stochastic", *Journal of Fixed Income* 3, pp. 58-66.

Tavakoli, J. M., 1998, "Credit Derivatives – A Guide to Instruments and Applications", *Financial Engineering*.

Varikooty, A. P., J. Liu and H. Huang, 1997, "Predictive Ability of Different Volatility Forecasting Techniques", in *Risk Management for Financial Institutions, Advances in Measurement and Control* (London: Risk Publications), pp. 127-42.

7

Some Estimations of the Value of Volatility

Shenglin Lu

Merrill Lynch

In the modern financial industry we see a constant flow of innovation and new products designed to serve the fast-growing investment world. Investors have a wider choice of products than ever before to improve their asset and liability management. Very often these are products with embedded options or derivatives offered by financial institutions. Products with embedded options and derivatives are created to decompose and restructure the risks embedded in the relevant underlying products. The options and derivatives market has already provided an additional dimension for many investors seeking a money management strategy. In more recent years efforts by financial institutions, academics and legal control departments to consolidate the derivative markets have enabled more investors to better understand, utilise and manage their financial operations. Options and derivative products have improved the liquidity of the financial economy.

As a result, the many sophisticated money-generating techniques of earlier years have gradually become the "transparent" arbitrage norm of present-day trading practices and the creation of a more dynamic market has emphasised the importance of volatility to the underlying. Volatility has become an important measurement of market strength and, consequently, is often regarded as a buy or sell market indicator.

The explosion in market volatilities, which produces uncertainty, requires fund managers and treasurers to use options for hedging purposes. Moreover, during periods when the yield curve is flat (ie, an expectation that future interest rates will be at levels similar to those at present) money managers use option positions to enhance yield and increase carry and estimating the value of volatility becomes a crucial task for financial professionals. As a result, new products are created to accurately record the behaviour of market volatility and research on volatility exposure has become more sophisticated, which we expect will bring more values to improve investment quality and achieve financial targets for investors.

Volatility is associated with almost every financial product. It is not the purpose in this chapter to exhaust any individual issue. Instead, I address selected topics related to volatility opportunities and provide some explanations from various approaches. First, I look into some techniques for estimating volatility. I discuss the well-known assumption that mean-reversion and jumps in the underlying asset have a tremendous impact on the estimation of volatility and how the volatility term structure is affected by the change caused by mean-reversion. In the second section, I consider some fundamental points that are closely related to option and volatility trading. For example, an investor may not be interested in having exposures in option markets by simply understanding the risks of option products. Many investors are afraid of paying too much time value, which they may never be able to recover. Volatility is a determinant of the time value of the associated option. Characterisation of the option premium in terms of its static and dynamic behaviours can specify risk factors and their relations explicitly for many standard options, and can therefore help to determine hedging cost and identify sources leading to mishedging. It is no surprise that many options can be decomposed into a weighted average of standard call and put options. In the third section, I present a few basic methods for capturing market opportunities using volatility strategies. During the past few years techniques created to capture the volatility values have enabled investors to use derivative products to obtain additional profits.

Most of the concepts used here, although generic, are based on a fixed-income market convention. When a mathematical formula becomes unavoidable, it is assumed that readers have a basic understanding of markets in terms of random walk.

Some basic techniques for estimating market volatility

Practitioners and researchers are constantly searching for new methods of estimating market volatility. The need for accurate interpretations of volatilities places constant pressure on the financial services industry. As an example, during the highly volatile period of the equity markets in 1997–98 the volatility swap became a popular investment vehicle.

The fundamental part of a volatility swap is an estimation of the actual volatility for the specified period of the swap. An accurate estimation of the actual volatility requires an excellent understanding of the underlying asset. I will examine the approaches of some methods and discuss the effect of their associated assumptions in relation to the dynamic behaviour of the underlying asset on the estimation techniques.

TRADITIONAL METHOD

Volatility is a measure of the standard deviation of security returns. Therefore, volatility estimators are basically variance estimators. The traditional approach uses close-to-close price changes. The sample prices of an asset is denoted by X_t, $t = 1, 2, ..., N + 1$ and the return is defined as $R_t = \log(X_{t+1}/X_t)$. The standard maximum likelihood variance estimator can be calculated as

$$\sigma = \sqrt{\frac{\sum_{i=1}^{N}\left(R_i - \overline{R}\right)^2}{(N-1)}}$$

$$\overline{R} = \frac{\left(\sum_{i=1}^{N} R_i\right)}{N} \tag{1}$$

This volatility estimate needs to be annualised on the basis of how the close-to-close price sample points are selected. Much estimation with slight modifications is used to take into account multiple daily observations as well as daily opening, closing, highest and lowest asset prices.

MEAN VARIANCE ADJUSTED METHOD

Mean-reversion is the major factor contributing to the term structure of volatility. Traders of long-dated options often witness empirical evidence of such a tendency. Although the level of mean-reversion is difficult to identify, financial economics suggests that market efficiency will settle market activity at its equilibrium. Intuitively, mean-reversion will bring down the long-period volatility relative to short-period volatility. In other words, day-to-day market observation will behave in a more volatile way than month-to-month market observation. In this section, we will try to find a technique to take into account the influence of mean-reversion in volatility estimation.

Asset price dynamics with mean-reversion but without volatility

Assume that the asset is fully predictable (ie, the next price move is determined by its historical performance) and that its return is completely determined by the previous

MEAN-REVERSION AND RANDOM WALKS

1. Mean-reversion describes a dynamic behaviour that possesses a series of embedded resistant and support levels that gradually move towards an average. The level of the mean-reversion indicates how the item moves lower when reaching resistance and moves higher when approaching the support level. Interest rate, credit spread, pre-payment speed and volatility demonstrate significant mean-reversion behaviour both in the short and long term and represent the attractiveness of the market and opportunities for money managers and other types of investors.

2. A random walk can be seen as dynamic behaviour based on the assumption that a future's position cannot be completely determined by the information available today. However, one can determine the *possible* positions in the future. The probability used to reach different positions is determined by how volatile the behaviour could be and what the expectation is. By using information provided by financial markets on actively traded options, futures and derivatives, one can project the future behaviour of the equity price, bond price, interest rate and credit spread.

return level. The return dynamics is described by

$$\frac{df}{dt} = \left[a - \alpha f\right], f(0) = f_0 \tag{2}$$

where f_0 is the initial return level, and a and α are, respectively, the expected return and mean-reversion strength of the asset. Solving this dynamic equation, we find that the return at any future time, t, is

$$f(t) = f(0)\exp(-\alpha t) + \frac{a}{\alpha}\left(1 - \exp(-\alpha t)\right) \tag{3}$$

Assuming that $\alpha > 0$, the equation states that after the return achieves a certain level it will retreat towards the previous level. As time passes, the initial return has a diminishing influence on the future return. And the equilibrium return, a/α, is independent of when one initially invests in the asset.

Asset price dynamics with mean-reversion and volatility

For an asset return with uncertainty of variance σ, its dynamics can be described as $df = [a - \alpha f]dt + \sigma dW(t)$, where $W(\ )$ is a standard Brownian motion. Probability textbooks refer to this stochastic process as an Ornstein–Uhlenbeck process (OUP). At each time t, the return is normally distributed with mean $f(0)\exp(-\alpha t) + \frac{a}{\alpha}(1 - \exp(-\alpha t))$ and variance

$$\sigma\sqrt{\frac{\left(1 - \exp(-2\alpha t)\right)}{2\alpha}}$$

(assuming that $f(0)$ is the current return). Its equilibrium distribution has mean a/α and variance $\sigma/\sqrt{(2\alpha)}$. Based on this analysis, the previous volatility estimation formula

$$\sqrt{\frac{\sum_{i=1}^{N}\left(f_i^T - f^{\bar{T}}\right)^2}{N-1}}$$

for the forward return volatility at time T obviously underestimates volatility if there is a positive mean-reversion.

We now estimate the volatility with possible mean-reversion based on the assumption that asset value grows lognormally. The stochastic differential equation (SDE) for a lognormal asset can be written as

$$dX_t = \mu X_t dt + \sigma X_t dW(t) \tag{4}$$

where parameter μ is the short-term return. The discretisation of (4) is

$$\frac{X_{t+\Delta t} - X_t}{X_t} = \mu \Delta t + \sigma \left(W(t + \Delta t) - W(t) \right) \tag{5}$$

An equivalent SDE, by Itô's calculus, is

$$d \log X_t = \left[\mu - \frac{\sigma^2}{2} \right] dt + \sigma dW(t) \tag{6}$$

which can be discretised as

$$\frac{\log X_{t+\Delta t}}{X_t} = \left[\mu - \frac{\sigma^2}{2} \right] \Delta t + \sigma \left(W(t + \Delta t) - W(t) \right) \tag{7}$$

Therefore, we now have a formula for daily volatility:

$$\sigma^2 \Delta t = 2 \left[\frac{X_{t+\Delta t} - X_t}{X_t} - \frac{\log X_{t+\Delta t}}{X_t} \right] \tag{8}$$

which becomes the following equation when applied to historical volatility estimation for the asset value held for a length of time T:

$$\sigma = \sqrt{ \sum_{i=1}^{N} 2 \left[\frac{ \left(\frac{X_{i+1}^T - X_i^T}{X_i^T} \right) - \log \left(\frac{X_{i+1}^T}{X_i^T} \right) }{\Delta t} \right] } \tag{9}$$

The advantage of this estimation is obvious. It is completely determined by the daily closing or opening price and allows for the time-dependence of the volatility and drift. And, most importantly, we do not need information about mean-reversion, which is required in the drift term to specify the asset dynamics in (4). Therefore, for an assumption of mean-reversion, we can actually calculate the implied market level of mean-reversion by using two different historical volatility estimations. This is because

$$\sqrt{ \frac{ \sum_{i=1}^{N} \left(f_i^T - f^{\bar{T}} \right)^2 }{N-1} }$$

is an estimator for

$$\sigma = \sqrt{ \frac{1 - \exp(-2\alpha T)}{2\alpha} }$$

and σ can be estimated from (9).

ESTIMATION OF VOLATILITY FOR ASSETS WITH JUMPS

For an asset price that jumps (caused by a dividend, credit, default, earning effect or market trend), two factors contribute separately to the total volatility. The first is the volatility from the smooth evolution of the asset. The second is the volatility to measure the scale of the jump. It should be noted that very often the jump is caused by non-systematic financial events. Its estimation requires extensive historical observations and is not reliable enough to be used for forecasting purposes, as the belief is that "nature" does not jump. Therefore, to estimate the volatility that only reflects the continuous part of the asset price dynamics, we should separate the continuous contributions from the total price performance by eliminating the jumps. For an asset with a possible jump in its price movement, the value of any investment with its cashflows relating to the asset price through a regular relation, F, can be expressed as

$$dF(X_t) = F'(X_{t-})dX_t + \tfrac{1}{2}F''(X_{t-})d\langle X\rangle_t$$
$$+\left[\Delta F(X_t) - F'(X_{t-})\Delta X_t - \tfrac{1}{2}F''(X_{t-})[\Delta X_t]^2\right] \qquad (10)$$

which is an application of standard Itô calculus to the jump–diffusion process. Here asset X allows jump $\Delta X(t) = X(t) - X(t-)$ at any instant t. This relation enables us to equate the total variance to the volatilities of the continuous and jump parts by

$$dX_t^2 = 2X_{t-}dX_t + d\langle X\rangle_t$$
$$\langle X\rangle_t = \langle X^c\rangle_t + \sum_{s\leq t}[X_t - X_{t-}]^2 \qquad (11)$$

In reality, practitioners estimate the volatility of the continuous part by clarifying the contributions from the jumps. What (11) suggests is that the variance from the continuous part can be calculated by subtracting from the total variance the square of the difference between the last closing date and today's opening when the difference appears relatively too large.

ESTIMATION AND MODELLING OF ACTUAL VOLATILITY
The actual volatility is an annualised standard deviation of future price movements between the present and a specific future date. And the implied volatility is the volatility level that is implicit in the market price of an option. In financial decision applications, the calculation of the Sharpe ratio and portfolio optimisation need an accurate risk/return estimation to determine the optimal asset allocation or risk attribution. This methodology has gradually been adopted to indicate portfolio hedging and risk management for an increasing number of markets. A refinement of this method can be used successfully to identify trading opportunities. The fundamental difference is that we need ex-ante computation for the investment decision instead of ex-post estimation for the performance evaluation. The predictability of actual volatility estimation plays an important role in the estimation of risk/return. Estimation based purely on historical statistics ignores market news, dynamics and expectations. Many successful results are based on advanced econometric models, particularly Garch models and their variants. Garch models and other econometric models have been applied to different markets with varying success in estimations of actual volatility. In option pricing applications, to characterise the momentum of the market option participants compare the actual volatility to the implied volatility.

Cost of carry, time value and volatility
The option premium is determined by the cost of replication for funding the forward delivery and part of this replication cost is used to follow market changes until the option expiration time. The time value in the option premium is represented by this part of the cost and volatility is crucial to determining time value. Intuitively, the time value is higher in a volatile environment because it is harder to trace price movements in a rapidly changing market. We will now take a look at topics relevant to the identification of time values.

COST OF CARRY, FORWARD PRICING AND PUT–CALL PARITY

A striking phenomenon of OTC or the structured derivative market is that exactly the same product is offered to investors at many different prices. Even more surprising, all are risk-free prices, and those who write the options can explain clearly why their offers are fair and safe. To investors the basic question is: by holding this product, what is the best possible value that can be added to their investments?

Stated simply, options provide leverage for the underlying asset. For asset and liability management, buying options may not be the only way to get this leverage, especially when the option happens to be expensive compared to the cost of owning the asset. If you have an attractive funding rate, you do not need to buy options to get the same leverage; for example, in the government agency market issuers do not have to buy swaptions to cover their short convexity position because they obviously have a funding advantage.

Essentially, we need to estimate the cost of carry and forward price. A forward contract is an agreement to buy or sell an asset in the future for a price specified today. If no cash is to change hands, the fair forward price is the price that can be agreed upon today. An option is an investment tool to measure the value of the future price relative to a specified strike price. From a replication point of view, a call option is equivalent to a long forward contract. The difference between holding the asset today and holding a forward contract is the cost of carry, which includes all the cashflows from the asset and the funding cost required to fulfil the forward delivery of the asset. The standard put–call parity is

$$\text{Call} = \text{Put} + \text{ITM} - \text{Carry}$$

where ITM is the "in-the-moneyness" of the asset relative to the given strike. The carry has been the main investment objective of many fund managers. When the carry is negative (ie, the yield curve is inverted or flat), investors take a short option position to increase the carry. To understand how the cost of carry affects the option, we will use a regular call option to explain the relationship between the cost of carry and the time value. The call premium can be decomposed into

$$\text{Call} = \text{Time value} + \text{ITM(Intrinsic value)}$$

and

$$\text{Value of call feature} = \text{Time value} - \text{Carry}$$

If the cost of the carry is greater than the time value, early exercise is plausible. The value of the option feature for a call option is the cost of unwinding the trade of the buy stock at the strike time (the put price), and it will indicate the early exercise if the put price is close to zero. If the forward price is far above the strike, the put option has no value. In this case an early exercise is executed if the time value is less than the carry. For a steep yield curve when the carry is positive, an early exercise is more likely. It should be noted that for most equity market products the carry is usually negative.

DYNAMIC AND STATIC DECOMPOSITION OF THE OPTION PREMIUM

The option premium is affected by three components: the market performance of the underlying, the expiration structure and the redemption structure. For a standard contingent claim, its value can be described by the following stochastic dynamics in a continuous-finance framework:

$$C\left(T, X_T\right) = C\left(t, X_t\right) + \int_t^T \frac{\partial}{\partial s} C\left(s, X_s\right) ds +$$

$$\int_t^T \frac{\partial}{\partial X} C\left(s, X_s\right) dX_s + \int_t^T \frac{1}{2} \frac{\partial^2}{\partial X^2} C\left(s, X_s\right) \sigma_s^2 X_s^2 ds \qquad (12)$$

Equation (12) relates the contingent value at time T to its value at time t along the passage of the price movement of the underlying asset, X. The second term is the theta, and the third and fourth are the delta and gamma adjustments along the passage. σ_s, $\mathsf{t} \leq \mathsf{s} \leq \mathsf{T}$, is the forward volatility structure.

In a classic Black–Scholes economy the volatility is constant across the term. If market movements can create a positive value through an effective delta–gamma hedge, the option produces a positive carry value. In more practical terms, if the actual volatility is higher than the implied volatility, we should go long on the option. The option premium depends on the payoff structure. For a generic payoff structure, the option premium's relationship to standard payoffs can be expressed as

$$
\begin{aligned}
C\left(X_T\right) = C\left(K\right) &+ \frac{d}{dX}C\Big|_{X=K}\left(X_T - K\right) \\
&+ \int_0^K \frac{d^2}{dy^2}\, C(y)\max\left(y - X_T,\, 0\right) dy \\
&+ \int_K^\infty \frac{d^2}{dy^2}\, C(y)\max\left(X_T - y,\, 0\right) dy
\end{aligned}
\tag{13}
$$

which suggests that many European options can be decomposed into a linear combination of standard puts and calls. The related Greeks are also a linear combination of the Greeks of calls and puts. It is therefore no surprise that some options, such as digital options, will have negative gamma and positive theta. The premium for a barrier option will not always increase along with volatility. An efficient utilisation of the payoff structure will enable money managers to unwind the risk caused by market changes by adding positions with specific payoffs to match investment needs accordingly. For example, barrier options are often chosen to "short" volatility. The efficient application of these two decompositions will certainly benefit the practice of structuring products, managing risk and searching for more trading opportunities.

TIME VALUE AND GAMMA LEVERAGE: IDENTIFYING THE ATTRACTIVE VOLATILITY OPPORTUNITY

As mentioned in the previous section, if the volatility is fairly priced, the delta–gamma hedge will offset the time decay of the option. The return from purchasing or selling options at the same volatility level is zero regardless of future price movements. This means that if implied volatility equals actual volatility, the gains (losses) from selling (buying) options exactly offset the profits (losses) caused by time decay.

In reality, we face a possible volatility overstatement and volatility term structure. A volatility over- or understatement may indicate a leading or a lagging market. Taking an option long, you pay theta and expect to gain through gamma. The value is therefore achieved by the exchange between actual volatility and implied volatility. If the actual volatility is the same as the implied volatility, then option value (gain/loss) with a delta–gamma hedge offsets the time decay. The premium paid to the implied volatility is received through actual volatility. This also explains where the time value comes from: it arises from the carry and optionality, the carry indicating the market trend and optionality characterising the local dynamics. Leveraging the time value and delta–gamma is a popular trading technique. For instance, a long delta-neutral at-the-money straddle trade is to buy an at-the-money straddle and keep delta-neutral. The purpose of this trade is to short implied volatilities and long actual volatility. If implied volatility remains unchanged, you gain from the realised volatility from the short theta. When prices are stable, the gain from selling the option offsets the time value. Taking an option long gains positive gamma. For an extraordinary volatility change, an option long will gain more in realised volatility than is paid in theta. Unfortunately, the implied volatility collapses when the extraordinary event has passed; therefore, the opposite short straddle gives you two risk exposures. The first is that the realised volatility can exceed the implied volatility and the potential loss can be unlimited. The second is that the implied volatility can jump further. Consequently, even if we observe market movements, time decay can absorb significant volatility profits. This partially addresses the question of why an option may have an abnormal return structure. The second risk is that you may realise an unlimited gain (or loss) by paying (receiving) a limited amount. In general, for a delta-neutral position the time decay profit – as we see from the dynamic decomposition – is given by $\frac{1}{2}$(Gamma $\times$ Price^2 $\times$ Implied volume^2). The gain from realised actual volatility is $\frac{1}{2}$[Gamma $\times$ Price^2 $\times$ (Actual volume^2 – Implied volume^2)]. After delta-neutral rebalancing the profit from an implied volatility change is Vega $\times$ (Current volume – Original volume). The relation between gamma and vega will be discussed further in a later section.

ADVANTAGE OF POSITIVE CONVEXITY AND OPPORTUNITY OFFERED BY
NEGATIVE CONVEXITY

Asset and liability managers are often faced with an obvious and difficult question – should they extend the duration of the asset to take advantage of an expected decline in long-term rates? The risk in such an undertaking is that, if rates rise, longer-duration assets lose their market value dramatically. The efficient management of asset duration requires quantification of the overall convexity. Positive convexity protects one from significant market movements. But history suggests that those willing to short convexity are paid well. Negative convexity will not only help to attain an attractive investment yield but it can also enhance returns. In a fixed-income market, convexity is used to determine the changes in the expected time of the full refund – the earlier the refund, the better the yield. For the issuer, early refunding means short convexity.

Convexity is a gamma-type concept (ie, change of duration relative to parallel curve change). Negative convexity will limit profits during a market rally. Products with super-convexity are actively traded in the market. Investors with access to option markets can buy or short volatilities to adjust their convexity positions without fear of physically holding the underlying cash instruments.

GAMMA AND VEGA LEVERAGE

Changes in price of the underlying asset are caused by many factors. Correctly identifying factors affecting actual volatilities and implied volatilities provides a guideline for choosing the proper investment strategy. Implied volatility often contains factors such as market expectations, supply and demand in the options market, the cost of options and market liquidity. The sustainability of these factors offers opportunities to investors in determining whether a gamma or a vega position will be the more attractive. Trading applications based on gamma and vega performance are well observed in the marketplace when the market displays an obvious trend and a sharp volatility swing. A typical trading practice is to identify the relative values of a long-dated option and a short-dated option using actual volatility and implied volatility. Obviously, gamma will benefit the short-dated options more because high actual volatility has a greater effect on the payoff distribution. For long-dated options the interest rate and vega dominate. Effectively leveraging gamma and vega can add relative value to actual volatility and implied volatility as well as provide an opportunity to gain from market trends. A typical example is to long a short-dated option and short a long-dated option. By doing so, we expect long-dated options to have gamma outperforming vega. In fact, gamma is inversely related to volatility and time to expiration. Therefore we can gain a long position in gamma by buying a short-dated option. Vega is proportional to time to expiration. We can short vega by selling a long-dated option when the market is going down and volatility is expected to be stable. Such a trade provides considerable profit because for a significant price movement in the near term with stable volatility, gamma will outperform vega. The determination of the payoff and expiration structure is important to this type of trade. The dominance of gamma over vega depends on how the option is structured.

PANEL 2

BLACK–SCHOLES, MERTON AND THE GREEKS

The classic Black–Scholes formula is used to value a call or put option which gives the option holder the right to buy or sell the equity or other financial products at a given time in the future for a price specified today. The uncertainty of the future price creates the need to use probability to ascertain the possibility of the future's price being higher or lower than the strike price. Therefore a price has to be paid to acquire the right to buy at some future date. The Black–Scholes formula defines explicitly how the price will be determined in terms of the asset price, expected return, strike level, uncertainty and time horizon. One of the fundamental successes of the Black–Scholes theory is the contribution of Robert Merton in the replication of the theory, which argues that any options and derivatives on the traded assets can be replicated using a portfolio of the assets and cash. Therefore options and derivatives become a leverage for a portfolio. If an asset manager holds a portfolio at risk, he or she can use an option as a leverage. The in-depth implication of Merton's theory is that the value of an option or derivative can be determined by the cost of replicating the option payoff. As a result, any option on financial products with liquidity or credit risk should be priced as the replication cost (hedging cost). The sensitivity of the option price to market inputs contains risks and is denoted by Greek characters. The Greeks are a group of factor sensitivities that indicate the exposure of a position or an entire portfolio. They can be summarised as follows:

Delta (Δ) – represents the price sensitivity of a derivative in relation to a change in the price of the underlying asset;

Gamma (Γ) – is a measure of the rate of change of the delta;

Rho (ρ) – denotes changes in the interest rate;

Theta (θ) – is the time period from the beginning of the option to the expiry;

Vega – represents changes in the volatility.

By building a hedge (replication) to mirror the asset portfolio, an investor can reduce its associated risks by adding or removing options as and when the Greeks indicate the rationale for doing so.

The performances of gamma and vega are very sensitive to the time to expiration and in-the-moneyness.

Understanding the basic value of volatility

Investors can make money from options by three different methods. The first is by correctly anticipating actual volatility levels (buying undervalued options and selling overvalued options). The second is by accurately estimating real volatility (predicting both the timing and the magnitude of a future price move). The last is by profiting through sheer luck by winning the lottery (buying overvalued and selling undervalued). One of the most important concepts in using volatility is that the value of volatility is not the same as the premium. The price you need to pay may not always be affected significantly by the change of volatility. To profit from a volatility opportunity, one needs to access those premiums that exploit the opportunity the most.

HISTORICAL/IMPLIED VOLATILITY RATIO AND EXPECTATION OF ASSET
PRICE MOVEMENTS

Implied volatility forecasts daily market movements. If the historical data for volatility suggest a different forecast, then using only historical volatility to evaluate an option will lead to misjudgement. A very high or low ratio implies that the options market is expecting the market change in the next time period to be vastly different from how it moved in the previous time period. Unwinding of the situation is inevitable for holders of options positions. High ratios imply that participants in the options market are anticipating a substantial move in the underlying market that cannot be predicted from historical prices. And option longs are losing more through time decay than they are making in trading through time value and gamma leverage. If actual volatility does not move to the level of implied volatility, those long options will have to be sold to buy back remaining time value. The same argument holds for low ratios and option shorts. When applying volatility ratio trading techniques, we assume that the market trending is fairly priced. One needs to remember that volatility is a directionless measure of the underlying asset. By tracking the ratio, one can observe the future volatility expectation versus the past.

MARKET BREAKEVEN LEVEL AND EXPECTED DELTA

Furthermore, we can use volatility data to retrieve the range of changes of asset price. In this favoured technique of investors and traders the expected actual market price movement is calculated to break even the time decay in a delta-neutral position. One calculates the expected range of price movents using implied volatility and identifies the predicted price movement using historical volatility. For example, consider a bond trading at a forward price of 100 with an implied volatility of 5.1%. This means that, in a year, with 68% probability the expected price range will be between 94.9 and 105.1 and the daily change will be 0.32. This is also known as a one standard deviation market range with a probability of 68%. For a standard deviation of 1.96 the probability is 95%, and for a standard deviation of 2.576 it is 99%. In general, the price range is computed as Forward price $\times \exp(\pm \text{Volume} \times \sqrt{T} \times \text{Standard deviation})$ with a given level of standard deviation and volatility. The daily change is therefore Forward price $\times 0.0051/16 = 0.32$, where 16 is the square root of 250. Extending this analysis, we can also calculate approximately the delta for the Black–Scholes option strike at 94.9, which is $(1 - 0.5 \times (1 - 0.68)) = 84\%$. This is because the delta for expiration in the money is the probability of the price in one year being above 94.9. This demonstrates the usefulness of delta as a measurement of the probability of an option expiring in the money. When we look at the confidence level at the expiration, deltas of in-the-money options drop in response to an increase in volatility or time because the expected future price range is increased. As such, a trader is not as confident (lower probability) that these options will ultimately expire in the money. Extended price ranges reduce the confidence of at-expiration results. The higher volatility and greater time imply that deltas of out-of-the-money options should rise. Since Black–Scholes theory compounds volatility on a continuous basis, increasing volatility has a greater effect on option valuations than increasing time. Doubling volatility doubles the expected future price range.

Using this technique and going one step further, we can invert the delta based on the target price range. For example, given the target price range

$$\log\left(\frac{\text{Target price} / \text{Forward price}}{\text{Volume} \times \sqrt{T}} \right)$$

one can obtain the number of standard deviations. By using a normal distribution table, we can find the probability of the market rallying to a high target price or better, or falling to a low target price or worse. As the method suggested, this probability is the proprietary delta.

In a fixed-income market, this breakeven market level will also be quoted on the basis of yield and in the calculation one needs to use yield volatility converted from price volatility.

In summary, the determination of the breakeven level relies on the assumption of market volatility. When volatility indicates an excessive market movement – especially before or after the economic release days – this technique can help to determine whether long or short options will fit one's investment objectives better.

RELATIVE VALUE OF VOLATILITIES

Volatility ratio and breakeven price calculation can reveal opportunities for asset/ liability managers to exploit attractive yields and profitable asset/liability matches. Many volatility-trading techniques are also based on the analysis of skews, smiles and the term structure of volatility. Relative volatility trading involves trading anomalies among the volatilities of options (or embedded options). The trades could be between different stock indexes in a single currency, between different equities or interest rates and so on. The method in this analysis is to establish the confidence bounds on the relative volatility levels and volatility spreads, and thereby to identify the current volatility spread level relative to the normal trading range. Trades can be made on the basis of the vega-neutral expectation that the abnormal volatility spread will disappear – if it is a cross-currency volatility spread. The trade needs to be based on a single currency. The drawback of this analysis is the possible misinterpretation of the cash value of the volatility. It is not unusual to pay a little to obtain the "sensitive" move in the market volatility.

A popular alternative technique in the fixed-income market is the asset swap method that operates by understanding the relative value of volatilities based on the cashflow equivalence quoted as a spread over the Libor rate. This application – which reveals the relative value of volatilities for assets with embedded options, traded options and default protection based on the asset swap technique – is gaining more attention in marketplaces. The asset swap allows one to express the asset value in terms of a synthetic floating rate instrument and therefore can be used to identify closely the basis risk and the relative values for the underlying asset, an asset with an embedded option and options linked to the underlying assets. For example, the volatility imbalances among swaptions, OTC treasury options, and callable and puttable debt papers have existed historically; with the help of an asset swap, investors can isolate the interest rate premiums and credit premiums for debts with embedded options. If investors are only interested in the protecting credit, the protection bought for an interest rate can be sold back to the market if one finds that the premium paid is low in relation to the market level. Historically, many puttable bonds are traded at the lower volatility level of 9% or below, while the equivalent swaption's volatility is above 14%. With this scenario, investors can sell the protection of basis risk by shorting the swaption using similar methods in order to improve the carry. Of course, an increased supply of swaptions in this manner will compress the swaption volatilities to a thinner volatility spread between puttable options and swaptions.

The same technique can be used for callable issues as well as for cross-currency and cross-credit products. By calculating the value with this technique, we are able to identify the relative value. As credit derivatives are expected to supply liquidity to credit trading, we expect that the relative value of the volatility will give a better understanding of the relations between assets with credit risk.

SOME ESTIMATIONS OF THE VALUE OF VOLATILITY

of any specific person who may receive this report. Investors should seek financial advice regarding the appropriateness of investing in any securities or investment strategies discussed or recommended in this report and should understand that statements regarding future prospects may not be realized. Investors should note that income from such securities, if any, may fluctuate and that each security's price or value may rise or fall. Accordingly, investors may receive back less than originally invested. Past performance is not necessarily a guide to future performance.

Foreign currency rates of exchange may adversely affect the value, price or income of any security or related investment mentioned in this report. In addition, investors in securities such as ADRs, whose values are influenced by the currency of the underlying security, effectively assume currency risk.

8

Risk-Sensitive Dynamic Asset Allocation

Tomasz R. Bielecki and Stanley R. Pliska

Northeastern Illinois University; University of Illinois at Chicago

This chapter develops and explains a new approach for making decisions on optimal asset allocation in a multiperiod setting. Macroeconomic and financial factors are explicitly modelled as stochastic processes that directly affect the mean returns of the assets. We employ methods of risk-sensitive control theory, thereby using an infinite horizon objective that is natural and features the long-run expected growth rate and the average volatility as two measures of performance – analogous to the mean return and variance, respectively, in the single-period Markowitz model. The optimal strategy is a simple function of the factor levels, and, even with constraints on the proportions of the portfolio, it can be computed by solving a quadratic program. Explicit formulas can be obtained, as is illustrated by an example where the only factor is a Vasicek-type interest rate and where there are two assets: cash and a stock index. The methods are further illustrated by a backtest study of US data with two assets and up to three factors.

Dynamic trading versus rolling Markowitz

Speaking in the I. E. Block community lecture at the 1998 SIAM annual meeting in Toronto, Robert C. Merton, a Nobel laureate in economics who is famous for his seminal contributions to financial theory, said that, "the portfolio selection process needs to be purged of its reliance on 'static' optimisation techniques, which are incapable, by their very nature, of evaluating intertemporal tradeoffs". The main point being made here is that, due to the well-known dependence of asset returns on macroeconomic factors such as interest and inflation rates, factors which themselves are stochastic in nature, a rolling Markowitz kind of strategy will leave money on the table. In other words, the naive approach where in each period the investor first makes updated forecasts and then makes asset allocations to optimise some single-period measure of performance will not be optimal in the long run.

A simple example will illustrate how a rolling Markowitz approach will produce trading strategies that are inferior to more dynamic strategies. This example also makes clear the limitations of the rolling Markowitz approach when there are factors (such as interest rates) whose movements are correlated with the returns of assets (such as stocks and long-term bonds).

Suppose that time is discrete and measured in years. There is a single macroeconomic factor that takes one of only two values: "Above average," denoted state A, or "Below average," denoted state B. There are also a single risky asset, whose returns are affected by the factor in a manner to be described, and a bank account, which has an interest rate (for simplicity) of zero. Finally, there are three investors, labelled RM, ARM and D. All three are portfolio managers who want a strategy that solves the same problem – namely, to maximise the long-run rate of return (ie, the portfolio's annual rate of return, averaged over many years) subject to the requirement that the long-run volatility

Table 1. Statistical data for rolling Markowitz example

Transition	P(transition)	Up return (%)	Down return (%)	P(up)	Mean (%)	Sigma (%)
A to A	0.48	10	−3	0.6	4.80	6.37
A to B	0.12	5	−8	0.5	−1.50	6.50
B to B	0.28	8	−10	0.4	−2.80	8.82
B to A	0.12	20	−10	0.6	8	14.70

does not exceed 5%. They all want to do this by following a strategy that divides their money between the risky asset and the bank account, rebalancing each year as required. For simplicity, there are no transaction costs.

Now, suppose that investor RM (which stands for "rolling Markowitz") is not aware that the macroeconomic factor affects the risky asset's returns but looks only at historical returns, thereby seeing a mean return of 2.3% and a volatility of 9.388%. Investor RM wants to choose the optimal value of the parameter π, the constant proportion of wealth to have in the risky asset in each and every period (the portfolio will be rebalanced in each period, if necessary, to restore this proportion). This optimal value is computed by solving a simple Markowitz problem. Since the interest rate is zero, the solution is simply $\pi = 5/9.388 = 0.5326$. Hence, at the beginning of each year investor RM will rebalance so as to proceed with 53.26% of the portfolio's value invested in the risky asset and with the balance in the bank account. The mean return under this strategy is 1.22%.

Meanwhile, investor ARM ("adaptive rolling Markowitz") notices that the conditional mean return and the conditional variance of the return depend on the state of the macroeconomic factor at the beginning of the year. Furthermore, this investor realises that one can do better than RM by letting the proportion in the risky asset vary with this state – say with π_A and π_B. So he (or she) collects some historical data and computes the conditional mean and conditional volatility for state A, obtaining 3.54% and 6.87%, respectively; in other words, for years that begin in state A, the asset's return will average 3.54% and the volatility will be 6.87%. The analogous numbers for state B are 0.44% and 11.99%. Investor ARM then solves a Markowitz problem for each state, obtaining $\pi_A = 5/6.87 = 0.7274$ and $\pi_B = 5/11.99 = 0.4171$. Thus, if a year begins with the factor in state A, investor ARM will rebalance so that 72.74% of the portfolio's value is in the risky asset; otherwise, ARM will proceed with 41.71% in the risky asset. Since in the long run 60% of the years will begin with the factor in state A, over many years ARM's portfolio will have an average return of 1.62%. This is, of course, better than investor RM achieves.

Finally, consider investor D ("dynamic"), who realises that correlations between the asset and the factor process mean that the optimal choice of π_A and π_B should be made simultaneously and not as the two separate calculations made by investor ARM. In particular, D observes that the factor process moves like a Markov chain, which means that next year's state depends on this year's state but otherwise is independent of states in preceding years. Moreover, D observes from historical data that if the current state is A, then, 80% of the time, the next state will also be A. Similarly, if the current state is B, the next state will be B 70% of the time. These probabilities are consistent with being in state A 60% of the time in the long run. Thus, four kinds of transitions are possible; and D observes, furthermore, that given the type of transition during a period, the asset's return during the same period will take one of only two values, as shown in Table 1. The long-run probabilities for the four types of transitions, as well as the conditional asset return means and standard deviations given the type of transition, are also shown in the table. For example, 48% of the transitions are from state A to itself, in which case either (with conditional probability 60%) the asset's return will be 10% or (with conditional probability 40%) the asset's return will be −3%, thereby giving a conditional mean of 4.8% and a conditional standard deviation of 6.37%. All these data are consistent with the already specified statistical estimates made by investors RM and ARM.

Now, investor D realises that the portfolio's mean return can be expressed as $2.12\pi_A + 0.18\pi_B$ and the corresponding variance can be expressed as $36.37\pi_A^2 - 0.76\pi_A\pi_B +$

Table 2. Key literature on the application of stochastic optimisation to portfolio management		
	No factors	**With factors**
Discrete time	Pliska (1997)	Lucas (1978)
Continuous time	Karatzas and Shreve (1998) Korn (1998)	Merton (1973) Brennan, Schwartz and Lagnado (1997)

$57.53\pi_B^2$. So investor D wants to choose π_A and π_B so as to maximise the first expression subject to the second expression being less than or equal to $25 = 5^2$. The solution is $\pi_A = 0.8910$ and $\pi_B = 0.0471$. Investor D implements this strategy just like investor ARM, only using these different proportions, thereby giving a mean return of 1.90%. Thus, investor D achieves a mean return that is much higher than both RM and ARM, although D's volatility is no greater than theirs. It is interesting to note that ARM's volatility is actually 5.14%, not 5.0%; this is because the variance of a convex combination of random variables is not necessarily equal to the same weighted combination of the variances.

This example illustrates the importance of making investment decisions that are based on a multiperiod rather than a single-period analysis, even if the single-period results are implemented on a rolling basis and with the parameter estimates also updated on a rolling basis. It has been known for years that various mathematical approaches, such as dynamic programming, can be used to solve, in principle, problems like this. Table 2 lists some key references in the literature, broken down by whether the underlying model has explicit factors and whether it is a discrete- or continuous-time model. The usual objective for these models is to maximise the expected utility of wealth or consumption. Unfortunately, however, realistic problems are usually computationally intractable. Although explicit results are known for a few, special cases, practical problems are difficult or impossible to solve, even with today's fast computers. This dilemma is why Merton also said in his SIAM address: "A fully satisfactory method of portfolio selection must come to grips with the large nonlinear systems of multivariate partial differential equations of dynamic optimality."

In summary, investors should seek a simple, tractable approach for asset allocation that features both multiperiod optimisation and explicit incorporation of underlying economic factors that are important for modelling asset returns. Existing portfolio optimisation approaches rarely meet these requirements, but a new approach developed by Bielecki and Pliska (1998a) and studied by Bielecki, Pliska and Sherris (1998) may fit the bill. This approach involves a new kind of objective for asset allocation problems: maximising the risk-adjusted growth rate. This objective will now be described.

Risk sensitivity saves the day

Consider a portfolio that grows as geometric Brownian motion with drift parameter μ and volatility parameter σ (this is the classical Black–Scholes model for the price of a stock). Then, for scalar parameter $\theta > 0$, which can be directly related to a risk-aversion parameter, consider the measure of performance $(\mu - \sigma^2/2) - (\theta/4)\sigma^2$. This should be interpreted as the portfolio's risk-adjusted growth rate because the portfolio's long-run growth rate, $\mu - \sigma^2/2$ (ie, the geometric mean return), is penalised by a term that is proportional to the square of the portfolio's volatility. The bigger the value of θ, the more risk-averse the investor. Moreover, using this as a measure of performance for a fixed value of θ, the optimal trading strategy will be the one which has the maximum growth rate for a particular level of volatility. Hence, as you vary θ you trace out the "asymptotic frontier". As displayed in Figure 1, this is perfectly

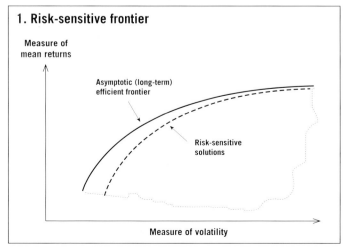

1. Risk-sensitive frontier

Measure of mean returns

Asymptotic (long-term) efficient frontier

Risk-sensitive solutions

Measure of volatility

analogous to the Markowitz efficient frontier except that now we are trading off infinite-horizon (ie, asymptotic) rather than single-period measures of average return and risk.

Generalising these ideas to the case where the portfolio's value process is a general stochastic process, not necessarily geometric Brownian motion, replace $\mu - \sigma^2/2$ by the portfolio's long-run growth rate, replace σ by the portfolio's average volatility, and one has the general risk-adjusted growth rate studied by Bielecki and Pliska (1998a). For a rigorous mathematical statement of their criterion, the *risk-sensitive* measure of performance is

$$J_\theta := \liminf_{t \to \infty} \left(\frac{-2}{\theta} \right) t^{-1} \ln E \, e^{-\left(\frac{\theta}{2} \right) \ln V(t)}$$

where $V(t)$ denotes the value at time t of the portfolio. However, although this expression may appear intimidating, a Taylor-series expansion of J_θ about $\theta = 0$ yields

$$J_\theta = \liminf_{t \to \infty} t^{-1} E \ln V(t) - \frac{\theta}{4} \limsup_{t \to \infty} t^{-1} \operatorname{var} \left(\ln V(t) \right) + O(\theta^2) \tag{1}$$

where $O(\theta^2)$ is an error term that converges to zero as the risk-aversion parameter θ converges to zero. Hence, J_θ has the same interpretation for a general portfolio process as for a lognormal portfolio: it is the long-run expected growth rate minus a penalty term that is proportional to the square of the volatility, plus an error that is proportional to θ^2. The penalty term is also proportional to θ, so θ should be interpreted as a risk-sensitivity or risk-aversion parameter. For θ close to zero the error term is negligible, and the general situation is again illustrated by Figure 1. For a fixed value of θ, choosing the trading strategy that maximises J_θ gives an approximate solution to the problem of maximising the portfolio's long-run growth rate subject to the requirement that the average volatility does not exceed a specified quantity.

While something is given up by allowing the error term $O(\theta^2)$ in the objective function, this is more than compensated for by the advantages of computational tractability. As shown by Bielecki and Pliska (1998a), this criterion allows one to apply risk-sensitive control theory to asset allocation models that have explicit underlying stochastic factors. Their paper presented the basic mathematical theory, while a second, by Bielecki, Pliska and Sherris (1998), considered how the model can be applied to asset allocation problems where the assets are either stock indexes or cash and where the factors are macro-economic variables such as interest rates. These methods are specialised even further in this chapter, the next section focusing on a simple asset allocation example where there is a single risky asset (a stock index) and a bank account that pays and lends according to a Vasicek interest rate.

Optimal asset allocation with Vasicek interest rates

Let us consider a model of an economy where the mean returns of the stock market are affected by the level of interest rates. Towards this end consider a single risky asset, say a stock index, that is governed by the stochastic differential equation

$$\frac{dS_1(t)}{S_1(t)} = \left(\mu_1 + \mu_2 r(t) \right) dt + \sigma \, dW_1(t) \quad S_1(0) = s > 0$$

where the spot interest rate, $r(\cdot)$, is governed by the classical "Vasicek" process

$$dr(t) = \left(b_1 + b_2 r(t) \right) dt + \lambda \, dW_2(t) \quad r(0) = r > 0$$

Here μ_1, μ_2, b_1, b_2, σ and λ are fixed, scalar parameters, to be estimated, while W_1 and W_2 are two independent Brownian motions. We assume $b_1 > 0$ and $b_2 < 0$ in all that follows.

The investor can take a long or short position in the stock index as well as borrow or lend money, with continuous compounding, at the prevailing interest rate. It is therefore convenient to follow the common approach and introduce the "bank account" process S_2, where

$$\frac{dS_2(t)}{S_2(t)} = r(t)\,dt$$

Thus, $S_2(t)$ represents the time-t value of a savings account when $S_2(0) = \$1$ is deposited at time 0.

Now let $h(t)$ denote an R^2-valued investment process (or strategy) whose components are $h_i(t)$, $i = 1, 2$. This process is defined as admissible if the following conditions are satisfied: $h_1(t) + h_2(t) = 1$; $\underline{h}_1 \le h_1(t) \le \overline{h}_1$; and $h(t)$ satisfies certain technical conditions, as explained by Bielecki and Pliska (1998a).

For an admissible investment process $h(t)$ we consider the solution, $V(t)$, of the stochastic differential equation

$$dV(t) = V(t)\big[h_1(t)(\mu_1 + \mu_2 r(t))\,dt + h_2(t)\,r(t)\,dt + h_1(t)\,dW_1(t)\big], \quad V(0) = v > 0 \tag{2}$$

The process $V(t)$ represents the investor's capital (or wealth) at time t and $h_1(t)$ represents the proportion of the time-t capital, $V(t)$, that is invested in the risky security at time t, so that $h_1(t)V(t)/S_1(t)$ represents the number of shares invested in this security at time t. The remaining proportion, $h_2(t) = 1 - h_1(t)$, of the time-t capital is invested in the bank account. The numbers $\underline{h}_1$ and $\overline{h}_1$ are arbitrary upper and lower bounds, which, for example, can be used to rule out short-selling.

Having in mind investment managers who are interested in long-term optimal capital management, we propose to investigate the following family of risk-sensitised optimal investment problems: *For a fixed θ, determine an investment strategy that maximises J_θ.*

In view of theorems 2.1 and 2.2 of Bielecki and Pliska (1998a), the optimal trading strategy is easy to work out. To this end one needs to consider the parametric quadratic programming problem

Minimise:
$$\left(\frac{1}{2}\right)\left(\frac{\theta}{2}+1\right)\sigma^2 h^2 - h\big(\mu_1 + \mu_2 r\big) - (1-h)r$$

Subject to:
$$\underline{h}_1 \le h \le \overline{h}_1$$

Let $H_\theta(r)$ denote the minimiser in the above problem. Then, the optimal investment proportions at time t are given as

$$h_1^\theta(t) = H_\theta(r(t))$$

and

$$h_2^\theta(t) = 1 - h_1^\theta(t)$$

That is, in this simple economy an investor maximising the risk-sensitised growth rate of his or her capital will do optimally by reacting to the changes in the spot interest rate and adjusting the proportions of the capital invested in the stock index and the bank account according to the above formulas.

In particular, if the upper and lower restrictions on the proportion $h_1(t)$ are removed, that is, if we set $\underline{h}_1 = -\infty$ and $\overline{h}_1 = \infty$, the minimiser $H_\theta(r)$ takes the (familiar) form

$$H_\theta(r) = \frac{\mu_1 + \mu_2 r - r}{\left(\dfrac{\theta}{2}+1\right)\sigma^2} \tag{3}$$

It is interesting to note the obvious similarity between this optimal strategy and the well-known results (Karatzas and Shreve, 1998; and Korn, 1998) for the case of conventional complete models of securities markets and power utility functions. In particular, when $\mu_2 = 0$, so that the mean returns of the stock market are independent of the interest rates, the expressions for the trading strategies are identical. Another special case of interest is when $\mu_2 = 1$, so that the "market risk premium", $(\mu_1 + \mu_2 r - r)/\sigma$, is constant. Here, however, the results are somewhat boring in that H_θ is constant with respect to r and $K_\theta(r)$ is linear in r.

For a complete discussion of the "Vasicek economy" presented in this section, we refer interested readers to Bielecki, Pliska and Sherris (1998). Models involving transaction costs have been studied by Bielecki and Pliska (1998b).

Generalisation and implementation

The Vasicek example presented in the previous section involved only two traded securities and a one-factor process. Bielecki and Pliska (1998a) consider a general problem of risk-sensitive dynamic asset allocation for a model of an economy involving several securities and several factors. Denoting by $S_i(t)$ the price of the ith security and by $X_j(t)$ the level of the jth factor at time t, they consider the following market model for the dynamics of the security prices and factors:

$$\frac{dS_i(t)}{S_i(t)} = \left(a + AX(t)\right)_i dt + \sum_{k=1}^{m+n} \sigma_{ik} dW_k(t) \quad S_i(0) = s_i > 0, \ i = 1, 2, \ldots, m \tag{4}$$

$$dX(t) = \left(b + BX(t)\right)dt + \Lambda dW(t) \quad X(0) = x \tag{5}$$

where $W(t)$ is a R^{m+n}-valued standard Brownian motion process with components $W_k(t)$, $X(t)$ is the R^n-valued factor process with components $X_j(t)$, the market parameters a, A, $\Sigma := [\sigma_{ij}]$, b, B, $\Lambda := [\lambda_{ij}]$ are matrices of appropriate dimensions, and $(a + Ax)_i$ denotes the ith component of the vector $a + Ax$.

As in the preceding section here, they denote by $h(t)$ an R^m-valued investment process or strategy whose components are $h_i(t)$, $i = 1, 2, \ldots, m$, and $h_i(t)$ represents the proportion of capital that is invested in security i. They allow for general constraints to be imposed on the investment strategies, and they define an investment process, $h(t)$, as admissible if the following conditions are satisfied: $h(t)$ takes values in a given subset, χ, of R^m, and $\sum_{i=1}^m h_i(t) = 1$; and $h(t)$ satisfies certain technical conditions, as explained in Bielecki and Pliska (1998a).

Bielecki and Pliska (1998a) demonstrate that under the condition of the lack of correlation between the residuals of the security price equations and the residuals of the factor equations (that is, under the condition that $\Sigma \Lambda^T = 0$), and under some other conditions imposed on the model parameters, an optimal investment strategy is given as a feedback on the levels of factors; that is:

$$h_\theta(t) := H_\theta(X(t)) \tag{6}$$

where $H_\theta(x)$ is a minimiser in the parametric quadratic programming problem

Minimise:
$$\left[\frac{1}{2}\left(\frac{\theta}{2} + 1\right)h^T \Sigma \Sigma^T h - h^T (a + Ax)\right]$$

Subject to:
$$h \in \chi, \quad \sum_{i=1}^m h_i = 1 \tag{7}$$

The general case when $\Sigma \Lambda^T \neq 0$ is currently under investigation, but it also leads to a parametric quadratic programming problem similar to the one presented above. For example, for a more general version of our "Vasicek economy":

$$\frac{dS_1(t)}{S_1(t)} = \left(\mu_1 + \mu_2 r(t)\right)dt + \sigma_1 dW_1(t) + \sigma_2 dW_2(t) \quad S_1(0) = s > 0$$

$$dr(t) = \left(b_1 + b_2 r(t)\right)dt + \lambda_1 dW_1(t) + \lambda_2 dW_2(t) \qquad r(0) = r > 0$$

the solution of the general parametric quadratic programming would lead to the process $h^\theta(t) = \left[h_1^\theta(t),\ 1 - h_1^\theta(t)\right]^T$, where $h_1^\theta(t) = H_\theta(r(t))$ and

$$H_\theta(r) = \frac{\mu_1 + \mu_2 r - r}{\left(\frac{\theta}{2} + 1\right)\sigma^2} + \left(\frac{1}{2}\right)\frac{\frac{\partial\phi}{\partial r}(r)\left(\lambda_1\sigma_1 + \lambda_2\sigma_2\right)}{\left(\frac{\theta}{2} + 1\right)\sigma^2}$$

gives the form of the optimal trading strategy. The function $\phi(r)$ that appears in the above formula for $H_\theta(r)$ is derived from a solution to a partial differential equation. Note that the second term in $H_\theta(r)$, sometimes called the hedging term, takes into account the presence of correlations between the residuals of the security price equation and the residuals of the factor equation (the spot rate equation).

To implement the above formulas so that actual investment decisions are generated in real time, one needs to make a discrete-time approximation and obtain estimates of the (typically unknown) market parameters a, A and Σ in the model (4)–(5). This leads to adaptive implementation of our optimal risk-sensitive strategy (6). This means that the estimates of market parameters are updated, perhaps with linear regressions, as time goes by and new market information is acquired, and subsequently the updated estimates are used instead of the "true" values of those market parameters in the formulas for optimal risk-sensitive investment rules generated according to (6)–(7).

In the next section we present empirical results that were obtained using such an adaptive implementation scheme.

Backtesting experiments with US data

In this section we backtest a model using data from the asset allocation study by Brennan, Schwartz and Lagnado (1997). They had monthly data from January 1974 to December 1994 for the Treasury bill short rate, a long-term Treasury bond rate, the monthly returns for an index of US equities and the dividend yields for the same equity index. We augmented these data with similar figures from January 1995 through November 1997. Thus, our data enable us to develop a model for the case of two assets – the stock index and a bank account which pays interest at the Treasury bill rate – and up to three factors: the short rate, the long rate and the dividend yield.

Our main objective is to illustrate how to implement our risk-sensitive asset allocation approach. A secondary objective for our empirical work is to see if risk-sensitive trading strategies do better than more conventional ones – in spite of the fact that, from a statistical standpoint, our choice of three factors is very poor for the purpose of predicting stock returns. When we regressed each month's returns against the three factor values at the beginning of each month, the R^2 and adjusted R^2 turned out to be only 0.038 and 0.026, respectively. Moreover, although the coefficients for the short rate and the dividend yield were statistically significant at the 95% level, the intercept and the coefficient for the long rate were not significant. So, if the risk-sensitive results presented here demonstrate any advantages over conventional strategies, it is reasonable to assume that a more astute choice of factors would lead to even better results.

We compare four kinds of trading strategies, each of which starts with $1,000 in January 1983. The data prior to 1983 were used for some of the strategies to make initial estimates of parameters. First are the constant-proportion strategies, where each month the division of wealth between the stock index and cash is rebalanced to a specified

Table 3. Constant-proportion strategies for US data

Stock proportion	Mean return (%)	Volatility (%)	Sharpe ratio	Final wealth ($)	Annual turn-over (%)
0.0	6.77	0.57	0.00	2,657	0.0
0.1	7.85	1.49	0.72	3,081	3.3
0.2	8.93	2.83	0.76	3,563	5.9
0.3	10.03	4.22	0.77	4,106	7.7
0.4	11.13	5.61	0.78	4,719	8.8
0.5	12.25	7.01	0.78	5,406	9.2
0.6	13.38	8.41	0.79	6,174	8.8
0.7	14.51	9.81	0.79	7,030	7.7
0.8	15.66	11.21	0.79	7,979	5.9
0.9	16.82	12.61	0.80	9,027	3.3
1.0	17.98	14.01	0.80	10,181	0.0
1.1	19.16	15.42	0.80	11,446	4.0
1.2	20.35	16.82	0.81	12,826	8.8
1.3	21.55	18.22	0.81	14,324	14.3
1.4	22.76	19.63	0.81	15,944	20.6
1.5	23.98	21.03	0.82	17,686	27.6
1.6	25.22	22.43	0.82	19,551	35.4
1.7	26.46	23.83	0.83	21,535	43.9
1.8	27.72	25.24	0.83	23,634	53.2
1.9	28.99	26.64	0.83	25,841	63.3
2.0	30.26	28.04	0.84	28,145	74.2

proportion. Different proportions, ranging between 0 and 2.0, were evaluated. Table 3 shows for each proportion the corresponding portfolio's mean annual return, volatility, Sharpe ratio, final (November 1997) dollar value and average annual turnover. The last measure is the percentage of the portfolio's value that is shifted between assets by the rebalancing process; it is included to give some indication of the possible transaction costs. Figure 2 is a graph of the mean annual return versus the volatility for values of the stock proportion ranging from about 0.13 to about 1.50.

The second kind of trading strategies are no-factor, risk-sensitive strategies. These are the strategies given by our model when one takes the matrix A = 0 in the asset's drift

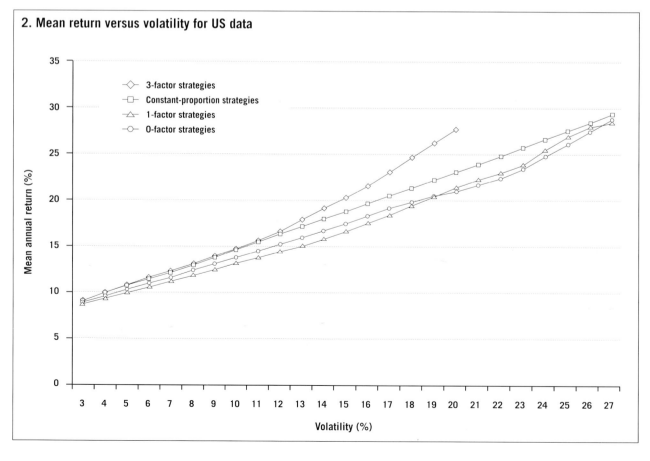

2. Mean return versus volatility for US data

Legend:
- ◇ 3-factor strategies
- □ Constant-proportion strategies
- △ 1-factor strategies
- ○ 0-factor strategies

y-axis: Mean annual return (%)
x-axis: Volatility (%)

coefficient. In particular, for the purposes of this section, this is the same as taking $\mu_2 = 0$ in the Vasicek model of the preceding section. Consequently, the optimal proportion reduces to the well-known formula, attributed to Merton, that results from the portfolio management problem where the investor's objective is to maximise expected isoelastic utility of wealth at a specified (finite) planning horizon (see Karatzas and Shreve, 1998, or Korn, 1998). For this reason, our no-factor risk-sensitive strategies can also be thought of as classical, Merton-type stochastic control strategies.

In our backtesting experiment we are interested in whether the Merton-type strategies fare better than the benchmark constant-proportion strategies. This may happen because the Merton proportion depends on, and thus fluctuates with, the short interest rate. If so, this would be evidence for the merits of the risk-sensitive control approach (and stochastic control theory approaches in general), irrespective of any opportunity to use factors for predicting asset returns. This is because the factor levels are ignored for the purpose of estimating the values of the parameters μ_1 and σ. In particular, only the stock index returns prior to 1983 were used for initial estimates of these two parameters. Moreover, each month, and on a rolling basis, the most recently observed return was added to the data set for the purpose of updating the parameter estimates, and then the new portfolio proportions were computed and implemented. However, to facilitate comparison with the benchmark constant-proportion strategies described earlier, we imposed lower and upper bounds on the stock index proportion of 0 and 2.0, respectively. This means that if the proportion coming from Merton's formula was lower (respectively, higher) than 0 (respectively, 2.0), the proportion actually implemented during the month was 0 (respectively, 2.0).

We backtested the no-factor risk-sensitive strategies for different values of θ, as shown in Table 4. Figure 2 is a graph of the mean return versus the volatility as θ ranges from about 1 to 23.

The third kind of strategy is our risk-sensitive control strategy where the short rate is the only factor, as in the preceding section. To backtest this kind of strategy we estimated σ as for the no-factor strategies, but now, instead of estimating μ_1 from just the sample of historical returns, we estimated both μ_1 and μ_2 by regressing in a rolling, month-to-month fashion the stock index returns of prior months against the Treasury bill short rate at the beginning of the corresponding months. The parameters μ_1 and μ_2 were taken to be the regression intercept and slope, respectively. This risk-sensitive control strategy was backtested for different values of θ, as shown in Table 5. Figure 2 is a graph of portfolio mean return versus volatility as θ ranges from about 2.5 to about 50.

Finally, the fourth kind of strategy we backtested is our risk-sensitive control strategy where there are three factors: both of the interest rates and the stock index dividend yield. We included this kind of strategy in spite of the fact that we are violating one of our assumptions. In particular, although the residuals of the two interest rate factors are

Table 4. No-factor risk-sensitive strategies for US data

Theta	Mean return (%)	Volatility (%)	Sharpe ratio	Final wealth ($)	Annual turnover (%)
0	29.47	27.62	0.82	26,071	89.3
1	28.53	26.81	0.81	24,162	122.5
2	26.45	25.25	0.78	20,082	138.7
3	24.76	23.90	0.75	17,217	138.3
4	22.89	22.57	0.71	14,365	139.3
6	20.29	18.71	0.72	12,027	119.3
8	18.23	15.96	0.72	10,050	104.2
10	16.19	13.33	0.71	8,216	84.6
12	14.80	11.42	0.70	7,113	69.0
15	13.34	9.40	0.70	6,068	54.1
20	11.82	7.26	0.70	5,091	39.6
25	10.87	5.91	0.69	4,541	31.2
30	10.22	4.99	0.69	4,191	25.8
40	9.39	3.81	0.69	3,773	19.1
50	8.88	3.08	0.69	3,533	15.1
75	8.19	2.11	0.68	3,226	10.0

Table 5. One-factor risk-sensitive strategies for US data

Theta	Mean return (%)	Volatility (%)	Sharpe ratio	Final wealth ($)	Annual turn-over (%)
0	28.86	27.43	0.81	24,492	123.1
1	28.30	26.76	0.80	23,563	151.3
2	28.02	25.97	0.82	23,528	177.0
3	27.14	25.12	0.81	21,912	196.9
4	25.85	24.15	0.79	19,469	199.9
6	23.13	22.05	0.74	15,215	205.3
8	20.49	19.05	0.72	12,232	197.2
10	17.80	16.25	0.68	9,432	175.9
12	15.99	14.16	0.65	7,855	154.2
15	14.27	11.70	0.64	6,600	123.6
20	12.53	9.04	0.64	5,470	92.2
25	11.44	7.37	0.63	4,832	73.5
30	10.70	6.22	0.63	4,426	61.2
40	9.75	4.74	0.63	3,941	45.7
50	9.17	3.84	0.63	3,663	36.5
75	8.39	2.61	0.62	3,309	24.4

Table 6. Three-factor risk-sensitive strategies for US data

Theta	Mean return (%)	Volatility (%)	Sharpe ratio	Final wealth ($)	Annual turn-over (%)
0	28.60	20.60	1.06	31,550	484.7
1	27.18	19.64	1.04	27,461	499.7
2	25.55	18.48	1.02	23,375	506.1
3	23.86	17.45	0.98	19,585	490.4
4	22.01	16.34	0.93	16,059	473.2
6	19.55	14.30	0.89	12,403	429.0
8	16.81	12.16	0.83	9,125	379.7
10	15.03	10.28	0.80	7,472	332.5
12	13.88	8.84	0.80	6,564	291.1
15	12.59	7.28	0.80	5,645	240.3
20	11.25	5.63	0.79	4,790	186.2
25	10.41	4.60	0.79	4,311	152.0
30	9.83	3.88	0.79	4,005	128.4
40	9.10	2.97	0.78	3,640	98.0
50	8.64	2.42	0.77	3,430	79.2
75	8.03	1.68	0.75	3,160	53.6

virtually uncorrelated with the residuals of the stock index, the residuals of the dividend yield factor are highly correlated with the stock index residuals, just as one would expect. Nevertheless, we thought that some interesting things might be learnt by proceeding with the backtest as if all the residuals were uncorrelated.

The backtest was conducted in the same way as the backtest of the one-factor, risk-sensitive strategies except that in this case the estimates of μ_1 and μ_2 (the latter now a three-component vector) were updated each month by conducting a regression with all three factors as independent variables. This kind of strategy was backtested for different values of θ, as shown in Table 6. Figure 2 is a graph of each portfolio's mean return versus its volatility as θ ranges from about 0 to about 50.

In conclusion, it should be clear that it is easy to implement risk-sensitive strategies in a practical way. The continuous-time theory is readily transformed to a discrete-time context by proceeding on a rolling basis to use statistical methods for updating parameters, using these updated parameters and new factor values to compute new asset proportions, and rebalancing accordingly. On the other hand, it remains unclear from these preliminary experiments whether risk-sensitive strategies with underlying factors do better than more conventional strategies, especially when transaction costs are considered. As can be seen from Figure 2, which ignores transaction costs, the three-factor strategies consistently did better than the others – and by margins which are noteworthy at higher volatilities. On the other hand, the no-factor and one-factor risk-sensitive strategies fared worse than the benchmark constant-proportion strategies at all levels of volatility. Apparently, the fluctuating proportions caused by fluctuating Treasury bill rates have a deleterious effect that is only mitigated when statistically significant factors are present.

Bibliography

Bielecki, T. R., and S. R. Pliska, 1998a, "Risk Sensitive Dynamic Asset Management", forthcoming in *Journal of Applied Mathematics and Optimization*.

Bielecki, T. R., and S. R. Pliska, 1998b, "Risk-Sensitive Dynamic Asset Management in the Presence of Transaction Costs", *Finance & Stochastics*, accepted subject to revision.

Bielecki, T. R., S. R. Pliska and M. Sherris, 1998, "Risk Sensitive Asset Allocation", *Journal of Economic Dynamics and Control*, accepted subject to revision.

Brennan, M. J., E. S. Schwartz and R. Lagnado, 1997, "Strategic Asset Allocation", *Journal of Economic Dynamics and Control* 21, pp. 1377–403.

Karatzas, I., and S. E. Shreve, 1998, *Methods of Mathematical Finance* (New York: Springer-Verlag).

Korn, R., 1998, "Portfolio Optimisation with Strictly Positive Transaction Costs and Impulse Control", *Finance & Stochastics* 2, pp. 85-114.

Lucas, R. E., 1978, "Asset Prices in an Exchange Economy", *Econometrica* 46, pp. 1429-45.

Merton, R. C., 1973, "An Intertemporal Capital Asset Pricing Model", *Econometrica* 41, pp. 867-87.

Pliska, S. R., 1997, *Introduction to Mathematical Finance. Discrete Time Case* (Oxford: Blackwell).

9

Developing and Implementing a Data Warehouse

John McCann

CIBC World Markets

In the past few years risk management has been characterised by a dramatic escalation in scope and complexity. Between 1980 and 1995 the number of trades booked daily in the larger firms has grown from the 10,000 range to the 1,000,000 range, a 100-fold increase. At the same time the diversity of markets and instruments has risen from around 20 to over 200, and the number of variables per trade from two to 10. The net effect (Figure 1) is a 5,000-fold expansion in volumes and complexity in fifteen years, outpacing even Moore's Law.[1] As the capacities and speeds of technology have increased, so has the desire to model more accurately the various components of risk associated with a given transaction in the financial markets and, indeed, to aggregate them in a variety of ways. This dynamic business requirement – to capture all transactions within a firm and allow virtually unlimited models and aggregations to be applied in a consistent manner and on a timely basis – is among the most demanding in the financial services world and, indeed, defines a situation in which a data warehouse may be the only viable solution.

This chapter first looks at what a data warehouse is, describes its components and indicates when a data warehouse solution is the appropriate choice. It then outlines a number of real-world issues and pitfalls and offers advice on how to approach design and deployment so as to minimise the inherent risks. Finally, it examines current trends and projects future directions for a number of the "degrees of freedom" that any data warehouse will need to recognise and accommodate.

What is a data warehouse?

To understand the concept and characteristics of a data warehouse, it is first necessary to review briefly the evolution of business automation.

The primary advantage of early automated systems in the 1960s and 1970s lay in their ability to speed up traditional transaction processing dramatically while increasing accuracy. Manual processes were translated directly into coded procedures and significant gains in efficiency were realised – especially for repetitive operations. Many of the products and services now taken for granted, such as daily interest savings accounts, were infeasible prior to automated banking systems. These systems, and their reporting, were operational in nature; the reports supported the accurate and timely processing of transactions and were rarely used by analysts and decision-makers. Information content was usually limited to that directly related to the transactions themselves.

Over time, businesses began to realise the potential secondary value of the data in their operational

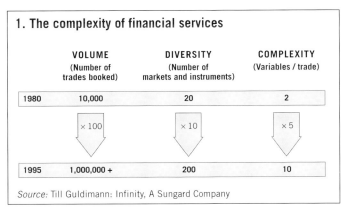

1. The complexity of financial services

	VOLUME (Number of trades booked)	DIVERSITY (Number of markets and instruments)	COMPLEXITY (Variables / trade)
1980	10,000	20	2
	× 100	× 10	× 5
1995	1,000,000 +	200	10

Source: Till Guldimann: Infinity, A Sungard Company

systems, and the demand for reports that correlated, analysed, summarised and compared the individual transactions grew steadily. Unfortunately, these types of reports were difficult to create and tended to degrade operational system performance. In response to this the information centre emerged in the 1970s: data from one or more operational systems were extracted into a separate database to be used exclusively for this type of analysis and reporting. This removed the burden from the operational systems, but it quickly led to a proliferation of information centres and did nothing to resolve the data inconsistencies between the various systems. Further, the data were replaced regularly – often daily – and there was no history retention or data archival. Finally, there were very few effective analysis and reporting tools to use on the information centres. The data warehouse emerged in the 1980s as a solution to these types of issues.

There are now a large number of definitions of a data warehouse. Fundamentally, it is an architecture – comprising the data, hardware/software platform, tools and processes required to provide a broad-spectrum facility for informed decision-making in a firm. We will examine the specific components of a data warehouse architecture in the next section, but first we need a more precise definition with which to work. One definition which has stood the test of time is that originated by Bill Inmon:[2]

> A data warehouse is a subject-oriented, integrated, time-variant, non-volatile collection of data in support of management's decision-making process.

The subject-orientated nature (as opposed to application-orientated) allows the users easily to locate and use the data they want, and because it is integrated they can correlate data from multiple applications. The non-volatile (read-only) and time-variant (maintains historical data) aspects support historical or trend analysis.

To help further grasp the essence of a data warehouse, Table 1 summarises some of the distinctions between a typical application system database and a data warehouse.

Table 1. Data warehouse – comparison with conventional database

Characteristic	Application system database	Data warehouse
Example	FX spot/forward trade capture	Enterprise risk management
Focus	Operational: current values of a limited amount of data in a basic, often legacy support system	Informational: accessing large amounts of data, often from multiple record systems, and involving analysis of those data over time
Performance sensitivity	High: throughput critical	Lower: computer-intensive
Demand on DBMS	Simple queries; schedulable	Complex queries; unpredictable
Data model	Application-specific	Enterprise perspective
Time horizon	Current; transient	Recent; persistent
Data management	Limited	Replication, archival
User-accessible	Possible, but affects performance	Purpose-built
Metadata	Non-existent	Critical aspect; high value
Perspective	Operation of a single business	Multidimensional, global coverage; historical patterns
Typical query	"What was the notional amount on that 6-month JPY forward we did with Barings on 15 January?"	"What is our all-product close-out exposure today to Daiwa?"
Value-add potential	Minimal	Data mining; business intelligence; data redistribution

Elements of a data warehouse

For ease of understanding, a data warehouse solution can be viewed as consisting of four functional groups of elements. Figure 2 illustrates the relationships between these major groups.

The input group extracts and loads the data from the source systems and performs basic editing and simple transformation on those data. The manage group contains the technical platform itself and performs the more complex editing, mapping, transformation and aggregation of the data and a variety of data management functions. The output group interprets, directs and manages the queries and their related responses, both scheduled and ad hoc, on behalf of the user community. Finally, the infrastructure group consists of tools and processes that underlie the whole data warehouse, ensuring the smooth and secure development and operation of the various components.

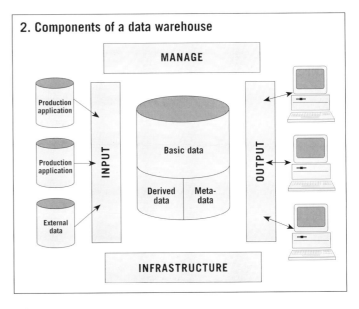

2. Components of a data warehouse

INPUT GROUP

The elements of this group deal with the initial extraction and loading of the data from the various source systems into the data warehouse. Table 2 summarises these elements, indicating the type of tool appropriate for each task, and identifies a typical product.

Data extraction often involves a "push" function from the source system, rather than a "pull" from the data warehouse. This ensures that the source system remains responsible for ensuring that the interface is unaffected by source system changes. As a result, the file creation process is embedded in the source system – often in custom code using the facilities of that system.

Once the file is created, it must be passed to the data warehouse. Unless your organisation has a global standard file transfer utility implemented, such as Network Data Mover, it is probably most efficient to use FTP (file transfer protocol) to move the files across your network.

Prior to (or, to some extent, during) loading, basic editing and transformation of the data can be performed. This is syntactic in nature, with no reference to the main data warehouse files, and is targeted at ensuring consistency in the input. There are a number of such "data mapping" products, which use metadata tables to perform the editing and simple transformation; this helps to ensure that the metadata themselves remain current.

The final step is to load the file into temporary tables in the data warehouse. This is often a time-critical task owing to the number of files to be dealt with and the ever-smaller overnight processing windows. Most database products have a very efficient load utility, which meets the requirement; some also provide limited editing capabilities.

Table 2. Elements of the input group

Element	Tools	Sample product (vendor)
Data-extraction programs	• Source system custom code • Commercial extract product	• System-specific • PowerBuilder (Sybase/Powersoft)
File transfer	• Low-level system tool • Data-movement tool	• FTP (various) • CONNECT:Direct (Sterling)
Data mapping/editing	• Data-mapping tool	• Prism Warehouse Executive (Prism Solutions)
Data load	• DBMSs fast-load utility	• Fast Load (Platinum)

Table 3. Elements of the manage group

Element	Tools	Sample product (vendor)
Client/server platform	• Data/application server(s) • Server operating system • Client PC • Client operating system	• Enterprise 10 000 (Sun Microsystems) • Solaris (Sun Microsystems) • DeskPro 6000 (Compaq) • Windows NT Version 4.0 (Microsoft)
Server data management	• Database management system	• Sybase version 11 (Sybase)
Data model	• Commercial data model • Proprietary model	• Eureka (Midas-Kapiti International) • Locally developed model
Complex editing/ transformation	• Custom solution • Data-scrubbing tool	• Custom C++ routines or stored procedures • Enterprise Integrator (Apertus)
Metadata creation/management	• Metadata tool • Custom solution	• Directory Manager (Prism Solutions) • Excel/Word (Microsoft)
Analytic engines	• Commercial products • Proprietary models	• RiskWatch (Algorithmics) • Custom C++ routines

MANAGE GROUP

The manage group contains the physical components that are most often associated with the term data warehouse: the various hardware and software components, and the data themselves. It often gets the most attention from those interested in the cost aspects of a data warehouse campaign although, in fact, far more is spent on the acquisition, transformation and transport of data.[3] The elements of this group are summarised in Table 3.

At the centre of the data warehouse architecture is the technical platform. For larger warehouses this will usually be based on a large multiprocessor machine, such as a Sun Enterprise 10 000 or a Hewlett Packard HP9000 server, or even a mainframe for very large installations. In most cases the vendor's standard operating system, such as Solaris or HP-UX, is used. Data storage requirements are among the most demanding in existence: some data warehouses are now in the 5–10 terabyte range (1 Tb = 1000 Gb) and are predicted to hit 100 Tb by 2000 in the retail industry as granularity continues to increase. This affects not only the sheer amount of storage space required but also archival and maintenance requirements. Typically, large disk arrays are used as online storage for the most recent data, with older data retained on optical disk for relatively rapid access when historical trend analyses call for it.

In the past couple of years the major database management system (DBMS) vendors, such as Oracle with Oracle8 and Sybase with Sybase version 11, have improved their generic products to the extent that it is no longer necessary to use specialty products, such as the AT&T/Teradata solution, for most situations.

In a similar sense, the dramatic improvements in power and stability on the user desktop have significantly reduced the need for special workstations to utilise the current generation of end-user software. In most cases a large Pentium PC with at least 64 Mb of memory running Windows NT 4.0 will handle the load.

The data model is critical to the success of the data warehouse. It must reflect the unique requirements of the organisation and its user base, while remaining so flexible as to accommodate most, if not all, future changes in requirements. For this reason it is often the case that a custom solution is required, even if this is based on a standard commercial product. (See Panel 2 on the DBMS design process for more details on how the specific business will influence the data model.)

Once the data have been loaded into the temporary tables, the more complex editing and transformation can be undertaken. These are quite specific to the organisation and its data and, again, often result in the requirement for a custom-coded solution. However, there are a number of data-scrubbing products, which parse and analyse the data. These can incorporate quite sophisticated approaches, including fuzzy logic and neural networks.

Table 4. Elements of the output group

Element	Tools	Sample product (vendor)
Managed reports	General-purpose query tool	Focus (Information Builders)
Managed queries	Purpose-built RDBMS query development tool	GQL (Andyne Computing)
Ad hoc queries	User-orientated query tool	Forest & Trees (Platinum)
Multidimensional analysis	Online analytical processing query tool	OLAP++ (SAS Institute)
Metadata queries	Specific metadata tools	Warehouse Directory (Prism)
Data mining/knowledge discovery	Data mining tool	KnowledgeSEEKER (Angoss)
Advanced presentation techniques	Data visualisation tools	Discovery (Visible Decisions)

When the final editing has been completed and the data are clean, required aggregations and other derived data can be generated and added to the data warehouse. These can be particularly effective at enhancing performance for complex queries that are made regularly. Any external analytic engines, whether packages or custom-coded, should also be run at this time. In enterprise risk management systems half or more of the spending on these analytical tools is on in-house, proprietary development.

Metadata are the "data about the data". They describe how information is structured in the warehouse, its source, any transformations or edits it has undergone, its meaning and its relationship to other data elements. Perhaps most importantly, they include a history of any changes to these aspects over time, which supports time-based analyses. A variety of tools exist to create and manage metadata, some related to the data-mapping products described in the previous section – Prism's Warehouse Directory and Warehouse Executive are an example of such symbiosis. Some organisations have chosen to use standard productivity-suite tools, such as Microsoft Word or Excel, to capture and manage metadata, although this is often for purpose-built data warehouses where the user community has limited interest in the metadata themselves.

OUTPUT GROUP
In the final analysis, the attraction of a data warehouse lies in its ability to provide valuable information to the end-user community. As with most information systems, this will require a number of routinely executed reports and queries, but one of the unique aspects of a data warehouse is its ability to respond to ad hoc queries and analyses. Each of these requirements differs in the demands it places on the system, and it is not surprising that a suite of products will be required to meet the full set efficiently. Table 4 summarises the various types of queries and sample products.

Managed reports and queries are those which run on a regular scheduled basis and which can be "tuned" to operate efficiently. A number of products exist to meet these needs and are able to operate against most of the major DBMS products. Their complexity sometimes makes them more appropriate for use by system developers.

Perhaps the greatest return on the investment in a data warehouse is its ability to support ad hoc queries. A successful product must be easy to use by non-technical staff, must interact smoothly with the metadata as well as the actual data themselves and should provide a variety of output forms and media. In a general-purpose data warehouse the metadata are a significant reference source; most of the data-mapping and metadata products have viewing and query facilities.

Multidimensional analysis tools allow the users to explore the data interactively online, analysing them in a number of dimensions at the same time. Whereas previously such analyses placed huge burdens on the database, tools such as OLAP++ from SAS can now operate effectively against the current releases of DBMS products.

DATA MINING TECHNIQUES

Data mining is a process which applies many of the techniques of artificial intelligence to data warehouses. Initial selection can involve sampling techniques and data preparation to reduce the volume, and a high-level review of the data using visualisation tools can help the user to become familiar with the "data landscape", select the best techniques and tools and decide where to start looking. Modelling products in this area typically support one or more approaches that analyse and structure the data. The main modelling techniques currently in use are outlined below, starting with the most machine-based and ending with the most user-driven.

Neural network
A machine whose architecture mimics the human brain. It builds internal representations of attribute patterns. These are adjusted as the data are reviewed, and certain patterns are reinforced. They thus "learn by example" and are effective at exploring complex data. They are not good, however, at explaining the rationale for the model that is developed and will often only accept numeric data.

Decision tree
The software automatically generates decision trees from the data, resulting in a sequence of rules – such as "If deal volume exceeds US$1B, assign client to segment 1". These rules are useful in predicting which records in a new group will yield a given result. This technique is good at identifying non-linear relationships and separating out the important variables.

Rule induction
Essentially the extraction from the data of if/then-style rules, selected on the basis of statistical significance.

Statistics
Utilises traditional statistical techniques, such as time-series forecasting, logistic regression and cluster analysis. These methods place more reliance on the interpretive ability of the user, but they do provide explanations for the observed patterns.

Visualisation
These techniques map and present the data visually on the basis of specific dimensions; only simple analytic techniques, such as clustering, are employed. The interpretation is largely in the user's hands (and eyes).

OLAP and query tools
These tools depend heavily on the user guiding the analytical process and navigating the data. The tools select and present requested data.

Newer tools combine multiple techniques and drive elements of the process by helping users to select the best approach in a given situation. A variety of new data-mining techniques continue to enter the marketplace. Some are existing techniques that are being put to new uses (fuzzy logic, case-based reasoning and genetic algorithms), while others are new (non-linear decision trees). In the near-term a number of promising approaches under development should add value: active software agents acting in place of users; reverse engineering of databases; and evolutionary sampling.

Data mining (Panel 1) is an expanding area of data warehousing technology. It entails examining data at a range of levels, searching for previously unseen patterns and relationships. Techniques such as induction, statistics and neural networks are employed in tools such as Intelligent Miner from IBM and Neural Connection from SPSS.

Presentation of the answer to a query is often overlooked as an area in which a quality tool can make a contribution. In fact, it is one of the techniques that is used in data mining to enhance the ability to recognise patterns and relationships. Modern tools, such as Discovery from Visible Decisions, provide striking, dynamic, three-dimensional views of the data and have proved popular in areas such as risk management and portfolio modelling.

INFRASTRUCTURE GROUP

The sheer scale of the data warehouse means that developing and maintaining the system components, as well as ongoing operation of the system, present a unique set of problems. It is not uncommon for a data warehouse to receive well over 100 files daily, which must be absorbed seamlessly into the system in a confined production window as the data warehouse is often at the end of the data food chain. Large numbers of summarisations, local and outboard analyses and scheduled reports need to be run, and ongoing maintenance, backup, tuning and enhancements must all be handled without affecting performance or availability. Unlike their mainframe predecessors, client/server systems were viewed until relatively recently as somewhat more informal and, accordingly, were run without the benefit of most of the painfully evolved automated support tools and management processes that are used in the mainframe world.

Development activities in data warehouses tend to centre on data capture/transformation and analytic engines, and most such development currently uses object-orientated (OO) techniques. OO can provide significant advantages in speed and accuracy over traditional coding methods. Similarly, due to the size and complexity of the system, automated testing and debugging tools are well advised.

A major data warehouse may be scheduled to undertake 2000 jobs a day – far exceeding the capacity of a human operator and even some of the simpler scheduling tools. An automated scheduler such as Autosys from Platinum Technology provides a broad set of features, allowing relatively sophisticated condition checking prior to releasing jobs, visualisation of the job streams and levels of operator notification in case something abnormal occurs. It can be closely integrated with an automated backup tool, such as Vault98 from CommVault Systems, to ensure the integrity of the data. Given the size and complexity of the data structures, automated backup and recovery using high-volume transfer technology is mandatory.

Monitoring and recording system usage in general, and the types and frequency of queries in particular, are required both to effectively charge back use of the system and to support the ongoing tuning efforts by the database administrator (DBA) and technical staff. As patterns of use change both the actual queries and the structure of the summary-level data can be tuned to maintain peak performance.

The data model is critical to the success of the data warehouse and, even if it is an off-the-shelf product, it will need to be maintained and extended over time. A development tool such as Erwin from Logic Works will help the DBA group in this task. Other tools such as DBArtisan help the technical staff to access and maintain the data structures within the DBMS.

Although the data warehouse should be seen as a global resource, it is likely that management will want to manage access to certain data closely; the combined security facilities of the operating system (such as Unix), the DBMS and the query tools should allow control of access down to the specific data element/end-user combination.

The data warehouse is a very complex structure and is highly vulnerable to unanticipated changes in its environment. The best defence is an effective change management system, whereby all changes are recorded and scheduled and their effect assessed by an automated system, like the Change Management Module of ServiceCentre from Peregrine

Table 5. Elements of the infrastructure group

Element	Tools	Sample product (vendor)
Automated development	Object-orientated development tools	Enterprise Developer (Symantec)
	Automated testing	Playback (Compuware)
	Debugging tools	Purify (Rational)
Operations management	Automated scheduling	AutoSys (Platinum)
	Automated backup/restore	Vault98 (CommVault)
Performance-tuning tools	Query monitor	Detector (Platinum)
	Usage audit/chargeback	Usage Tracker/Cost Tracker (Pine Cone)
Data management	Data model creation/ maintenance	Erwin (Logic Works)
	DBA support tools	DBArtisan (Embarcadero)
Security/integrity	Permissioning/monitoring	Operating system + DBMS + query tools
	Change control process/system	Change Management Module in ServiceCentre (Peregrine)
Documentation management	Automated documentation generator	StoryBoard (Vision)

Systems. It tracks all changes, helps identify dependencies between changes and system components and supports levels of sign-off on change requests, all in the name of ensuring continuity of operation.

Finally, documentation of the system will tend to be extensive and complex. Even such a simple tool as Lotus Notes will assist in ensuring that the documentation is current and consistent; a more comprehensive solution such as StoryBoard from Vision Software Tools offers more features, such as simulated form transitions and slide shows, in addition to comprehensive documentation and screen captures. Table 5 summarises the above and gives a sample product in each category.

Why use a data warehouse for risk management?

Having established what a data warehouse is, the natural question is why would one want to use this large and complex solution for risk management. To answer this question, we will first review the evolution of risk management as a discipline. With that as background, we can summarise the characteristics of a typical global risk management solution, examine the attractions and challenges in using a data warehouse solution, and finally suggest some questions to ask in determining the suitability in your particular case.

BACKGROUND: THE EVOLUTION OF RISK MANAGEMENT

Risk management as a scientific discipline has been evolving steadily since its inception in the late 1970s, when early asset and liability management involved analyses – often done manually – of liquidity and funding gaps. Credit risk dominated then, in response to a rapid growth in international banking and loans to less-developed countries. As the 1980s progressed there was a shift towards market risk as LBOs (leveraged buyouts) and asset securitisation became major activities. During the 1990s the explosive growth in financial market activities further increased the importance of market risk, but it has also brought ongoing refinement in the measurement of other, correlated exposures, including credit risk and operational risk. At present there is a strong trend to aggregatable risk measures, which work across products, markets and customers, allowing consistent global perspectives on all risk dimensions.

As a direct result of these developments the sophistication of the models of both market and credit risk has evolved. As shown in Figure 3, credit risk measurement initially amounted to tracking the notional amount of the instruments involved. Although this was adequate for conventional loans it was very simplistic, and it became increasingly conservative (and unacceptable) as derivative products were introduced. In response to that, a series of percentage multipliers was applied to the notional amount in recognition of the fact that the exposures to a FX forward, a FX option and a FRA were inherently different. This measure was static and failed to recognise the evolution of counterparty risk over time, and, more recently, a dynamic measure has been adopted whereby one component recognised the cost of replacing the deal in the current market (mark-to-market), while the other modelled the set of future risks during the remaining life of the deal (future exposure). Finally, the most progressive institutions are moving to a standardised, aggregatable measure that will be valid across all products and risk types.

In a very similar way, the measurement of market risk has changed over time. Figure 4 shows the evolution of the measurement of the future risk component of credit risk, and it serves equally well to illustrate the evolution of market risk as well as the increasing complexity of the credit risk model. The first improvement on the original notional amount approach was the use of a basis point value (BPV) approach, in which the reaction of the market value of an instrument to a one basis-point shift in the benchmark rates was calculated and used to measure exposure to market movements. It was soon deemed too simplistic, and was replaced by a probability-based measure which incorporated market volatility – the first basic value-at-risk (VAR) model. The primary drawback of this measure was that it ignored correlation between instruments and the entire portfolio effect. This was remedied through a more sophisticated model that took into account the natural offsets between instruments in a given portfolio. More recently, further advances have been made to incorporate stress-testing techniques into the model to take into account the fact that the basic models have certain boundaries of applicability.

The complexity of these risk management models has increased exponentially and is likely to continue to do so for the foreseeable future. Furthermore, the categories or dimensions of risk continue to grow: the main types currently include market and credit (each with several sub-categories[4]), liquidity, operational, regulatory and human factor.

CHARACTERISTICS OF A RISK MANAGEMENT SYSTEM

Global risk management by its nature needs to capture all transactions that entail risk. As has just been noted, there is a wide variety of risk types, so that virtually every transaction involving a cash flow entails one or more categories of risk. With this and the previous section as background, we can now describe the major characteristics of a global risk system.

Volume of input

As shown at the outset, since the advent of desktop computing there has been a many-thousandfold increase in the volumes of data associated with the daily business of large securities firms.

In addition to the basic transaction data from every transaction-processing system in the firm, a wide range of "dimension data"[5] elements are necessary to support the suite of risk calculations and aggregations required. This information is often not included in the transaction itself and needs to be captured separately. For each way in which two transactions could be combined, the corresponding dimension data must be available. As

3. Evolution of the measurement of credit risk

1 Notional amount

2 Static — Notional x constant %

3 Dynamic — Mark-to-market plus future exposures

4 Portfolio level — Aggregatable measures

INCREASING SOPHISTICATION

Source: Dr Robert Mark, CIBC

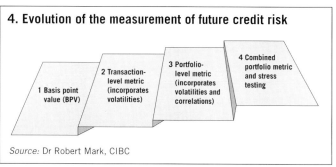

4. Evolution of the measurement of future credit risk

1 Basis point value (BPV)

2 Transaction-level metric (incorporates volatilities)

3 Portfolio-level metric (incorporates volatilities and correlations)

4 Combined portfolio metric and stress testing

Source: Dr Robert Mark, CIBC

DBMS DESIGN PROCESS

The fundamental challenge facing a database designer is to create a database that will support a wide range of unknown queries in the future. The solution is to design a structure to support the business process, not just the known queries. This means that the design should not need restructuring as the query profiles evolve. Most queries will be based on the facts (typically the transactions) within the data warehouse. Unlike the dimensions (or reference data), these facts do not change over time. This makes the fact data suitable for storing at the centre of a "star schema" structure – physical database structures that store factual data in the "middle", with the dimension reference data ranged around them.

Step 1: Identify facts and dimensions

The first step in designing the database is to identify the facts and the dimensions. In practice, this can be challenging. It is best to approach the task from the perspective of the business process. Identify the basic transactions that drive the business. Then, use current query requirements and entity-relationship models to help identify the primary dimensions for each transaction. Next, ensure that a potential fact is not really a dimension with embedded facts – to take a banking example, a customer address table could contain a series of dates relating to when each of his accounts was opened: it is probably better to structure these dates as a separate fact table. Finally, review the potential dimensions to weed out any that are, in reality, facts. Here, the decisions will be based on the intended primary focus of the data warehouse. To illustrate, a marketing DW would view the customer as a fact, whereas a sales analysis warehouse would view the customer as a dimension, to be used as a basis for analysis.

Step 2: Design the fact tables

Having identified the facts and dimensions, the analyst next designs the fact tables. Here

a minimum, a variety of customer, product and organisational data elements are needed; however, the scope for analysis using the data warehouse is directly related to the scope of these reference/correlation data. In a typical data warehouse such secondary data will represent about 30% of the total content.

Multiplicity of source systems

In most large financial services organisations a data warehouse has to operate with a disconcerting number of source systems. For several reasons that were compelling at the time, little consideration was given to alignment with existing systems when choosing a system to support a new business line or product. Indeed, it is quite common to find multiple systems processing the same product in different business lines – or even in different locations of the same business line. The consequences are multiple data models, hardware/software platforms, DBMS choices, telecommunications protocols and geographic locations. At CIBC our risk management data warehouse currently (mid-1998) receives over 400 files nightly from 26 systems on seven legacy platforms in 10 locations, with a daily data volume that can amount to 2–3 Gb.

Range of performance demands

Given the range of users who can be expected to access a risk management data warehouse, it is not surprising that the demands in terms of response time will also vary widely. Once the sheer size of the database is factored in, the difficulty increases dramatically.

The first hurdle is the daily load and update process. As indicated above, it is not the difficulty is in trading off the business value of the query output against the cost of generating it. The resulting decisions include the level of detail retained and for how long it is held. There are several approaches to making these decisions. In some situations, using statistical sampling techniques can reduce the amount of detail retained. A business-view analysis of how long a detailed data element will remain relevant on its own will suggest when aggregations can reduce volumes. The number of (column) items retained in a given transaction can be reduced by removing those which are unlikely to be used in decision support; control fields, intermediate results and many aggregations and reference data fall into this category. Reduce the size of those retained as much as possible because the vast numbers of rows give this technique high leverage. If the query profile suggests a regular need for analyses by the time of a transaction in addition to its date, it is usually best to store time values in the fact table rather than reference them in dimension tables using a foreign key within the fact table. Finally, intelligent partitioning of the fact tables can help significantly.

Step 3: Design the dimension tables
The third step is to design the dimension tables. Generally, these are structured on the basis of knowledge of the query profiles. Entities which are accessed regularly should be duplicated (denormalised) into a star schema dimension table. For example, a table of banking products could contain name, business line, product family and location. The less active elements should be arranged in a series of separate, normalised tables. This approach provides most of the requested information in one table, reducing the number of joins while limiting the amount of excess baggage in the active tables.

Finally, the designer needs to recognise that in the real world it will be necessary to allow some crossover between dimensions. For example, banks may have regional differences in pricing for services. This means that, rather than accessing the product dimension table for a price, we must look at the intersection of product and region. So long as this causes no user confusion and the crossover areas remain relatively small, this is an acceptable situation. They will tend to reduce over time as the dimension structures evolve.

uncommon for more than a gigabyte of data in 150 files to arrive each day. This must be processed during an overnight window that is steadily shrinking: typically, less than four hours are available from the arrival of the last input file until the system has to be ready for user access again. During that time the update cycle must be run – including the creation of aggregations and other derived results – and a substantial number of scheduled reports and queries created.

Once the system is available to the users again in the morning, the demand profile shifts radically. Instead of bulk processing of input and report generation, the system must now respond rapidly to an unpredictable load of ad hoc queries from a broad user base. At one extreme an analyst might ask for a full RAROC[6] evaluation on the firm's ten largest customers, and would be willing to wait 10 minutes for a response. At the same time a trader may make an enquiry on whether adequate credit is available to do a US$50,000,000 FX spot transaction with a foreign bank – and wants a response within a few seconds.

Each of the above situations requires the DBMS to be tuned in a different manner. The challenge for a systems designer is to be able to meet all these demands without incurring unacceptable levels of cost. Panel 2 outlines the steps involved in creating an appropriately structured database. Although somewhat more technical in content, it provides some insight into the process and some of the design tradeoffs required.

Complexity and scope
As was shown in the section on the evolution of risk management, the complexity of risk modelling has risen in recent years and more types of risk are being independently

modelled each year. The number of financial services products that are being tracked can already exceed 200, and new and ever more complex products are created almost daily by the traders. Finally, the ability to define a portfolio in almost any way extends both the amount of dimension data required and the complexity of the analyses.

As a result, a global risk management system sets requirements for volume, scope, complexity and performance that are among the most demanding in the business world.

ADVANTAGES OF A DATA WAREHOUSE
There are a number of compelling reasons for using a data warehouse solution for global risk management. At the highest level, it might be said that the demands of a world-class global risk management system are such that only a data warehouse is sufficiently robust to support them. The design of a data warehouse pays particular attention to the acquisition and management of vast quantities of data on a powerful, flexible delivery platform. Besides this natural alignment of requirements and design characteristics, there are several other reasons for selecting a data warehouse solution. We examine several below.

Optimal technology
A data warehouse embodies the optimal technology for the volumes and pace of such a system; the large and flexible hardware architecture supports the size of the database and the ad hoc nature of query access. The same is true of the current generation of DBMS products. The data structure is focused on providing flexible correlation and aggregation of data elements and is designed to support complex analytic engines and retain their results.

Consistent, current, credible data
As with any measuring or monitoring system, the integrity of the data in a risk management system is paramount if the credibility of the process is to be maintained. This places a heavy emphasis on the acquisition, editing, scrubbing and homogenisation of the data input to the data warehouse. By design, it is updated regularly (at least daily), so that the data – both basic and derived – remain current. The intent is that it has a feed from every customer transaction-processing system in the firm, which is exactly what a risk management system needs.

Support for derived data
A significant portion of the value of a data warehouse lies in its derived or calculated data, and it is optimised to support the algorithms and summarisations required to create these efficiently. In risk management it is critically important to be able to relate transactions to each other reliably on a variety of bases, in support of aggregation, correlation, netting and a wide variety of portfolio structures.

Facilitates central treasury function
The data warehouse's ability to support reliable aggregation right to the top of the organisation provides a credible basis for a centralised treasury function. In effect, the treasurer will be able to hedge the firm's overall position.

Ideal platform for data redistribution
One of the more common complaints about a risk management group is that it is a sort of "black hole" for data: they demand input from all business lines, yet provide only a limited set of monitoring reports. The global reach and consistent data (including history and metadata facilities) of a warehouse all support a broad remarketing of the firm's data.

Unique store of history
One of the significant differences between a data warehouse and a conventional operational database is its intelligent time dimension. By design, the metadata "remember" the significance of each value of each data element over time, even as meanings and value ranges evolve, enabling meaningful historical and trend analyses. The data warehouse is

thus a unique store of market history, trading patterns and results since it can remove the effect of data differences between systems and well as structural changes in the data themselves over time.

Basis for RAROC

The data warehouse, owing to the broad scope of its data, is uniquely positioned to provide, on a consistent basis, all of the cost/benefit/risk aspects of a RAROC calculation. The expense and burden elements come from the (external) financial system(s),[7] while the various risk elements are available from the risk management component.

Opportunities for data mining

A relatively new field, data mining supports the identification of new ways of competing. It uses sophisticated trend- and pattern-recognition techniques to identify previously unseen relationships. These can be exploited in helping design new products or marketing campaigns.

CHALLENGES OF A DATA WAREHOUSE

In the best tradition of "no free lunch", it is important to realise the issues and negative effects that must be accepted and dealt with in undertaking a major data warehouse initiative. First and foremost, it is so large in scope that it will place demands on virtually every system in the firm. Ensuring the willing and timely cooperation of so many other groups can be one of the biggest obstacles to implementation. An examination of specific challenges follows.

Expensive

A true enterprise-level data warehouse has the potential to be one of the most expensive IT projects ever undertaken by a firm.[8] Much effort has been expended in trying to develop cost/benefit justifications for these projects – with limited success. While almost any enlightened business-line executive will readily acknowledge the high value of the data resource that a proper data warehouse represents, it is often difficult to convince that same executive to contribute funding to such a project if it means that a project for one of his revenue-generating systems has to be postponed. As a result, it is often difficult to get solid sponsorship at a business-line level.

Management of expectations difficult

It is very tempting for the beleaguered project manager of a data warehouse to describe the things it could do in future rather than the somewhat modest scope the initial implementation is likely to have. Users can readily understand the image of a global, historically consistent, firm-wide transaction database of absolutely clean data, with a vast selection of correlation data and powerful, user-friendly query tools. They need little encouragement to think of the ever more complex queries and analyses they have always wanted to do. This is fatal. What they have then come to expect may never be available, and certainly will not be in the near-term; thus, even a successful initial implementation can lead to profound disappointment for the end-users.

It is imperative that user expectations be managed: so, underpromise and overdeliver. To the non-technical user the concept of a data warehouse appears deceptively simple, and he or she must be regularly reminded of the difficulties of creating such a powerful information resource.

Service-level management

A cousin of the above issue is that, even if the initial implementation has been configured technically to meet the very demanding performance requirements of a data warehouse, it is by nature and design dynamic. The challenge is to maintain that level of performance over time in a system characterised by terabytes of data, algorithms and models of meteorological complexity and by an unpredictable, but ever more challenging, workload.

Data quality

Data are the single most intractable problem in data warehousing. It is an industry axiom that the data in a particular system will only be (not quite) as good as is required to support basic system operation. Thus, there are already problems even within a single system – usually with data which, because of their use in that system, are free-form or unedited. Unfortunately these data often form part of the dimension data required in a data warehouse. The problem increases exponentially when this type of data is used to correlate transactions between systems (say, by customer or product type). The growth of independent systems, and fragmented ownership, make the problem worse. Finally, although most systems have a history-retention process, this will sometimes contain only a subset of the original data, and almost never a history of the metadata for that system.

Four examples will provide an appreciation of the scale of the data problem:

❏ A large insurance firm, on first examining its various systems, discovered that it had more than 300,000 correspondent companies on file. After a painstaking data clean-up, it turned out that the actual number was less than 30,000, each company having an average of 10 'synonyms' in use.

❏ A Canadian bank undertook some years ago to create a central information file on its retail customers. On analysing its major customer transaction systems, the bank identified 8,000,000 distinct accounts. Extensive use of a sophisticated data-scrubbing service resolved 80% of the account names as either unique or conclusively equivalent to one or more others. The remaining 20% had to be resolved manually, primarily by the individual branches of record. This task took over 150 staff-years to complete.

❏ One US company discovered that its files contained 127 variants on how it identified AT&T.

❏ CIBC World Markets currently has 818 active synonyms for Chase Manhattan in automated systems where Chase is acting as an issuer; the count is higher if counterparty-only products (such as repos) are included.

In a word, data quality is tough to get and easily lost. The credibility of a system hinges on the consistency of the data. It usually requires a monumental effort to clean up an enterprise's data in the early stages of a data warehouse, but most staff can relate to the potential benefit. An equally large problem comes after implementation. In most cases the clean-up effort happens "in transit" – outside the actual source systems; it is very difficult to force legacy source systems to change their data structures and editing criteria in support of a data warehouse. Thus, unless vigilance is maintained, the data will tend to get "dirty" again. This is because the original problems tend to be concentrated in the free-form or unedited fields that were of minor importance to the source system; in the absence of improved systemic edits in those systems, those creating the input will continue to enter "values of convenience".

Data overload

The good news is that the more people use a warehouse, the more they appreciate its value and potential. The bad news is that this almost always increases the data they want to have included in the warehouse, both in terms of retention of history on existing fields and in the addition of new fields. This can lead to growth rates in the hundreds of per cent range and will affect performance adversely.

A variant of the same problem is the need to reduce the raw data to more meaningful information. Otherwise the end-users will be trying to take an "information sip" from a veritable firehose of data.

Risky technologies

One of the reasons that a data warehouse is successful is that it combines the best of a number of powerful, relatively new, and thus risky, technologies. Many large solutions use a client/server architecture, have a large and complex data model, are critically dependent on an effective LAN/WAN (local/wide area network) structure and push VLDBMS (very large database management systems) technology to the limits. The problems arise both from the multiple complex technologies themselves and from the need to support and exploit those technologies (see next item).

Staffing challenges

Notwithstanding what has just been said about the challenges of the technology, in the end a successful data warehouse project will depend 10% on technology and 90% on experience. The firm itself must supply a deep and broad knowledge of the internal environment, both technical and business. This usually requires the most experienced senior staff from the main source systems. Unfortunately, most senior users and senior technical staff look on a data warehouse project as a rather dull and uninteresting one. It may be difficult to convince either group that senior staff should be attached to an extended, non-revenue-generating project.

The technologies involved are relatively new, and the talent pool available – both within the firm and off the street – is limited. In both cases global projects with non-negotiable deadlines – the biggest being Year 2000 and EMU – compete for the same resource pools.

DETERMINING SUITABILITY: KEY INDICATORS

The foregoing discussion suggests that, in many situations in which a global risk management solution is required, a data warehouse may be the answer. The question then becomes: How can one determine whether it is the correct solution in a particular situation?

Listed below are a number of key indicators that a data warehouse could be the appropriate solution in the given situation, and the subsequent section lists situations in which a data warehouse may not be advisable.

Commitment to global risk management

A firm which has a genuine commitment to risk management on an enterprise level will recognise the scope of the undertaking and will be less likely to flinch at the resources required to create an appropriate technical platform. Often in such firms there will be a separate risk management division, providing a ready-made sponsor with global clout.

Evolving risk models

One of the great strengths of a data warehouse is its flexibility in reliably correlating and aggregating data using dimension data. Another is that it is designed to support and exploit powerful analytical routines to generate some of its derived data. The complexity and sophistication of risk models is constantly increasing, and if your firm plans to stay current, these two strengths will help it to respond effectively to this evolution.

Broad line of products and services

In general, the broader the range of business in which a financial services firm engages, the greater will be the range of transaction-processing platforms and data models used.[9] The discipline and consistency that a data warehouse brings to its input data stream is extremely valuable in such situations.

Clear ownership/sponsorship

Ironically, the fact that a properly designed data warehouse will have appeal for most business areas in the firm can also be a source of problems. Many such areas would find conflicts of interest arising if they were the sole owner/sponsor of the project, particularly in issues concerning data standards and design. In practice, data warehouses are often sponsored by a group with a very broad mandate – such as finance, marketing or risk management or an empowered steering committee. Whatever the case, clear, unambiguous ownership of the project is essential for the its success. Avoid the temptation to identify the IT organisation as the owner or sponsor – this invites a technical success/business failure scenario: a beautiful, functional product that the business staff will not adopt and use.

Senior executive support

The scope of a data warehouse project is so broad, and its impact so extensive, that it must be understood and supported by the highest levels of management. The project timeline and budget conspire to make it a tempting target for other, more obviously revenue-generating projects: both funding and staffing can be vulnerable without an executive champion. In addition, the project may require some difficult design decisions, particularly in the data area, and gaining agreement from senior business-line management is dramatically easier when the top of the house is onside.

Broad potential interest in output

In the absence of a compelling classic cost/benefit justification, a broad user base is one of the stronger selling points for such a project. In the case of a risk management data warehouse, direct access to the measurement/monitoring/performance information by the business lines can be a powerful incentive to support the project, most especially if the intention is to institute RAROC performance measurement or to use the facility for capital attribution. The global reach and accessibility of a data warehouse architecture suits this situation well.

Growth in information centre solutions

If the firm is at the stage of evolution where there are a growing number of information centres (see page 142 for a definition), it is an indication of increasing interest in data analysis. Experienced users of such centres will have encountered some of their limitations and could well be attracted by the scope and power of a data warehouse facility. In many cases, the potential to consolidate or eliminate many of these information centres can provide a significant portion of the financial justification for a warehouse project.

Organisational patience

If the firm has no previous experience of a data warehouse, it is often wise to use a disposable prototype approach the first time. This is doubly true if the firm has limited experience with client/server technology. Such a project will of necessity be something of a voyage of discovery. It is very important that management realise the need for a degree of organisational patience and tolerance of an activity that is quite limited in scope, will be thrown away, and represents an effort to come to grips with several new technologies.

DANGER SIGNS

If yours is a small firm with a well-defined market niche and a limited line of products, a data warehouse may be overkill; it is possible that an information centre approach could meet the requirements. This will be particularly true if the plans for risk management are modest. In most cases, however, an ambitious move into global risk management is best supported by a data warehouse solution. Outlined below are a number of danger signs – indicators that there may be trouble ahead for such a project. While no individual indicator need be a reason to abandon the project, each will require a clear and specific response to mitigate its effect.

Lack of clear executive support

This is one of the primary reasons for the failure of any big project. It is especially true in one such as this, where there is no clear business driver – the system will not (directly) generate revenue and could even be viewed as a "big brother" monitoring system. In such cases the budget and staff will be highly vulnerable to poaching by other, more pressing projects.

Unreasonable expectations

The motto "underpromise and overdeliver" captures the essence of the type of expectation management that must be practised with such a project. Pressure for fast delivery will tend to lead to critical design compromises, and unrealistic performance demands will almost certainly never be met in any economically acceptable way. If this describes the situation in your firm, an extensive marketing/education campaign will be needed before the project starts, and specific provision should be made in the budget for this to be pursued on a continuing basis.

Inadequate technical infrastructure

The majority of financial services firms are not so far beyond the "*son et lumière*" environment that characterised the trading floors of the early 1980s. Despite a superficial appearance of technical sophistication, until well into the 1980s most trader stations were essentially a bank of telephone lines and proprietary data-distribution monitors with modest technical intelligence. The explosive growth of PCs and workstations, new products and systems and global telecommunications in the past decade has catapulted the industry to levels of complexity that it took the mainframe world nearly 30 years to reach. This reaches its peak with global client/server architectures. Unfortunately, the technical infrastructure – especially networks and server architectures – has not usually kept up. Worse, the knowledge levels of support and operations staff, along with automated support tools for them to use, are often inadequate. Major potential problem areas include a lack of detailed knowledge of the particular DBMS, Unix, network and desktop operating systems, along with a dearth of automated tools for problem management, change control, usage/capacity monitoring, workflow/job scheduling, software distribution and version control, and for file backup and restore. These facilities and knowledge bases are clearly out of scope for most data warehouse projects, but their absence can be catastrophic. The best approach is to ensure that the firm's technology group undertakes to address these issues on a timely basis for the project.

The data warehouse project: real-world challenges and solutions

Let us now assume that the decision has been made that a data warehouse is the right solution to support your firm's risk management initiative. In the section "Challenges posed by a data warehouse", we discussed a number of challenges facing the project management team in such a situation. We will now revisit each of them and offer suggestions as to how to mitigate their effects. Finally, a group of "generally good ideas, tips and war stories" are presented at the end of the section.

CHALLENGE/RESPONSE

Listed below are the challenges identified in the section just referred to, together with a discussion of the strategies and tactics that can be used to minimise the associated risk. Table 6 provides a summary.

Expensive

Any non-philanthropic firm will very probably demand a full business case for a project on the scale of a data warehouse. Spend the money upfront to develop a comprehensive costing document. Be especially thorough with the project plan. It is difficult to overestimate the effort involved – almost impossible in the case of data clean-up. Plan for phased, incremental delivery, and sell that as a series of optional exit ramps for use if the project fails to meet expectations at any point. Target a high-pain business area of modest scope initially to increase support and deliver high-profile benefits.

Since such a project can rarely be justified on the basis of regulatory or legislative demand, or on revenue generation, you will need to be somewhat innovative on the benefits side. Do not sell the project as an "act of faith" – this will not hold up, and will result in some very tough questions in the medium term.

Industry survey statistics can be quoted, although they very often reveal a pre-

Table 6. Risk mitigation

Issue	Risk	Mitigation
Expensive project	Business case scrutiny: benefits seen as"soft"	• Upfront spending to develop comprehensive document • Phased development plan • Leverage vendor relationships • Target high-pain area first • Alternative metrics: Business volume enabler Better capital attribution Platform for RAROC
Expectation management	Users come to expect the unachievable – boundless queries	• Develop (funded) marketing plan, including presentations, demos, newsletters • Tightly scripted demos: emphasise phased deliverables, acknowledge limitations
Service levels	Data volume and growth in user load bring system to knees	• Specific performance parameters in service-level agreement. Be conservative initially, review regularly • Maximum flexibility in storage and compute capacity • Buy/build DBMS-tuning expertise • Monitoring tools for data and queries
Data quality	Difficult to establish and maintain	• Very senior owner/sponsor • Empowered DBA • Publicise contents, metadata, to encourage interest in source system owners
Data quantity	Users overwhelmed by volume of data; effects on system performance	• Scrutinise data retention requirements • Monitoring tools for data usage: Migrate little-used data to CD Identify new summaries
Risky technologies	Threat to development schedule; ongoing cost and performance issues	• Strategic alliances with vendors, including technology transfer • Specific budgets in plan for training, support tools
Staffing difficulties	Project seen as dull; staff not attracted	• Educate staff beforehand on technical scale and scope • Start with high-profile technical staff – others will want to work with them • Visible training plan and budget • Completion bonus structure

dominance of non-quantifiable factors. In a 1997 survey of data warehouse users by Sentry Market Research, 30% of respondents identified faster and better data access as the biggest benefit, as against 16% who realised a competitive advantage and only 6% who identified cost savings. More concretely, International Data Corporation (IDC) conducted case studies with 41 organisations in 1996 to estimate the return on investment over three years on their successful warehouse projects: the overall average was 401%, with an average payback period of 2.3 years and an average development cost of US$2.2 million. More than 80 of the top 100 US banks use a data warehouse solution for risk management.

It may be possible to view the project as a business enabler. For example, the centralisation of credit limits management in a warehouse can either reduce the internal cost of funding the various credit positions or allow higher business volumes within existing global limits.

The warehouse could support improved capital attribution and thus reduce operating costs for the businesses. It could also be the enabler of innovative measurement and compensation schemes, such as RAROC.

If possible, form strategic alliances with suppliers. Hardware and DBMS vendors do this regularly now, providing specialised design and development expertise from their resource base (see "Risky technologies" later in this section). They can be expected to contribute materially to the project, thus reducing the costs borne by the firm itself.

Management of expectations difficult

In describing the capabilities of a data warehouse, it is very easy to allow users' imaginations to generate expectations that the actual facility may never be able to meet. The concept of a database of all the firm's transactions – each with clean, consistent data values and able to be correlated in a vast number of ways – is beguiling. The reality is more likely that the warehouse will initially be relatively limited in scope and the data will be neither comprehensive nor perfect.

The best approach to this situation is to have a specific marketing plan for the project, complete with defined resources and a schedule. The goal is to convey an accurate picture of what the system can do, ensuring that the user community has the proper perspective on the warehouse. If this is done correctly, the initial users can become advocates for the data warehouse after the fact.

One method is to provide relatively conservative, tightly scripted demonstrations of the planned capabilities, with some emphasis on the restrictions or exclusions of the initial implementation. Another is to institute a frequent newsletter which provides regular reinforcement of the types of queries that will be possible with the initial version, as well as review and discussion of the planned regular reports. Yet another is to encourage users with questions about potential queries to contact the project team for clarification. If the particular query is possible, let them know; if not, add it to the future requirements list. Although this may place an additional burden on the analytical team, it is effective in clarifying for users (and sometimes for the project team) what the system can, and cannot, do. It also helps to foster a sense of ownership in the users, which encourages them to better understand, and even promote, the system.

Service-level management

The item above concerns what the warehouse will be capable of doing; this item relates to when and how fast – ie, availability and response times. It addresses two of the most challenging aspects of running a data warehouse environment: the pressures on the overnight production update window; and the effect of unmanaged queries from users during the day.

This is another expectation management situation, and the best solution is to document it in a service-level agreement (SLA). The first version of the SLA should be very conservative in assigning actual numbers; for example, commit initially only to have the system and reports available to users by 8 am if they sign off the last of the source systems by 8 pm the previous evening. After several months of operation – including at least one month-end cycle – the numbers can be tightened up and, on the basis of experience, extended to include average response times for managed online queries. Ad hoc queries should be supported on a best-effort basis only.

The technical design of the data warehouse should be as flexible as possible since, by their nature, the requirements will change in a largely unpredictable way. This is where a strategic partnership with the hardware and DBMS vendors can pay dividends. The hardware vendor must commit to ensuring expandability of the three key platform areas: central processing units (CPUs), memory and disk space. The DBMS vendor has experts who, through knowledge of the internals of their product, are able to strike the best compromise between theoretical and practical design of the data structure; they must minimise as far as possible any built-in limitations to adding new indices or data elements.

Finally, using a query-monitoring tool will allow regular "weeding of the garden". Some queries will fall into disuse, others will be added, and the usage patterns of existing queries will change. All these can change the optimum set of summarisations required to meet performance expectations: some that are no longer needed can be dropped, while adding new summarisations to speed up the response to newly popular queries can make material contributions to performance.

Data quality

Ownership of the data warehouse should be vested at a very senior level to maximise the span of interest of the owner and remove as many specific business-line biases as possible. Responsibility for the actual data should be given to an empowered DBA who is authorised to define and enforce consistent standards. This should extend to requiring that any new systems be aligned with these standards and that legacy systems at least improve their editing rules wherever feasible.

Providing broad availability of the metadata will also encourage the use of existing data elements rather than the generation of new fields in one of the source systems when a new need arises.

Data overload

Careful analysis of proposed additional data needs can help to screen out those which will provide limited value. For instance, users will often ask for far more historical retention than is actually justified. Better to sell the users on the 80–20 rule: retain only enough historical data to support 80% of the projected queries. In a large finance application at a Canadian bank the users were asked how much monthly reporting should be retained online. They responded on the basis of their experience with regulatory retention – 24 months in this case. A short discussion with the unit heads involved quickly revealed that, in practice, they almost never went back further than three months. This resulted in a reduction of over 85% in the disk requirements for the report-browser server.

Once the data are there you need to track the actual usage, and be prepared to use this to determine whether and when to trim back the retention period. In the discussion of tools in the "Infrastructure" section we indicated that monitoring system usage, including types and frequencies of queries and fields accessed, supported ongoing tuning efforts by the DBA and technical staff. As patterns of usage change, some data tend to fall into disuse (indeed a startling amount is used only once or twice at the outset and then never again). These "dormant data" need to be removed to second-level storage, such as CD-ROM, where they will still be accessible if needed but will not affect online performance.

In a similar manner, the initial data model should include most of the appropriate summaries and calculated/derived data based on usage patterns observed at the outset. Again, over time, usage changes and the above monitoring tools will help to identify potential new summaries to reduce the volumes of raw data that users need to access regularly.

Risky technologies

As mentioned earlier, a data warehouse architecture brings together a number of relatively new technologies, with the attendant risks. One effective way to mitigate these risks is through strategic alliances with the major vendors whereby they provide in-depth technical knowledge through their own staff on the project. Included in the agreement should be a technology transfer clause which stipulates that a portion of the time and effort provided by the vendor is directed at training the firm's staff in the use of the particular technology. This usually appeals to the internal staff and will shorten the period of dependency on vendor staff measurably.

The project plan should include a specific budget component for training; it is not enough to assume that regular departmental training budgets or "osmosis" will provide the training the staff need to develop and support the application.

Similarly, the project should ensure that adequate infrastructure support tools are available; if they are not available and not forthcoming from the IT budget, they must be explicitly identified and budgeted in the project plan.

Staffing challenges

Acquiring top-notch internal staff for a data warehouse project can initially prove difficult. It may be viewed as less attractive than, for instance, a front-line dealing system project. Presentations to technical staff on the conceptual design and scope of the project, with due emphasis on the technologies to be used, can help with that. A mandate from the project sponsor to assign one or two of the top technical staff can make the project more attractive to the rest. A generous training budget is a powerful attractor: staying current in leading-edge technologies ranks high on the Maslow[10] scale for technical staff. Judicious use of completion bonuses can provide the clincher.

SOME GENERAL SUGGESTIONS

Considerable benefits can be had from actively managing the volume of data in the warehouse. Consider purchasing a tool to monitor usage at an individual data element level. So-called "dormant data" increase over time, and they significantly degrade performance. These data can arise from an initial design that included lots of additional fields to cater for potential future needs, from end-users dramatically overestimating the required retention of history, and from end-users creating one-time summary data which are not used again. Dormant data should be periodically removed to a lower-availability storage medium, such as CD-ROM, where, while still available, they do not affect online performance. The monitoring tool can also be linked to a chargeback allocation mechanism.

A data warehouse is a different type of application, but it is also a different type of project. It is never static, and must be designed for constant change. It defies the traditional, "straight-ahead" approach to a project: the full requirements include future needs – which can only be guessed at the outset. Professional project management and experienced design consultancy are both well worth the cost.

Even though one of the most powerful aspects of a data warehouse is its "memory", it will prove very difficult to convert anything reliably except recent history. Detail history may not be available in some systems, and it is rare that the corresponding metadata history is available and comprehensive. Finally, it can be difficult to scrub historical data successfully. The upshot: avoid converting historical data where possible.

Having selected a vendor or vendors experienced in your industry, emphasise and exploit partnerships with them. This is especially important with hardware and DBMSs. They have a large pool of staff with strong technical knowledge, and most are very aware of the power of an intimate business relationship in ensuring customer loyalty. Most organisations undertaking enterprise-level data warehouse projects, especially in risk management, are large and global. A strategic partnership in creating a data warehouse encourages the vendor to provide top talent at little or no cost given the marketing value of such a high-profile project if successful.

A clean-up of legacy data is the most labour-intensive and expensive aspect of a data warehouse project. An intensive analysis at data level of all the source systems at the outset can pay significant dividends. It will determine the value of specific data elements, along with the "cost-to-clean". This can be helpful in designing the warehouse effectively, as well as suggesting process changes which can improve the quality of both present and future data. A number of data-auditing firms work closely with scrubbing/mapping firms in defining the optimal path in navigating the data jungle.

Invest in metadata. They capture the etymology of each data element, including its historical evolution, and are vital input to all operational aspects of the warehouse, including data loading, editing and updating, as well as query generation and historical trend analyses. Metadata are used by many tools, and it is important that these tools be able to exchange them seamlessly (see the next point). If properly accessible, metadata are also a valuable research base for business analysts who are trying to formulate a new query: they need to understand a particular data element completely to ensure that they select the right targets for their query.

Usually, very little can be done to improve the alignment between the multiple source systems that feed a data warehouse, so the project must deal with existing data models and their lack of integration. However, when choosing the toolkit for the data warehouse there is an opportunity to ensure at least pairwise component integration. For example, tools that support the Metadata Interchange Format (MIF) from the Metadata Coalition will be able to exchange metadata easily, eliminating the need for further mapping and transformation exercises. In the absence of such alignment, one option is to define your own metadata standard and ensure that the tools are able to meet that standard.

As mentioned previously, a data warehouse is politically vulnerable since most business users view it initially as a major cost only and, even if they recognise the potential information value of such a facility, are unlikely (or unmotivated) to convert that to a solid, attributable revenue projection. One way to defuse this situation is to proactively repackage and "market" the data in the warehouse. Most business heads and their analysts are attracted to any type of customer- and product-orientated trend information, and providing this to them can sometimes win friends.

Finally, a data warehouse is critically dependent on quality components. Using a world-class, intuitive query tool to investigate unreliable and inconsistent data is guaranteed to focus attention on an inadequate data strategy; similarly, quality data that are only accessible using a complex, poorly understood query engine will ensure that network and DBMS capacity are never fully exploited because user interest will stagnate or die. The answer: buy the best, build the rest. Invest in those things which are so unique to your situation that no off-the-shelf product suits. This is more likely to be in such areas as data models, metadata tools and analytic engines.

Trends and issues

Risk management is one of the most dynamic fields in financial services. The products it measures, the models it uses to do that measurement, the regulatory framework and the technology it employs all meet or exceed Moore's Law. Outlined below is a snapshot of the various dimensions of change of which a global risk management data warehouse must be aware, along with some projections of developments over the next couple of years.

PRODUCTS

Risk management got seriously complex when derivatives began to appear in significant numbers and notional values. They are well-established products now, and their complexity will, almost of necessity, continue to increase. The successful financial products firm today offers a "one-stop" type of service: the solution to a particular business finance situation may involve half a dozen or more individual products and services, all packaged so as to be seen as a single solution by the client. "Financial engineering" is a term that is used to describe this phenomenon: the building-block products are integrated and combined to create a unique financial solution for the specific combination of client and situation. This is a very profitable business when done correctly; unfortunately, few current risk management systems are able to handle this "portfolio effect" truly well.

Portfolio trading, in which a collection of securities is assembled so as to optimise the net effect of their responses to market movements, is similar to the above in that it is highly individualised and the interactions to be modelled are complex. It continues to grow, and seems only to be limited by the ability of the traders involved to conjure up new structures.

The trend to securitisation will continue. This, in effect, converts the projected cash-flows of some element of the balance sheet into a marketable security and thereby transfers the related risk to the purchasers of that new security. These products are more difficult to model because each one is unique.

RISK MEASUREMENT

The mandate of risk management as a discipline is, colloquially speaking, to keep up with the Masters of the Universe. Risk managers must strive always to stay at least one step ahead of the traders and financial engineers: their perspective on risk must be at enterprise level.

All aspects of risk modelling are becoming more sophisticated. Notional amount has evolved into aggregatable measures based on sophisticated algorithms. Value-at-risk (VAR), the dominant aggregatable measure of risk today, is itself evolving. Originally built to recognise volatilities at an individual transaction level, it has evolved to incorporate the correlations inherent in a portfolio. Current work is directed at recognising the limitations of any statistical model and accommodating them through such techniques as stress testing and scenario analysis.

This evolution from simplistic to sophisticated which has occurred with market and credit risk could well repeat itself with operational risk – an area that is now receiving considerable attention. Several other types of risk have been identified, including liquidity, regulatory and human factor risk, although these have not yet been studied to the same extent.

The goal for global firms is a credible, consistent, standard unit of risk. Several firms are aggressively moving towards that goal, defining product- and customer-independent measures which can be assigned at the transaction/instrument level and aggregated almost without restriction. The attraction of such enterprise-level risk management is undeniable. Meridien Research estimates that in 1997 this was a US$572 million market.[11]

The creation and acceptance of a standard risk measure sets the stage for new measures of performance. In his soul, any banker would love to be able to choose on the basis of relative risk levels between two transactions that appear to offer similar returns. RAROC offers such a possibility – it defines an easily understood measure of performance which is independent of instrument type or counterparty and can be aggregated in virtually unlimited ways. Leading firms are moving in this direction since it offers an attractive method for allocating capital or credit, as well as for measuring the profitability of products, staff, clients and business lines. This performance measurement aspect could have profound effects on the behaviour of the organisation and so should be deployed only with much forethought and great caution.

Public risk is a reality: RiskMetrics and CreditMetrics from JP Morgan moved standard-model risk values into the public domain. For second-tier players, these provide an inexpensive tool for industry-standard risk monitoring; for industry leaders, they raise the bar, as well as providing a "sanity check" for any proprietary measurement processes. Those who believe that first-rate risk management can provide strategic advantage will inevitably need to develop ever more sophisticated techniques.

Netting, a very powerful approach to reducing exposure, has evolved from bilateral settlement netting, through novation, to closeout netting. Multilateral netting, in which a clearing-house process takes place, dramatically reduces risk – directly through the netting process, but also through the "exchange effect" of the clearing entity itself. In each of these cases the leverage (and the complexity) increases.

Timeliness is everything: credit risk is often available on a real-time basis, monitoring exposures to counterparty, currency and country. Market risk is moving in that direction. It is likely that, given its nature, operational risk will too.

REGULATION

It was the regulators who created one of the first de facto standards after the initial "notional amount" approach to risk measurement. The Bank for International Settlements defined a set of percentages to be applied to the notional amount for a given instrument to determine its credit risk exposure. This trend continues. The basis for assigning risk has evolved from asset size to market value volatility, and will continue to add sophistication. The principle of RAROC, as implemented in the bigger institutions, must be attractive to the regulatory agencies, as are the various portfolio effects: cross-product, cross-business and cross-risk types. Backtesting is being advocated by the regulators as a means of verifying that the current models agree with the recent past: apply the models to the conditions in effect then and determine whether the predicted results are aligned with what actually occurred. Operational risk is now being studied by the Federal Reserve, among others, and will continue to grow in prominence. Finally, the move from batch to real-time monitoring has already been endorsed by agencies like the Federal Reserve in the US, and will probably become a requirement in the near future.

Pressure from the regulators on smaller financial services firms to implement a risk management solution will increase; given their inability to afford either internally developed solutions or those custom-built by top-tier consultants, the market for application packages should benefit over the next few years. Regulators are also sensitive to the need for bifurcation: leading-edge modelling for the major firms, effective industry-standard solutions for the rest.

In summary, regulatory measurement is closing in on the industry-leading practices of the premier firms: the gap between the introduction of a new management or monitoring practice and its adoption by regulators is shrinking. Continuing consultations between the regulators and the industry are seen as vital by both groups; these discussions will tend to align internal management risk reporting and regulatory reporting.

TECHNOLOGY

The increases in raw horsepower delivered by Moore's Law have mostly been sufficient to support the demands of all but the most exotic risk management systems. There is no guarantee, however, that this geometric increase will by itself be able to keep up with the growth in such demands; for example, the increase in sophistication of the models is probably closer to exponential in terms of processing requirements, and the complexity of ad hoc queries is likely to proceed the same way.

Fortunately, technology improvements continue to appear in areas other than just computing power and storage density. Two specific areas that have also made significant contributions to performance are in DBMS capabilities and hardware architecture.

In the early days of data warehousing, large installations required a purpose-built DBMS to handle the volumes and performance needed. The strongest partnership was that between NCR and Teradata; their high-profile work with the Bank of America in the mid- to late 1980s established that very large data warehouses were possible, although beyond the capabilities of the mainstream portable DBMS products. This began to change with the introduction in the mid-1990s of products like Oracle 7 and Sybase 11. Vendors were responding to the unique demands of this growing market with improvements in bulk data loading, query optimisation, parallel operations (I/O, queries, backup), data partitioning and specialised indexing. Such improvements will almost certainly continue to appear, both to improve the efficiency of data selection and movement and to take advantage of platform improvements; the release of Oracle8 in 1997 supports this contention.

The advent of parallel hardware technology is probably even more important than developments in DBMS products. Having multiple CPUs in the same machine means that more than one job can be run simultaneously; most importantly, the same job can be run simultaneously on several CPUs. Given the relatively modest cost of additional CPUs, this dramatically expands the range and scope of economically feasible queries. It is currently the best bet in the battle to keep up with the growth in data volumes. Research continues in this area, as does concurrent DBMS research in constructing and optimising parallel queries.

Partnerships and consolidation in the vendor community, both within and across product lines, will continue, increasing the levels of integration – a welcome development. The challenge comes in the frequent cases where a large, well-established firm (such as a software conglomerate or a consulting firm) buys a small, entrepreneurial specialist firm (such as a risk-modelling or analysis tool developer). The culture of the small firm can be smothered by the larger firm, with the result that the fundamental assets of the smaller firm decide to move on.

Data mining represents the use of a data warehouse with potentially the highest return. Identifying a market for new product or service, or a previously hidden purchasing pattern in a given customer segment, could lead to new lines of business or dramatically increase the effectiveness of targeted marketing campaigns. The sophistication of the tools and techniques will continue to increase, especially in statistics, induction, neural networks, fuzzy logic and visualisation. There is a trend to the use of multiple techniques within a particular tool to increase the chance of identifying new patterns.

The designs of data warehouses are now entering the second generation. Initially, the emphasis was on just getting the data into the warehouse, usually without much regard to integrating those data. The second generation deals with many more data, focuses on their integration (a difficult, manual, high-return process that can account for more than 70% of the cost of a project), uses much more sophisticated access and analysis tools, recognises the value of metadata and is starting to incorporate data marts into the design. Data marts are logical subsets of data from the warehouse that are designed to support the

PANEL 3

DATA WAREHOUSE EXAMPLE: CIBC RISK MANAGEMENT

The Canadian Imperial Bank of Commerce (CIBC) is (in June, 1998) the largest bank in Canada, in terms of assets, and the seventh largest in North America. In recent years CIBC World Markets, its investment banking component, has moved aggressively into new businesses, including derivatives, high-yield debt and securitisation. It was decided at the outset that a strong, proactive approach to market risk management was required. The bank has developed a leading-edge solution based on a data warehouse architecture. It incorporates advanced VAR analytic models and covers all CIBC World Markets (formerly known as CIBC Wood Gundy) desks worldwide – of which there are more than 180. The risks covered include interest rate, equity, foreign exchange and commodity. There are over 100 mappings from legacy systems, resulting in more than 400 incoming files nightly; these contain over 150,000 transactions and add about 2–3 Gb of data daily. More than 100 classes of instrument are supported and more than 700 programs are run each night.

The approach taken was to "buy the best and build the rest". Strategic partnerships were formed with HP, Sybase and Prism. The components of the system, known as the Frontier system, are listed below by method of acquisition, and a summary diagram is presented in the accompanying figure.

Buy

Client/server hardware and software (HP 9000)
Data-mapping tool (Prism Executive Suite)
Ad hoc query tool (Andyne GQL)
DBMS (Sybase SQL Server 11)
Automated scheduling (Tivoli Maestro)
Object-orientated development tools (Rogue Wave Tools.h++)

Build

Data model (proprietary)
Analytic engine (DGVT Calculator)
Input bridges (via Prism)
Metadata (Microsoft Office: Excel and Word; looking at Prism web access and OLAP-based metadata management tools)
Other analytic engines (proprietary)
Documentation/presentation tools (Microsoft Office)

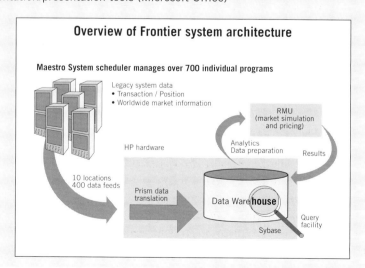

Overview of Frontier system architecture

Maestro System scheduler manages over 700 individual programs

Legacy system data
• Transaction / Position
• Worldwide market information

RMU
(market simulation and pricing)

HP hardware

Analytics
Data preparation   Results

10 locations
400 data feeds

Prism data
translation

Data Warehouse

Query
facility

Sybase

unique business needs of a specific group or application. The usual approach is to locate the data mart on a departmental-level server dedicated to that user group and use replication-type processes to ensure data consistency.

Metadata always held the promise of being the key to more incisive analysis and knowledge generation. The second generation of warehouses marks the passing of the era of centralised metadata. It has been recognised that, with the growth in data marts, there is a need to retain and manage metadata at the local server level. This leads to a distributed metadata architecture and the emergence of metadata exchange tools and standards.

Traditional DBMSs have historically been limited in their support of non-traditional data types, including images, video and audio. Much work is being done on so-called object-relational DBMSs, which store complex data types as objects and can manipulate and "compare" the substantial data structures found in object-orientated environments.

New access tools are constantly being developed. The Internet/intranet explosion has resulted in web technology access tools starting to dominate warehouse purchasing plans. The warehouse is evolving from being a semi-closed source for a limited set of "information druids" to becoming a foundation for traditional executive information systems (EIS) and decision support systems (DSS); as a result, tools from those disciplines – such as Essbase, a multidimensional analysis tool from Arbor Software – are being used with data warehouses.

The Internet has already begun to make risk measures a public-domain commodity: the initial breakthrough by JP Morgan in releasing RiskMetrics set the stage. Recently, a joint venture between three vendors with limited traditional overlap resulted in the debut of a more broadly applicable product. A website called riskview.com uses Dow Jones data on equities and indexes, Infinity's portfolio analysis and presentation software, and an IBM platform (web hosting) to provide virtually free state-of-the-art risk management to individual and institutional investors.

Middleware is a rapidly growing technology product area. Although definitions vary dramatically, it can be regarded as a platform for managing the processing life of a business transaction. The main features include intelligent message publication, navigation and guaranteed delivery, and validation/transformation/enhancement of the message content, supported across all of the firm's technical infrastructure. It offers exciting possibilities for relieving data warehouse projects of their traditional burden as the agent for enterprise-wide data standardisation. Middleware provides assured delivery of transactions between applications, along with data mapping and transformation. Judging from current industry experience, this could reduce the budget for a major data warehouse project by two thirds or more, simply by delivering clean, consistent data on a timely basis.

Panel 3 (page 165) provides an overview of the CIBC risk management data warehouse known as "Frontier".

More than 40 person-years of development went into Frontier in the first three years, creating a basic level of full functionality, and work continues. The use of a standardised measure (the RMU, or risk measurement unit) across products has revolutionised the reporting and perception of risk. This concept is being extended to include credit and operational risk. The system is also being extended to be the basis for real-time credit limit monitoring and for calculations on regulatory and economic capital.

1 *Moore's Law, first articulated in 1965 by Gordon Moore, one of the three founders of Intel Corp, states that the density of components on a microchip doubles approximately every 18 months while the cost halves. It is regularly applied to a number of other similar metrics as well: cost per MIPS (million instructions per second), storage capacity per unit area, data transfer rates across a WAN, etc. In this case, a complexity increase on the order of 1000 would be predicted.*

2 *W. H. Inmon, author of the seminal work* Building the Data Warehouse *(QED Press, Wellesley, MA), is widely recognised as the father of the concept. He has published 36 books and more than 350 articles in major computer journals. He co-founded Prism Solutions and currently heads Pine Cone Systems, a Colorado-based firm he founded, which specialises in monitoring and management tools for Data Warehouses.*

3 *Estimates vary, largely due to differences in definition, but Meridien Research, in a paper published in May 1997 (Williams, D., "Vendor-Provided Enterprise Risk Technology Solutions", Meridien Research, Needham, MA), defines the integration component of a risk management solution as that which provides data transport, formatting and workflow. It estimates that this segment constitutes 65% of the US$572 million ERM market. For 1998, the market size estimate rose to US$890 million.*

4 *For instance, market risk can be broken down into equity, currency, commodity and interest rate risk (which can itself be subdivided into trading risk and gap risk).*

5 *Dimension data is a term used to describe the reference data elements of a data warehouse, as opposed to the fact data (eg, the transactions themselves). Product hierarchy, customer information and branch information are examples of dimension data.*

6 *RAROC – risk-adjusted return on capital – is a performance measure that is being introduced by several leading financial institutions. It includes the costs, as well as the risks, associated with a given transaction. The direct and indirect revenues are reduced by direct and indirect expenses and by expected losses. A further refinement also risk-adjusts the capital (RAROraC) by including additional capital needed to cover unexpected credit and market losses. These measures can be used to assess the performance of traders, business lines, products, customers or regions, and can actually drive compensation.*

7 *Note that one of the major challenges facing a firm as it moves to a RAROC program is the difficulty in attributing costs and, especially, losses at an instrument level. Much research has been invested in modelling aggregatable instrument-level risk; the same is not true for the burden aspects of a deal.*

8 *One survey of 250 information systems organisations in the United States found an average data warehouse investment of US$2 million in hardware and US$1 million in software alone. For the top 100 banks, the average is closer to US$10 million over 5 years. Estimates of the overall size of the data warehouse market vary due to imprecision in the definitions, but range as high as US$6 billion.*

9 *This can be a significant contributor to operational risk. Each separate system will require a separate support knowledge base, both technical and operational. Shortened product life cycles and increasing product complexity exacerbate the problem.*

10 *Abraham Maslow (1908–70), a US psychologist, is most famous for his theory on man's hierarchy of needs. These range from the basic physiological requirements for security, love and esteem and, at the top, self-actualisation. As each need is satisfied the next higher level dominates consciousness. A person who lacks food is not concerned with love; however, a person who has the esteem of others can still feel incomplete.*

11 *Williams (1997; see note 3). It is interesting to note that the component relating to data acquisition, transformation and transport, which Meridien terms the integration layer, constitutes 65% of the total.*

GLOSSARY

This glossary provides short definitions of terms and abbreviations that are used, often without further explanation, in the risk management industry. The glossary has been designed for general reference, so not all of the terms defined below are used elsewhere in this book. Longer definitions are available in an industry-standard glossary entitled *The Chase/Risk Magazine Guide to Risk Management*, which is also available from Risk Publications.

Accreting swap Swap whose notional amount increases during the life of the swap (opposite of amortising swap (qv))

Accrued benefit obligation Present value of pension benefits that have been earned by an employee to date, whether "vested" in the employee or not. It can be an important measure when managing the asset/liability ratio of pension funds

Add-on factor Simplified estimate of the potential future increase in the replacement cost (qv), or market value, of a derivative transaction

All-or-nothing Digital option (qv). This option's put (call) pays out a pre-determined amount (the "all") if the index is below (above) the strike price at the option's expiration. The amount by which the index is below (above) the strike is irrelevant; the payout will be "all" or nothing

American option Option exercisable at any time up to expiration (*see also* European option)

Amortising option Option whose notional amount decreases during the life of the option, such as an amortising cap, collar or swaption

Amortising swap Swap whose notional amount decreases during the

life of the swap (opposite of accreting swap (qv))

Annuity swap Swap where, on the fixed payment side, the principal amount is amortised over the life of the swap

Arbitrage The simultaneous buying and selling in different markets of two or more equivalent securities undertaken to exploit price disparities for a riskless profit

Arch (autoregressive conditional heteroscedasticity) A discrete-time model for a random variable. It assumes that variance is stochastic and is a function of the variance of previous time steps and the level of the underlying

Asian option *see* average price (rate) option

Asset Probable future economic benefit obtained or controlled as a result of past events or transactions. Generally classified as either current or long-term

Asset & liability management (ALM) The practice of matching the term structure and cashflows of an organisation's asset and liability portfolios to maximise returns and minimise risk

Asset allocation Distribution of investment funds within an asset class or across a range of asset classes for the purpose of diversifying risk or adding value to a portfolio

Asset securitisation The process whereby loans, receivables and other illiquid assets in the balance sheet are packaged into interest-bearing securities that offer attractive investment opportunities

Asset swap Swap involving cashflows on assets

Asset-backed security A financial instrument that is collateralised by bundled assets such as mortgages, real estate or receivables

Asset-risk benchmark Benchmark (qv) against which the *riskiness* of a corporation's assets may be measured. In sophisticated corporate risk management strategies the dollar risk of the liability portfolio may be managed against an asset-risk benchmark

Asset-sensitivity estimates Estimates of the effect of risk factors on the value of assets

At-the-money An option with a strike price which is the same as the price of the underlying security

Average cap Also known as an average rate cap, a cap on an average interest rate over a given period rather than on the rate prevailing at the end of the period (*see also* average price (rate) option)

Average price (rate) option Option on a currency's average exchange rate or commodity's average spot price in which four variables have to be agreed between buyer and seller: the premium, the strike price, the source of the exchange rate or commodity price data and the sampling interval (each day, for example). At the end of the life of the option the average spot exchange rate is calculated and compared with the strike price. A cash payment is then made to the buyer of the option

that is equal to the face amount of the option times the difference between the two rates (assuming the option is in the money; otherwise it expires worthless)

Average worst-case exposure The expression of an exposure in terms of the average of the worst-case exposures over a given period

Back-testing The validation of a model by feeding it historical data and comparing the results with historical reality

Backwardation Description of a market in which commodity forward prices are lower than the spot price

Balance sheet Statement of the financial position of an enterprise at a specific point in time, giving assets, liabilities and stockholders' equity

Bank holding company (US) A company that owns or controls one or more banks but does not engage directly in banking activities

Barrier option Option where the ability of the holder to exercise is activated or, alternatively, extinguished if the value of the underlying reaches a specified level. Also known as a limit option or trigger option

Basis swap Interest rate swap between two counterparties with floating-rate debt issued on two different bases – eg, three-month Libor, six-month Libor, US commercial paper, US Prime

Basket option Option based on an underlying basket of bonds, currencies, equities or commodities

Bear One who believes that prices will decline

Bear market A market in which prices are declining

Benchmark Criterion against which

to measure the performance of any of a variety of variables, including interest-rate, foreign-exchange, liability and pension-fund portfolios. They can be used to judge the performance of risk managers or fund managers

Beta The sensitivity of a stock relative to swings in the overall market. The market has a beta of one, so a stock or portfolio with a beta greater than one will rise or fall more than the overall market, whereas a beta of less than one means that the stock is less volatile than the market

Bid/ask (offer) spread Difference between the buying price and the selling price of an asset at a particular moment in time

Bilateral netting The ability to offset amounts owed to a counterparty under one contract against amounts owed to the same counterparty under another contract – for example, where both transactions are governed by one master agreement. Also known as "cherry picking"

Blended interest rate swap Result of adding a forward swap (qv) to an existing swap and blending the rates over the total life of the transaction

bpv Basis point value. The price movement due to a one basis point change in yield

Break forward Forward contract which the customer can break at a predetermined rate, allowing him or her to take advantage of any favourable exchange rate movements

Bull One who expects prices to rise

Bull market A market in which prices are rising

Business intelligence tools Term used to describe the latest generation of access tools, which are expected to support both data extraction and subsequent analysis

CAD The European Union's Capital Adequacy Directive

Call option Contract that gives the purchaser the right to buy an underlying at a certain price on or before a certain date (*see also* put option)

Call price The price at which the issuer can call in a bond or preferred stock

Cancellable swap Swap in which the payer of the fixed rate has the option, usually exercisable on a specified date, to cancel the deal (*see also* swaption)

Cap Ceiling on the price level of an underlying (eg, commodity or interest rate), constructed from a strip of European options (qv). For example, if on prescribed reference dates a standard interest rate such as Libor or US Treasury bills is above a rate agreed between the seller of the cap and the buyer, the seller pays the buyer the extra interest costs until the next reference date. The opposite of a floor (qv)

Capped option Option where the holder's ability to profit from a change in value of the underlying is subject to a specified limit

Caption Option on a cap (qv)

Central line theorem The assertion that as sample size, *n*, increases, the distribution of the mean of a random sample taken from almost any population approaches a normal distribution

Cherry picking *see* bilateral netting

Close-out netting The ability to net a portfolio of contracts with a given counterparty in the event of default. (*See also* bilateral netting)

CMTM Current mark-to-market value (*See also* current exposure and replacement cost)

Collar Combination of the purchase of a cap (qv) and the sale of a floor (qv), or vice versa, to create the desired band within which the buyer of the collar wants the price of the underlying (eg, interest rate costs) to be held

Commodity swap Swap where one of the cashflows is based on a fixed value for the underlying commodity and the other is based on a floating index value. The commodity is often oil or natural gas, although copper, gold, other metals and agricultural commodities are also commonly used. The end-users are consumers, who pay a fixed rate, and producers

Compound option Option on an option, the first giving the buyer the right, but not the obligation, to buy the second on a specific date at a predetermined price. There are two kinds. One, on currencies, is useful for companies tendering for overseas contracts in a foreign currency. The interest rate version comprises captions (qv) and floortions (qv)

Comptroller of the Currency An official of the US Treasury Department responsible for the primary supervision of banks in the US

Contango Description of a market in which the forward price of a commodity is higher than the spot price

Contingent option Option where the premium is higher than usual but is only payable if the value of the underlying reaches a specified level. Also known as a contingent premium option

Contingent premium option *see* contingent option

Controlled foreign company (CFC) In US tax parlance, a CFC is a foreign corporation where 50% of the total combined voting power of all classes of stock entitled to vote, or of the total value of the stock of the corporation, is held by US shareholders

Correlation matrices Statistical constructs used in the value-at-risk (qv) methodology to measure the degree of relatedness of various market factors

Corridor Collar (qv) on a swap using two swaptions (qv)

Cost of carry The cost of financing an asset relative to the interest received, it is positive when the cost of financing is lower than the interest received

Cost volatility Volatility relating to operational errors or the fines and losses a business unit may incur. Reflected in excess costs and penalty charges posted to the profits and losses. (*See also* revenue volatility)

Counterparty risk weighting *see* risk weighting

Country risk The risks, when business is conducted in a particular country, of adverse economic or political conditions arising in that country. More specifically, the credit risk of a financial transaction or instrument arising from such conditions

Credit (or default) risk The risk that a loss will be incurred if a counterparty to a derivatives transaction does not fulfil its financial obligations in a timely manner

Credit derivatives Financial contracts that involve a potential exchange of payments in which at least one of the cashflows is linked to the performance of a specified underlying credit-sensitive asset or liability

Credit-equivalent amount As part of the calculation of the risk-weighted amount (qv) of capital the Bank for International Settlements (BIS) advises each bank to set aside against derivative credit risk, banks must compute a credit-equivalent amount for each derivative transaction. The amount is calculated by summing the current replacement cost (qv), or market value, of the instrument and an add-on factor (qv)

Credit risk (or default risk) exposure The value of the contract exposed to default. If all transactions are marked to market each day, such positive market value is the amount of previously recorded profit that might have to be reversed and recorded as a loss in the event of counterparty default

Credit spread The interest rate spread between two debt issues of similar duration and maturity, reflecting the relative creditworthiness of the issuers

Credit swaps Agreement between two counterparties to exchange disparate cashflows, at least one of which must be tied to the performance of a credit-sensitive asset or to a portfolio or index of such assets. The other cashflow is usually tied to a floating-rate index (such as Libor) or a fixed rate or is linked to another credit-sensitive asset

Credit value-at-risk (CVAR) *see* value-at-risk (VAR)

Cross Two non-dollar currencies in relation to each other – eg, Deutschmark and yen

Cross-currency swap Also known as a (cross-) currency coupon swap, an interest rate swap with the fixed rate payable in one currency and the floating rate in another

Cumulative default rate *see* probability of default

Currency option The option to buy or sell a specified amount of a given currency at a specified rate at or during a specified time in the future

Currency swap Swap where payment (typically a default or credit downgrade) occurs. It can be linked to the price of a particular security, set at a

predetermined recovery rate, or it can take the form of an actual delivery of the underlying security at a predetermined price

Current assets Assets which are expected to be used or converted to cash within one year or one operating cycle

Current exposure *see* replacement cost

Current liabilities Obligations which the firm is expected to settle within one year or one operating cycle

Daily range The difference between the high and low points of a single trading day

DEaR Daily earnings at risk

Default correlation The degree of covariance between the probabilities of default of a given set of counterparties. For example, in a set of counterparties with positive default correlation, a default by one counterparty suggests an increased probability of a default by another counterparty

Default probability *see* probability of default

Default risk *see* credit risk

Default risk exposure *see* credit risk exposure

Deferred payout option American option (qv) where settlement is at expiry

Deferred start options Options purchased before their "lives" actually commence. A corporation might, for example, decide to pay for a deferred start option to lock into what it perceives as current advantageous pricing for an option that it knows it will need in the future

Deferred strike option Option where the strike price is established at a future date on the basis of the spot foreign exchange price prevailing at that future date

Defined benefit plan Contractual obligation established between a corporation and its employees to provide them with an agreed level of financial support at their retirement

Delegation costs Incentive costs incurred by banks in delegating monitoring activities

Delta A measure of the price movement of an option based on the price change in the underlying security

Derivative A financial instrument whose value changes with the value and characteristics of another market variable, known as the underlying (qv)

Diffusion effect The potential for increase over time of the credit exposure generated by a derivative: as time progresses, there is more likelihood of larger changes in the underlying market variables. Depending on the type and structure of the instrument, this effect may be moderated by the amortisation effect (qv)

Digital option Unlike simple European and American options, a digital option has fixed payouts and, rather like binary digital circuits, which are either on or off, pays out either this amount or nothing. Digital options can be added together to create assets that exactly mirror index price movements anticipated by investors. (*See also* one touch all-or-nothing)

Direct risk Risk of loan default on the lending of money. (*See also* credit risk)

Discount When an option trades for less than its intrinsic value it is trading at a discount. A future is trading at a discount when it trades for less than the price of the underlying security

Discount swap Swap in which the fixed-rate payments are less than the

internal rate of return on the swap, the difference being made up at maturity by a balloon payment

Dividend discount model
Theoretical estimate of market value that computes the economic or the net present value of future cashflows due to an equity investor

Down-and-in option Barrier option (qv) where the holder's ability to exercise is activated if the value of the underlying drops below a specified level. (*See also* up-and-in option)

Down-and-out option Barrier option (qv) where the holder's ability to exercise expires if the value of the underlying drops below a specified level. (*See also* up-and-out option)

Drill-down capabilities The methodology/system used to calculate future exposure when a potential future credit exposure profile reveals that an institution's exposure could become unacceptably high, providing a clear breakdown of the types of potential market event that are responsible for the result

Dual currency option Option allowing the holder to buy either of two currencies

Dual currency swap Currency swap where both the interest rates are fixed rates

Dual strike option Interest rate option, usually a cap or a floor, with one floor or ceiling rate for part of the option's life and another for the rest

Duration Measurement of the percentage change in the market value of a single security given a 1% change in the underlying yield of the security

Duration gap Measurement of the interest rate exposure of an institution

EAFE Europe, Australia and the Far East Equity Index

Early exercise The exercise or assignment of an option prior to expiration

Efficient frontier method Technique used by fund managers to allocate assets

Embedded option Interest rate-sensitive option in debt instrument that affects its redemption. Such instruments include mortgage-backed securities and callable bonds

Employee stock option programme Plan tying a portion of the compensation of a company's employees to its long-term performance

Equity The residual interest in the net assets of an entity that remains after deducting the liabilities

Equity options Options on shares of an individual common stock

Equity warrant Warrant (qv), usually attached to a bond, entitling the holder to purchase share(s)

Equity-linked swap Swap where one of the cashflows is based on an equity instrument or index, when it is known as an equity index swap

ERISA Employee Retirement Income Security Act

European option Option that can only be exercised at expiry. (*See also* American option)

Exchange rate agreement Contract for differences or synthetic agreement for forward exchange (qv) that does not reflect changes in the spot market

Exercise The act of a call (put) option holder buying (selling) the underlying product. (*See also* American option and European option)

Expected (credit) exposure Estimate of the most likely future replacement cost, or positive market value, of any given derivative transaction, expressed

as a level of probability. More exactly, it is the mean of all possible probability-weighted replacement costs, where the replacement cost in any outcome is equal to the mark-to-market present value if positive, and zero if negative

Expected (credit) loss Estimate of the amount a derivatives counterparty is likely to lose as a result of default from a derivatives contract, with a given level of probability. The expected loss of any derivative position can be derived by combining the distributions of credit exposures (qv), rate of recovery (qv) and probabilities of default (qv)

Expected default rate Estimate of the most likely rate of default of a counterparty expressed as a level of probability

Expected rate of recovery *see* rate of recovery

Exposure profile The path of worst-case or expected exposures over time. Different instruments reveal quite differently shaped exposure profiles due to the interaction of the diffusion (qv) and amortisation effects

Extinguishable option Option in which the holder's right to exercise disappears if the value of the underlying passes a specified level. (*See also* barrier option)

Federal Reserve System The central bank of the US, composed of a seven-member Board of Governors, 12 regional Reserve Banks, and depository institutions that are subject to reserve requirements

Floor Series of European call options protecting the buyer from a fall in interest rates below a specified rate; the opposite of a cap (qv)

Floortion Option on a floor (qv)

Forward Agreement to exchange a predetermined amount of currency, commodity or other financial instrument at a specified future date and at a predetermined rate

Forward band Zero-cost collar (qv); that is, one in which the premium payable as a result of buying the cap (qv) is offset exactly by that obtained from selling the floor (qv)

Forward break *see* break forward

Forward exchange agreement (FXA) Contract for differences or synthetic agreement for forward exchange that also reflects changes in the spot market

Forward rate agreement (FRA) Short-term interest rate hedge. Specifically, a contract between buyer and seller for an agreed interest rate on a notional deposit of a specified maturity on a predetermined future date. No principal is exchanged. At maturity the seller pays the buyer the difference if rates have risen above the agreed level, and vice versa

Forward swap Swap arranged at the current rate but entered into at some time in the future

Forward/forward Short-term exchange of currency deposits. (*See also* forward/forward deposit)

Forward/forward deposit Agreement by one party to make a deposit with another at a specified future date and at a predetermined rate

Fraption Option on a forward rate agreement (qv). Also known as an interest rate guarantee

FTSE-100 (Footsie 100) Index comprising 100 major UK shares listed on The International Stock Exchange in London. Futures and options on the index are traded at the London International Financial Futures and Options Exchange (Liffe)

Function In information technology (IT), that part of an organisation with specific responsibilities, such as credit control, human resources, finance, etc. (*See also* process)

Future Obligation to buy or sell a standard amount of currency, commodity, financial instrument or service at a predetermined price and at a specified date. Futures are normally traded on exchanges and involve margin payments (daily payments to or from the holder of the position that vary according to the profit or loss of the position)

Future benefit obligation (FBO) Present benefit obligation (PBO) (qv) of benefits earned by employees plus an estimate of the present value of future PBO that current employees will accrue, assuming that they keep working for the company until retirement

Future exposure *see* potential exposure

Gamma A measurement of the rate at which delta changes, based on a unit change in the price of the underlying security

Gap ratio Ratio of interest rate-sensitive assets to interest rate-sensitive liabilities; used to determine changes in the risk profile of an institution with changes in interest rate levels

Gapping Feature of commodity markets whereby there are large and very rapid price movements to new levels followed by relatively stable prices

Garch Generalised Arch (qv)

GIC Guaranteed investment contract

Gold warrant Naked or attached warrant exercisable into gold at a predetermined price

Hedge A strategy to reduce risk by effecting a transaction that offsets an existing position

Herstatt risk *see* settlement risk

High coupon swap Off-market coupon swap (qv) where the coupon is higher than the market rate. The floating-rate payer pays a front-end fee as compensation. Opposite of low coupon swap (qv)

Historical simulation methodology Method of calculating value-at-risk (VAR) (qv) using historical data to assess the likely effect of market moves on a portfolio

Implied volatility A measurement of the volatility of a stock using current rather than historical price. If the price of an option rises with no corresponding rise in the price of the underlying security, the implied volatility has risen

Index option An option whose underlying security is an index. Index options enable a trader to bet on the direction of the index

Indexed notes Contract whereby the issuer usually assumes the risk of unfavourable price movements in the instrument, commodity or index to which the contract is linked, in exchange for which the issuer can reduce the cost of borrowing (compared with traditional instruments without the risk exposure)

Interest rate cap *see* cap

Interest rate floor *see* floor

Interest rate guarantee Option on a forward rate agreement (qv). Also known as a fraption

Interest rate option Option to pay or receive a specified rate of interest on or from a predetermined future date

Interest rate swap (IRS) Swap where the cashflows exchanged are based on two different ways of calculating interest, most commonly where one is a fixed rate and the other a floating rate

Intermarket spread A spread involving futures contracts in one market spread against futures contracts in another market

In-the-money A call option with a strike price below the price of the underlying equity, or a put option with a strike price above the price of the underlying equity

Intrinsic value The amount by which an option is in-the-money

IRS Internal Revenue Service

ISE International Stock Exchange of London

Issuer risk Risk to an institution when it holds debt securities issued by another institution. (*See also* Credit risk)

Knock-in option Option where the holder's ability to exercise is activated if the value of the underlying reaches a specified level. (*See also* barrier option)

Knock-out option Option where the holder's ability to exercise is extinguished if the value of the underlying reaches a specified level. (*See also* barrier option)

Lambda A measure of the effective leverage of an instrument, defined as the percentage change in the market price of a derivative for a 1% move in the underlying

Lender option Floor (qv) on a single-period forward rate agreement (qv)

Leptokurtosis Refers to a probability distribution that has a larger mass on the tail (qv) and a sharper hump than a normal distribution

Level payment swap Evens out those fixed-rate payments that would otherwise vary, for example, because of the amortisation of the principal

Leverage The ability to control large amounts of an underlying variable for a small initial investment

Liability Probable future sacrifice of economic benefit due to present obligations to transfer assets or provide services to other entities as a result of past events or transactions. Generally classed as either current or long-term.

Limit option *see* barrier option

Liquidation Any transaction that closes out or offsets a futures or options position

Liquidity Ease and speed with which assets can be converted into cash with minimal risk of capital loss. The volume of turnover in a market

Loan-equivalent amount Description of derivative exposure which is used to compare the credit risk of derivatives with that of traditional bonds or bank loans

Lognormal distribution The assumption that the log of today's interest rate, for example, minus the log of yesterday's rate is normally distributed

London interbank offered rate (Libor) Rate of interest at which funds are offered in the London interbank market for maturities ranging from overnight to five years. Three- and six-month Libor are widely used as reference rates for payments on floating-rate loans

Long position When the number of contracts bought exceeds the number sold

Long-dated forward Forward foreign exchange contract with a maturity of greater than one year. Some long-dated forwards have maturities as great as 10 years

Long-term assets Assets which are expected to provide benefits and services over a period longer than one year

Long-term liabilities Obligations to be repaid by the firm more than one year later

Lookback option Option that allows the purchaser, at the end of a given period of time, to choose as the rate for exercise any rate that has existed during the option's life

Low coupon swap Tax-driven swap, in which the fixed-rate payments are significantly lower than current market interest rates. The floating-rate payer is compensated by a front-end fee. Opposite of high coupon swap (qv)

Mapping The process whereby a treasury's derivative positions are related to a set of risk "buckets"

Margin The minimum amount of money required to buy or sell a security when the investor is using borrowed money

Margin call The demand by a broker to an investor to put up money because of a decline in the value of owned securities based on minimum amounts of capital required by the broker or the exchange

Marginal default rate *see* probability of default

Market comparables technique Technique for estimating the fair value of an instrument for which no price is quoted by comparing it with the quoted prices of similar instruments

Market-maker Market participant who is committed, explicitly or otherwise, to quoting bid and offer prices in a particular market

Market risk Risks related to changes in prices of tradable macroeconomic variables, such as exchange rate risks or interest rate risks

Mark-to-market To calculate the value of a financial instrument or portfolio on the basis of current market rates or prices of the underlying

Minmax option One of the strategies for reducing the cost of options by forgoing some of the potential for gain. The buyer of a currency option, for example, simultaneously sells an option on the same amount of currency but at a different strike price

MLIV Maximum likely potential increase in value

Momentum The strength behind an upward or downward movement in price

Monetised equity collar Transaction comprising three stages. First, a protective put option is purchased that guarantees the client a minimum value on the underlying equity position. Second, a call option is sold to reduce the cost of the put in exchange for sacrificing some of the potential appreciation of the stock. Third, there is an advance of cash equal to a percentage of the value of the put strike price. The transaction enables the client to retain some equity exposure to major moves in the underlying stock

Monte Carlo simulation Technique used to determine the likely value of a derivative or other contract by simulating the evolution of the underlying variables many times. The discounted average outcome of the simulation gives an approximation of the derivative's value. Monte Carlo simulation can be used to estimate the value-at-risk (VAR) (qv) of a portfolio. Here, it generates a simulation of many correlated market movements for the markets to which the portfolio is exposed, and the positions in the portfolio are revalued repeatedly in accordance with the simulated scenarios. This gives a probability distribution of portfolio gains and losses from which the VAR can be determined

Mortgage-backed security (MBS) Security guaranteed by pool of mortgages. MBS markets include the US, UK, Japan and Denmark

Moving average convergence/divergence (MACD) The crossing of two exponentially smoothed moving averages that oscillate above and below an equilibrium line

Multi-index option Option which gives the holder the right to buy the asset that performs best out of a number of assets (usually two). The investor would typically buy a call allowing him or her to buy the equity index that has performed best over the life of the option

Negative divergence When at least two indicators, indexes or averages show conflicting or contradictory trends

Net present value (NPV) Technique used to assess the worth of future payments by looking at the present value of those future cashflows discounted at today's cost of capital

Noise Fluctuations in the market which can confuse or impede interpretation of market direction

Novation Replacement of a contract or, more usually, a series of contracts with one new contract

Offer The price at which an investor is willing to sell a futures or options contract

Off-market coupon swap Tax-driven swap strategy, in which the fixed-rate payments differ significantly from current market rates. There are high and low coupon swaps (qv)

One touch all-or-nothing Digital option (qv). This option's put (call) pays out a predetermined amount (the "all") if the index goes below (above) the strike price at any time during the option's life. How far below (above)

the strike price the index moves is irrelevant; the payout will be the "all" or nothing

Operational risk Risk of loss occurring due to inadequate systems and control, human error or management failure

Opportunity cost Value of an action that could have been taken if the current action had not been chosen

Option Right, but not the obligation, to buy or sell a given commodity, stock, interest rate instrument or currency in the future at a mutually agreed price, known as the strike price (qv). The right is given in exchange for a premium

Option on Libor An interest rate option (cap or floor) that uses Libor (qv) as the benchmark

Option-dated forward contract Or option forward. Forward foreign exchange contract with an option on the date of exchange

Options Clearing Corporation (OCC) The issuer of all listed options on all exchanges

Ornstein–Uhlenbeck equation A standard equation that describes mean reversion. It can be used to characterise and measure commodity price behaviour

OTC *see* over-the-counter

Out-of-the-money A call with a strike price above the price of the underlying equity, or a put with a strike price below the price of the underlying security

Over-the-counter (OTC) Customised derivative contracts that are usually privately arranged with an intermediary such as a major bank, as opposed to a standardised derivative contract which is available on an exchange

Over-the-top warrant Warrant with the same characteristics as an up-and-out option (qv)

Participating forward Also known as a profit-sharing forward, an adaptation of the range forward (qv) in which only a floor (qv) is fixed. Instead of paying a premium, the owner undertakes to pass a percentage of any gain to the seller. The percentage (known as the seller's participation rate) varies in direct proportion to the level of the floor. For a low participation rate, the buyer must accept a low floor. The buyer is allowed to choose the level of either the participation rate or the floor. Based on his choice, the seller fixes the other variable

Participating option Option where the holder forgoes a predetermined percentage of any profits in return for paying a reduced premium

Participating swap Swap where a counterparty incurs lower costs in return for giving up a percentage of any gain on the swap

Passive foreign investment company (PFIC) In US tax parlance, a foreign corporation that has either 75% or more of its gross income as passive income or at least 50% of its assets held for the production of passive income

Path-dependent option Generic term for options where the payoff, or sometimes the exercise style, depends, not just on the current price of the underlying asset or commodity but also on the path it follows

Peak exposure If the worst-case or the expected credit risk exposures of an instrument is calculated over time, the resulting graph reveals a credit risk exposure profile. The highest exposure marked out by the profile is the peak exposure generated by the instrument

Periodic resetting swap Swap where the floating-rate payment is an average of floating rates that have prevailed since the last payment, rather than the interest rate prevailing at the end of the period. For example, the average of six one-month Libor rates rather than one six-month Libor rate

Portfolio variance The square of the standard deviation (qv) of a portfolio's return from the mean

Positive cashflow collar Collar (qv) other than a zero-cost collar

Potential exposure Estimate of the future replacement cost, or positive market value, of a derivative transaction. Potential exposure should be calculated using probability analysis based on broad confidence intervals (eg, two standard deviations) over the remaining term of the transaction

Premium The amount above the intrinsic value of the option paid to the writer of an option by the purchaser.

Present benefit obligation (PBO) Measure of the present value of pension benefits earned by employees to date, adjusted for the estimated salary level at which the actual payouts of the benefits will be calculated. It can be an important measure when managing the asset/liability ratio of pension funds. (*See also* future benefit obligation)

Pre–settlement risk As distinct from credit risk arising from intra-day settlement risk (qv), this term describes the risk of the loss that might be suffered during the life of the contract if a counterparty to a trade defaulted and if, at the time of default, the instrument had a positive economic value

Price–earnings ratio A ratio giving the price of a stock relative to the earnings per share

Probability of default The likelihood that a counterparty will not honour an obligation on a timely basis when it becomes due

Probit procedures Methods for analysing qualitative dependent methods where the dependent variable is binary, taking the values zero or one

Process In information technology (IT), the detailed set of activities that each function (qv) in an institution performs or is required to perform

Projected benefit obligation (PBO) Or accrued liability. The steady-state (going concern) actuarial liability of a pension fund

Put option A contract that gives the purchaser of the option the right to sell a security at a specified price for a specified period of time

Quanto options (quantos) Options in which the strike price for the underlying is denominated in a second currency. A common example is a foreign currency Bund option

Quasi-American options These allow the option holder to exercise at agreed times other than maturity

Range forward Forward contract in which, instead of an individual spot rate for exchange, a range is agreed, allowing for exchange at any rate prevailing within that range at maturity. If the spot rate at maturity is outside that range, the exchange takes place at the end of the range nearest that rate. The buyer of the contract fixes only one end of the range, the seller retaining the right to fix the other

RAPM Risk-adjusted performance measurement

RAROC Risk-adjusted return on capital. The expected spread (in dollar terms) over economic capital, calculated for individual assets or portfolios

Rate of recovery Estimate of the percentage of the amount exposed to default – ie, the credit risk exposure (qv) – that is likely to be recovered by an institution if a counterparty defaults

Reduced-cost option Generic term for options for which there is a reduced premium, either because the buyer undertakes to forgo a percentage of any gain, or because he or she offsets the cost by writing other options (eg, minimax, range forward). (*See also* zero-cost option)

Relative performance option Option whose value varies in line with the relative value of two assets

Replacement cost The present value of the expected future net cashflows of a derivative instrument. Aside from various conventions dealing with the bid/ask spread, synonymous with the "market value" or "current exposure" of an instrument

Return on assets The net earnings of a company divided by its assets

Return on equity The net earnings of a company divided by its equity

Return on value-at-risk (ROVAR) An analysis conducted to determine the relative rates of return on different risks, allowing corporations to compare different risk capital allocations and capital structure decisions effectively

Revenue volatility Volatility reflecting the extent to which each business unit is exposed to financial loss as a result of a mismatch between the variability of income and costs in each financial year. (*See also* cost volatility)

Reversal The act of switching from a fixed to a floating basis in a swap, or vice versa

Rho Measure of an option's sensitivity to changes in interest rates

Risk contribution A measure of the undiversified risk of an asset in a portfolio

Risk weighting When calculating the amount of capital that the Bank for

International Settlements (BIS) advises should be set aside to cover the credit risk generated by derivative transactions, banks first calculate a "credit equivalent amount" (qv) and then multiply this figure by the appropriate counterparty "risk weighting" (eg, 20% for OECD incorporated banks). The product of this calculation is the final "risk-weighted amount"

Roller-coaster swap Swap in which a counterparty alternately pays a fixed and then a floating rate

S&P 100 *see* Standard & Poor's 100

S&P 500 *see* Standard & Poor's 500

Secondary market A market in which securities are traded after their initial public offering

Sensitivity analysis Analysis of the possible loss of future earnings, fair values or cashflows arising from selected hypothetical changes in market rates and prices

Settlement risk The risk that occurs when there is a non-simultaneous exchange of value. Also known as "delivery risk" and "Herstatt risk"

Sharpe ratio Measure of the attractiveness of the return on an asset by comparing how much risk premium the investor can expect it to receive in return for the incremental risk (volatility) the investment carries. It is the ratio of the risk premium to the volatility of the asset

Short position When the number of contracts sold exceeds the number bought

Skew Biased introduced in calculating probability when there are more observations in the left or right tail (qv)

SLA Savings and Loan Association

Slippage The difference between estimated and actual transaction costs, usually made up of commissions and price differences

SOLB LPF Salomon Brothers Large Pension Fund Bond Index

SPDA Single premium deferred annuity

Spot price Price paid for commodities when they are offered for immediate payment and physical delivery

Spread lock Fixes a given spread over, for example, US Treasuries for a borrowing at some time in the future

Spread lock swap Swap with an option to fix the floating-rate payment at a given spread over a benchmark fixed rate, such as US Treasuries, at some time or for some period in the future

Spread strategy An option strategy that involves holding long and short options on the same underlying security

Standard & Poor's 100 (S&P 100) Index of 100 US stocks, whose average performance gives an indication of broad stock market trends. The index comprises transport, financial and utility stocks

Standard & Poor's 500 (S&P 500) Index of 500 US stocks whose average performance gives an indication of broad stock market trends. It consists of 400 industrial stocks plus those in the S&P 100 (qv)

Standard deviation Single number representing the deviation or dispersion from the mean. (*See also* portfolio variance)

Step-down swap Swap in which the fixed-rate payment decreases over the life of the swap

Step-up swap Swap in which the fixed-rate payment increases over the life of the swap

Stock index future Future on a stock index, allowing a hedge against, or bet on, a broad equity market movement

Stock index option Option on a stock index future

Stock option Option on an individual stock

Straddle The sale of a put and a call with the same strike price on the same underlying and with the same expiry. The strike is normally set at the money. For purchasing two premiums, the purchaser benefits if the underlying moves enough either way. Straddles therefore enable the purchaser to hedge against an expected increase in volatility in the underlying

Stress testing Analysis that gives the value of a portfolio under a range of worst-case scenarios

Strike price The price level of the underlying asset at which an option may be exercised

Structured note Structured notes are OTC products that bundle several disparate elements to create a single product, generally by embedding options in a debt instrument such as a medium-term note

Swap The exchange of one sort of cashflow for another. (*See also* asset swap, cancellable swap, commodity swap, currency swap, interest rate swap and swaption)

Swaption Option to enter into a swap at a future date and predetermined fixed rate. The terms "payer's option" and "receiver's option" indicate whether the owner has the right, but not the obligation, to pay or to receive fixed-rate payments. (*See also* cancellable swap)

Synthetic agreement for forward exchange (SAFE) Contract for differences on the spread between two currencies between two future dates

Synthetic option Replicating the payment of an option using cash or, more often, futures

Tail probability Low-probability event

Tax-exempt swap Swap where the fixed-rate cashflows are in line with those of tax-exempt bonds, especially US municipal bonds

Termination Cancellation of a swap agreement, with settlement based on the current value of the swap

Theory of economic capital Theory that economic or risk capital is the equity capital required to support unexpected losses

Theta A measurement of the decay of an option's price for every one day that passes

Time value The value of an option in addition to its intrinsic, due to the amount of time remaining until expiration of the contract

Tobit procedures Methods for analysing qualitative dependent methods where the dependent variable is censored and assigned a zero value if the event does not occur

Total return swap Swap agreement in which the total return of bank loans or credit-sensitive securities is exchanged for some other cashflow, usually tied to Libor, or other loans, or credit-sensitive securities. It allows participants to effectively go long or short the credit risk of the underlying asset

TPS Transfer pricing system

Traded option Option that is listed on and cleared by an exchange, with standard terms and delivery months

Transaction risk Extent to which the value of transactions that have already been agreed is affected by market risk (qv)

Translation risk Foreign currency assets and liabilities of a firm have to be translated into the domestic currency at the end of the firm's financial year. Translation risk is the risk that this translation will dramatically affect the value of the company's assets and liabilities due to exchange rate fluctuations

Trigger option *see* barrier option

Tunnel option Set of collars, typically zero-cost, covering a series of maturities from the current date. They might, for example, be for dates six, 12, 18 and 24 months ahead. The special feature of a tunnel is that the strike price on both sets of options, not just on the options bought, is constant

Uncovered option When the writer of the option does not own the underlying security. Also known as a naked option

Underlying The asset on which an option is based and which must be bought or sold on the exercise of the option contract

Underwriting risk Risk of loss occurring from underwriting an issue for sale or unexpected levels of claims (insurance)

Unexpected default rate The distribution of future default rates is often characterised in terms of an expected default rate (eg, 0.05%) and a worst-case default rate (eg, 1.05%). The difference between the worst-case default rate and the expected default rate is often termed the "unexpected default rate" (ie, 1% = 1.05 − 0.05%)

Unexpected loss The distribution of credit losses associated with a derivative instrument is often characterised in terms of an expected loss (qv) or a worst-case loss (qv). The unexpected loss associated with an instrument is the difference between these two measures

Up-and-away option *see* up-and-out option

Up-and-in option Type of barrier option (qv) which is activated if the value of the underlying goes above a predetermined level. (*See also* down-and-in option)

Up-and-out option Type of barrier option (qv) that is extinguished if the value of the underlying goes above a predetermined level. (*See also* down-and-out option)

Value-at-risk (VAR) Formally, the probabilistic bound of market losses over a given period of time (known as the holding period) expressed in terms of a specified degree of certainty (known as the confidence interval). Put more simply, the VAR is the worst-case loss that would be expected over the holding period within the probability set out by the confidence interval. Larger losses are possible but with a low probability. For instance, a portfolio whose VAR is $20 million over a one-day holding period, with a 95% confidence interval, would have only a 5% chance of suffering an overnight loss greater than $20 million

VAR *see* value-at-risk

Variance–covariance methodology Methodology for calculating the value-at-risk (qv) of a portfolio as a function of the volatility of each asset or liability position in the portfolio and the correlation between the positions

Vega A measure of the change in an option price for a 1% change in volatility

Vested benefit obligation (VBO) Measures the present value of pension benefits that have been earned by, and are due to, the employee regardless of whether he or she continues working for the firm. It can be an important measure when managing the asset/liability ratio of pension funds

Volatility Measure of the variability (but not the direction) of prices or rates

Warehouse Applies principally to swaps. To run a book without matching transaction for transaction. The object is to allow the management of a book as a whole rather than as a set of individual deals. In theory, all market-makers should warehouse

Warrant Certificate, often issued as part of a package together with a bond, giving the purchaser the right, but not the obligation, to buy a specified amount of a given asset, such as the issuer's equity (equity warrants), bonds (debt warrants), currency, oil, gold or other commodity, at a specified price during the course of a given period of time

Warrant-driven swap Swap with a warrant attached allowing the issuer of the fixed-rate bond to go on paying a floating rate in the event that he or she exercises another warrant allowing him or her to prolong the life of the bond

Worst-case (credit risk) exposure Estimate of the highest positive market value a derivative contract or portfolio is likely to attain at a given moment or period in the future, with a given level of confidence

Worst-case (credit risk) loss Estimate of the largest amount a derivatives counterparty is likely to lose, with a given level of probability, as a result of default from a derivatives contract or portfolio

Worst-case default rate The highest rates of default that are likely to occur at a given moment or period in the future, with a given level of confidence

Worst-case rate of recovery *see* rate of recovery

Write To sell an option is to write it. The person selling an option is known as the writer

GLOSSARY

Yield curve Graphical representation of the term structure of interest rates, usually depicted as spot yields on bonds with different maturities but with the same risk factors plotted against maturity

Yield-curve option Option that allows purchasers to take a view on a yield curve without having to take a view about a market's direction

Yield-curve swap Swap in which the index rates for the two interest streams are at different points on the yield curve. Both payments are refixed with the same frequency whatever the index rate

Zero-premium option Generic term for options for which there is no premium, either because the buyer undertakes to forgo a percentage of any gain or because he or she offsets the cost by writing other options. (*See also* reduced-cost option)

Zero-cost collar Purchase of a put option at a desired strike price and the simultaneous sale of a call at a strike set so that the premium collected on the call matches the premium paid for the put. This results in a zero-cost transaction

Zero-cost option *see* zero-premium option

Zero-coupon bond Bond on which no coupon is paid. It is either issued at a discount or redeemed at a premium to face value

Zero-coupon swap Swap converting the payment pattern of a zero-coupon bond (qv) either to that of a normal, coupon-paying fixed rate bond or to a floating rate

INDEX